TRIGGER WARNINGS

Jeff Sparrow is a writer, editor, and broadcaster. He writes a fortnightly column for the *Guardian*, and contributes regularly to many other Australian and international publications. Jeff is a member of the 3RRR Breakfasters team and the immediate past editor of the literary journal *Overland*. He is also the author of a number of books, including *No Way But This: in search of Paul Robeson* and *Money Shot: a journey into porn and censorship*.

D0892823

TRIGGER WARNINGS

POLITICAL CORRECTNESS AND THE RISE OF THE RIGHT

JEFF SPARROW

SCRIBE
Melbourne • London

Scribe Publications
18–20 Edward St, Brunswick, Victoria 3056, Australia
2 John St, Clerkenwell, London, WC1N 2ES, United Kingdom
3754 Pleasant Ave, Suite 100, Minneapolis, Minnesota 55409 USA

First published by Scribe 2018

Copyright © Jeff Sparrow 2018

Typeset in 12.35/17 pt Bembo by the publishers

Printed and bound in Australia by Griffin Press

Scribe Publications is committed to the sustainable use of natural resources and the use of paper products made responsibly from those resources.

9781925713183 (Australian edition)
9781911617075 (UK edition)
9781947534698 (US edition)
9781925693133 (e-book)

CiP records for this title are available from the National Library of Australia and the British Library.

scribepublications.com.au
scribepublications.co.uk
scribepublications.com

To Steph, for all the reasons

Contents

Introduction

> Nothing is more anti-American, anti-freedom, anti-truth,
> and anti-reality than political correctness. It is a noose
> around America's neck, growing tighter each day … It is
> a communal tyranny, not dissimilar to the one America
> fought a revolution over.

This passage comes from a volume published in 2015 under
the title *Retaking America: crushing political correctness.*[1] There
was nothing particularly unusual about it. Rather, it was a
boilerplate example of a popular genre in what was often
called 'culture war'. On Amazon, readers could find a wide
assortment of books making an almost identical pitch: *The
Intimidation Game: how the left is silencing free speech*; *The
Silencing: how the left is killing free speech*; *Bullies: how the left's
culture of fear and intimidation silences Americans*, and many,
many others.[2]

 If *Retaking America* was in any way different, it was only
because of its author, a man called Nick Adams. For, despite

his book's title, Adams was not American at all. He was an Australian who'd launched his political career in the inner-Sydney suburb of Ashfield.

Back in 2004, Adams had become the youngest councillor in Australia, winning election for the Liberal Party while still at school. His policies included support for portraits of the Queen, opposition to multiculturalism, and the extermination of the suburb's pigeons.[3]

'Ashfield should be inhospitable to pigeons,' he told a perplexed council meeting as he presented a plan to protect the region from avian flu.[4]

Adams' career in local government came to an end when his verbal abuse of a journalist led to a six-month suspension from the Liberal Party. Undaunted, he decamped to the US and reinvented himself as a motivational speaker and conservative commentator. Soon, he would be prosecuting the culture war on Fox News and similar platforms.

By good luck or by good timing, Adams' second coming coincided with the rise of a certain Donald J. Trump. In fact, in *Retaking America*, Adams presented a model inauguration address written for a hypothetical but distinctly Trump-like president.

'Of all enemy combatants, political correctness is the most dangerous,' announced Adams' imaginary statesman. 'It endangers our homeland and our culture. It emboldens our enemies and critics. It denies reality and encourages mediocrity … That's why my first act as President is to announce from this day forward an end to political correctness.'[5]

During the 2015 primaries campaign, Donald Trump was grilled by Fox News personality Megyn Kelly, who quizzed him about his long history of sexism.

'You've called women you don't like fat pigs, dogs, slobs, and disgusting animals,' Kelly began. 'Your Twitter account has several disparaging comments about women's looks. You once told a contestant on *Celebrity Apprentice* it would be a pretty picture to see her on her knees. Does that sound to you like the temperament of a man we should elect as president, and how will you answer the charge from Hillary Clinton, who is likely to be the Democratic nominee, that you are part of the war on women?'

Trump didn't hesitate.

'I think the big problem this country has is being politically correct.'[6]

Sections of the crowd in the studio erupted into whoops and cheers.

Kelly had highlighted a record of misogyny sufficient to sink the electoral chances of a traditional politician. But Trump neither apologised nor explained. Rather, he implied that the question itself was out of line, symptomatic of a broader national dysfunction — and many in the audience, it seemed, thought so, too.

In *Retaking America*, Adams explained that he'd left Australia to escape oppression by political correctness.

'From identity politics and secularism,' he argued, 'to the all-powerful welfare state and the war against national identity, every problem in America today is compounded by this suffocating regime of thought control.'[7]

After 9/11, the US government passed the USA
PATRIOT act, rolling back traditional freedoms in the
name of fighting terror. The CIA established a network
of 'black sites', secret prisons located all over the globe, in
which suspects could be detained without charge or trial after
being snatched from the street. American agents established
elaborate protocols for 'enhanced interrogations', sometimes
involving the practice known as 'waterboarding' — a torture
technique used by Stalin, Hitler, and Pol Pot. Successive
presidents embraced a program of assassination, in which
the commander-in-chief signed off on 'kill lists' handed to
drone operators so that the death sentences could be carried
out remotely by sophisticated robots. The National Security
Agency and other agencies worked to establish a total
surveillance of all electronic communications, compelling
every major American internet service provider to hand over
the content of their users' records. According to Edward
Snowden, in a single month in early 2013, one National
Security Agency unit collected data on more than 3 billion
telephone calls and emails that had passed through the US.[8]

Those developments — reminiscent of the darkest sci-fi
dystopia — didn't trouble Adams in the slightest. For him,
it was political correctness that constituted an Orwellian
tyranny. He wasn't alone. Throughout the Republican
primaries, almost all the major candidates denounced PC.
Ben Carson explained that PC was 'destroying our nation',
Ted Cruz said that it was 'killing people', Jeb Bush declared
that it needed 'to be shattered', and Carly Fiorina insisted
that it was 'choking candid conversation'.[9]

4

Like most mainstream pundits, the Democrat strategists assumed that anti-PC obsessives were unelectable. The Clinton campaign actively tried to boost the fortunes of those it called 'the Pied Piper candidates' — the 'culture war' populists likely, according to the conventional wisdom, to lead their party into the wilderness. Chief among them, of course, was Donald Trump, a man whom the Democrats privately identified as their preferred opponent.[10]

In many ways, Trump behaved exactly as they hoped.

Following Kelly's tough questioning, Trump hinted to the public that she was probably menstruating. During a later feud with Ted Cruz, he implied that Cruz's father had helped assassinate JFK.[11] He threatened to imprison Hillary Clinton, mocked the spasticity of a disabled reporter, and boasted on tape about sexual assaults ('Grab them by the pussy!').[12]

Yet Trump's faux pas did not destroy his campaign. The crasser his conduct, the more his fans enthused. For them, the gaffes weren't scandals at all but evidence of a welcome hostility to the political correctness 'killing our country'. Trump's boorishness became a performative rejection of an entire philosophy: with each sneer, he proved himself a walking, talking rebuke to the PC agenda.

The US election in 2016 came, of course, after a series of other political earthquakes, events that spectacularly upended the liberal consensus. In Britain, the electorate voted to leave the European Union, its 'No' campaign spearheaded by UKIP's Nigel Farage, a man whose 'Little Englander' persona manifested itself as an opposition to political correctness distinctly reminiscent of Trump (whom he later befriended). In Australia, Pauline Hanson and her anti-PC One Nation party staged an unexpected resurrection.

Those results were noteworthy for many reasons, not least because, for the first time in years, the language of class made itself heard. Again and again, candidates said they represented 'the working class' — a group previously rarely mentioned in mainstream politics. Yet, again and again, these candidates were, it seemed, enlisting workers for the right, rather than the left.

In the second decade of the 21st century, the developed world endured shocking levels of social inequality. A new Gilded Age, some called it, with the contrast between the haves and the have-nots stark and getting starker. Oxfam reported that the world's eight richest billionaires controlled as much wealth as the poorest half of the planet's population, a disparity of resources and political power unknown to any previous generation.[13] In the United States, it was even worse, with the nation's three richest men together holding more wealth than the bottom 50 per cent.[14]

Looking at those statistics, a historian of the future might assume that the left was ascendant: that the injustice under which the planet groaned would be fuelling radical ideas and egalitarian alternatives to the status quo.

Such a historian would be wrong.

Donald Trump worked from an office serviced, quite literally, by a golden elevator. For decades, he had constructed a persona based on conspicuous consumption and crass excess — and then won the presidency on an anti-establishment ticket. The most powerful man in the world's most powerful nation, he somehow presented himself as the scourge of the elites.

Almost everywhere, the right claimed the language of radicalism, a vocabulary weaponised against a left accused of representing a loathed status quo. Not only did progressives fail to make gains in circumstances that should have, on paper, favoured social justice and equality, but the populism that flourished explicitly targeted progressive ideas and slogans. The radical right attacked immigrants, refugees, Indigenous people, and so on — but it also campaigned against the perfidy of 'cultural Marxists', liberal elitists, social-justice warriors, and so on.

Not surprisingly, many progressives found politics suddenly well-nigh unintelligible.

In August 2015 — shortly after Trump's Megyn Kelly interview — the basketball legend and anti-racist campaigner Kareem Abdul-Jabbar discussed what he called the 'apocalyptic backlash' against political correctness. Yes, he acknowledged, sometimes campaigners went too far; yes, on occasion, so-called PC measures were annoying or silly. Nevertheless, the aim of erasing 'centuries of bias in our country's collective unconscious' was, he said, worthy and valid — and what the right attacked as PC was, for Abdul-Jabbar, generally 'a benign combination of good old-fashioned manners and simple sensitivity toward others'.[15]

Around this time, the alt-right provocateur Milo Yiannopoulos — a British journalist working for the Trump-supporting *Breitbart* — was building a high-profile career with an online fan base of almost fanatical loyalty. He was doing so by mocking precisely the traits that Abdul-Jabbar identified as self-evidently important.

'Your professors are cunts, on the whole,' Yiannopoulos told students in Oregon. 'Limp-wristed, pacifistic, sandal-wearing weirdos.'

Feminism was a 'cancer', he said elsewhere. Lesbians were 'horrendous, quivering masses of horror', birth control was 'a mistake', women were 'happier in the kitchen', and so on.[16]

Yiannopoulos eventually flamed out. But the anti-PC sentiment that he'd tapped into — the hostility to so many ideas associated with the left — continues to bubble away. The *New York Times*' Bari Weiss writes of the so-called 'Intellectual Dark Web', a network of remarkably popular personalities (the New Atheist Sam Harris, the psychologist Jordan Peterson, the right-wing 'feminists' Ayaan Hirsi Ali and Christina Hoff Sommers, the commentator Ben Shapiro and others) united mostly by their visceral hatred for measures that liberals see as self-evidently decent.[17]

It's not just that the left and right consider each other repellent. It's also that they find each other almost incomprehensible.

Understanding the political landscape of today is not easy — and intervening in it is even harder. The peculiar positions taken by left and right — and the strange arenas on which they fight over them — only make sense in the context of a long and complicated history.

This book offers a particular explanation of that history. It suggests that the anti-elitist right has successfully reshaped the frame through which even people on the left understand politics. As a result, the usual response by progressives to populist provocateurs and charlatans not only fails to combat them, but often leaves them stronger.

In many ways, the right depends, almost parasitically, on the left, in ways that the left consistently fails to understand.

The chapters that follow unpick the dynamics of contemporary culture wars, the methodology through which the right reinterprets social class. They retrace the recent history of the left, so as to put into context the strange phenomenon of political correctness, and they examine the evolution of anti-elitism before concluding with an argument about the wrong and the right ways to respond to social inequality in the age of Donald Trump.

A 'trigger warning' is, of course, an alert given to readers about distressing or upsetting material, allowing them to prepare themselves for what they might encounter. As we've come to expect in the so-called culture wars, the media attention devoted to trigger warnings bears little relationship to their actual prevalence. When a tiny number of courses in a tiny number of universities offered students notice about potentially disturbing content (a courtesy not so different from that given to viewers by commercial television networks), conservative culture warriors seized on the development as further evidence of generalised PC tyranny.

In a later chapter, I analyse that particular furore for what it reveals about politics today. The title of this book does not imply that trigger warnings are, in and of themselves, of particular significance, except insofar as they exemplify the contemporary tendency for debates to fixate on the relatively trivial.

But the term feels appropriate in part because any discussion of political correctness and related issues will, inevitably, be controversial. The culture wars, almost by design, touch on subjects (such as race, gender, religion, and sexuality) about which people feel very strongly. It's difficult to unpick the arguments around PC without causing some offence to someone, particularly when presenting a case that is at odds with the mainstream left as well as the right.

So that's one reason for a warning. But there's another.

This book is a polemic, a deliberate attempt to challenge conventional wisdom. But it's not meant as empty contrarianism or as a provocation. On the contrary, it's predicated on the notion that, despite the silliness of people like Nick Adams, politics in the 21st century matters a great deal.

We live, after all, in a time of warnings. As this book goes to print, scientists from the US National Oceanic and Atmospheric Administration have announced the 400th consecutive month of above-average temperatures.[18] It's a grim reminder of the urgent challenges confronting the planet.

But just as economic inequality hasn't spontaneously generated movements for egalitarianism, we need to recognise that environmental catastrophe will not, in and of itself, spur environmental action. The denunciations of political correctness that helped Donald Trump win office are also a standard tool for climate denialists and oil moguls.

That's a second reason for the title. However challenging we find these debates — however much they trigger us or others — we need to persist with them, simply because they touch on tremendously urgent problems.

CHAPTER ONE

Inventing PC

Political correctness never really existed — at least, not in the way that conservatives claim.

As we saw with Nick Adams, right-wingers portray PC as an Orwellian scheme to end freedom of speech, a deliberate strategy to impose a progressive orthodoxy. In reality, radicals coined the term as a joke. The phrase first emerged within the American New Left as an ironic homage to Stalinist rhetoric, adopted by progressives to mock censorious comrades and to chaff the overly earnest.[1] In Australia and Britain, the preferred term was 'ideologically sound', but the gag worked the same way.[2] When an activist declared a particular film or book or person 'PC' (or 'ideologically sound'), she did so with her tongue firmly planted in her cheek. It was never serious. By describing a friend as 'very PC', a radical didn't imagine herself to be identifying incipient tyranny. She was just suggesting that they might lighten up.

What was originally a satire on totalitarianism somehow

became, for the right, a signifier of totalitarianism. The quite strange process by which this happened illuminates important trends in modern politics.

The story began in the United States in 1964, when, over the course of a year, thousands of Berkeley students embraced civil disobedience in massive protests for free political expression on campus.

'[T]here's a time,' student leader Mario Savio said, in his iconic speech at the demonstrations, 'when the operation of the machine becomes so odious — makes you so sick at heart — that you can't take part. You can't even passively take part. And you've got to put your bodies upon the gears and upon the wheels, upon the levers, upon all the apparatus, and you've got to make it stop. And you've got to indicate to the people who run it, to the people who own it, that unless you're free, the machine will be prevented from working at all.'[3]

The campaign — a major win for free speech — and the rhetoric that accompanied it inspired a generation of New Leftists. Perversely, though, it also played a major role in the career of that doyen of modern conservatism, Ronald Reagan, and the eventual campaign against PC.

Originally a Hollywood liberal, Reagan had shifted to the right during the Cold War. His political career really took off, however, when he capitalised on the backlash against free speech at Berkeley in a run for governor. Campaigning in 1966, he denounced the 'small minority of beatniks, radicals and filthy speech advocates [who] have brought such shame to ... a great university'.[4] Then, in 1969, activists tried to establish a free-speech area ('People's Park') on vacant university land. Reagan duly placed Berkeley under martial law, and deployed helicopters, the National Guard, and riot police, who killed one man and wounded several others.

The governor showed no remorse. 'Once the dogs of war have been unleashed, you must expect things will happen,' he said.[5]

In *Retaking America: crushing political correctness*, Adams explained his hostility to PC as support for freedom of speech. '[P]olitical correctness,' he declared, 'acts as a heavy blacksnake, whipping us into submission. Pushing us into line. Cutting us down. It squelches debate and polices speech.'[6]

In reality, the campaign against PC began with the so-called 'education wars' launched during Reagan's second term as president in the late 1980s. The Reaganite right who led that effort were not promoting free speech. In the wake of his confrontation with the Berkeley activists, Reagan believed deeply in censorship — and actively campaigned for more of it. The 1984 Republican National Committee platform, on which he ran for re-election, promised: 'We will vigorously enforce constitutional laws to control obscene materials which degrade everyone, particularly women, and depict the exploitation of children.'[7]

Adams also made the familiar claim that PC was 'a disease of the elites', something that he, a man of the people, instinctively despised. 'You'll never catch me eating kale, seaweed or tofu,' he boasted. 'When a waitress offers me a gluten-free menu, I decline almost immediately ... [It] will be ribs, brisket, chicken fried steak, mac 'n' cheese, fries and onion rings, washed down with beer and soda, followed by pie, all the way.'

But the education reformers of the 1980s were not opposing elitism. On the contrary, they were angry that the universities weren't elitist enough.

The key text of the 'education wars' was 1987's *The Closing of the American Mind*, by the University of Chicago's Allan Bloom, an idiosyncratic neoconservative philosopher.[8] Bloom originally called his manuscript *Souls Without Longing*, a title that conveys something of the peculiarity of his project: a chatty, discursive summation of the ideas of Leo Strauss (Bloom's teacher, and the inspiration for a generation of neoconservatives).

To analyse the America of the 1980s, Bloom looked back to the ancient world, where, he said, philosophy and reason developed in opposition to society and politics, in an antagonism exemplified by the execution of Socrates. The classical tradition showed that the university needed to resist the democratic and commercial imperatives of the modern world, existing 'for the sake of the freedom of the mind'. That freedom was (or should be) an elite project, enabling select students to confront their own natures and grapple with eternal truths.

In Bloom's presentation, philosophy involved eros as well as intellect, awakening in the best young people a love for learning and a love for virtue that enabled them to become complete people ('souls without longing', no less). But this project had been threatened by the social and intellectual levelling unleashed by the 1960s, with objective values giving way to rampant relativism and young people seeking erotic solace not in Plato but in rock music and MTV.

'Nothing noble, sublime, profound, delicate, tasteful or even decent can find a place in such tableaux,' Bloom sniffed.

Bloom's publisher did not expect *Closing* — an oddball polemic by a man previously known mostly for translations of Plato and Rousseau — to do particularly well. To their astonishment, it became an international sensation, remaining on the *New York Times* bestseller lists for non-fiction for four months, and eventually selling over a million copies: a remarkable achievement under any circumstances, but particularly so for an eccentric meditation on the role of philosophy in the late 20th century.

More importantly, *Closing* sparked a prolonged and intense debate about the state of the modern university, a debate furthered by E. D. Hirsch (*Cultural Literacy*), Roger Kimball (*Tenured Radicals*), Dinesh D'Souza (*Illiberal Education*), and many others.[9]

Why did such a book find such an audience? Whatever Bloom's intentions, he was read less for his thoughts about philosophy than for his critique of academic leftism. A few years earlier, secretary of education William Bennett had announced that students were graduating from American institutions lacking 'even the most rudimentary knowledge about the history, literature, art, and philosophical foundations of their nation and their civilization'.[10] Bloom offered a similar argument, albeit on a more sophisticated (and slightly strange) basis.

For him, a liberal education identified those rare individuals capable of absorbing the dangerous and esoteric truths conveyed by classical philosophy — truths that, by their nature, bore no relationship to the whims of the populace. Not surprisingly, he judged the contemporary university to be largely bankrupt:

> The university now offers no distinctive visage to the young person. He finds a democrat of disciplines — which are there either because they are autochthonous or because they wandered in recently to perform some job that was demanded of the university ... Equality for us seems to culminate in the unwillingness and incapacity to make claims of superiority in the domains of which such claims have always been made — art, religion and philosophy.[11]

If read carefully, *Closing* offered an argument directed against the free-market right as much as against the left. His demand that the university provide a place in which 'scholars and students [could] be unhindered in their use of reason' constituted an implicit critique of the commercialisation of higher education, a process subsequently far more important in destroying the scholarly contemplation that Bloom advocated than any machinations by the left.

But *Closing* wasn't read carefully. Rather, Bloom's critique was boiled down to a central claim: that the objective values embodied in the Western canon — the great works of European thought — were being menaced by intellectuals' embrace of diversity, inclusion, and postmodernism. In particular, he condemned the aesthetic 'relativism' that, he said, led academics to elevate African-American or female writers in place of those they dubbed 'Dead White Men'. What was needed was a return to 'the good old Great Books approach, in which a liberal education means reading certain generally recognized classic texts'.

Expressed like this, the message was entirely compatible with the nostalgia underpinning the Reagan revolution. Reagan's promise of 'Morning in America' invoked a vanished greatness, an Edenic period prior to the social and political excesses of the 1960s — excesses he particularly associated with the radical students he fought at Berkeley. For Reagan and Reaganites, Bloom added academic heft to the president's own longheld belief that universities were (as he'd once explained) hotbeds of 'communist sympathisers, protesters and sex deviants'.[12] Ungrateful students needed to knuckle down and learn something; the university itself should abandon leftist fads and become, once more, an intellectual idyll where Great Men contemplated Great Ideas.

Bloom's denunciation of populism became, for many readers, a kind of populism itself. When he mocked the postmodernism taught by radical professors, he did so by invoking the objective truths embodied in the philosophical and literary canon. Readers, however, judged the zany po-mo profs from the perspective of 'sound common sense' — a quite different position, but one that facilitated an emerging distinction, in the education wars, between, on the one hand, honest, everyday Americans and, on the other, overeducated and arrogant leftists.

As a result, the 'mac 'n' cheese' anti-elitism of Adams derived historically from the classical elitism of Bloom. As Michael Berube put it: 'Bloom's odd book was the jab that allowed the right to set up the haymaker it's delivering now.'[13]

But Bloom himself didn't mention 'political correctness'. It wasn't until 1990 — three years after *Closing*'s publication — that those words came to dominate the debate.

On 28 October 1990, Richard Bernstein published an article in the *New York Times*' 'Ideas and Trends' section entitled 'The Rising Hegemony of the Politically Correct'.[14] The piece focused, in particular, on debates over the curriculum at the University of Texas, with conservatives making the Bloomite claim that the achievements of Western civilisation were under threat.

Bernstein, however, contributed a new vocabulary. His article began:

> The term 'politically correct', with its suggestion of Stalinist orthodoxy, is spoken more with irony and disapproval than with reverence. But across the country, the term PC, as it is commonly abbreviated, is being heard more and more in debates over what should be taught at the universities.

Even though he acknowledged that 'political correctness' (and the associated 'politically correct person' or 'pcp') was 'not used in utter seriousness', Bernstein claimed that a certain cluster of opinions had come to define 'a kind of "correct" attitude towards the problems of the world, a sort of unofficial ideology of the university.'

In digital databases of mainstream American publications, the term 'politically correct' barely featured prior to 1990. As the *Guardian* writer Moira Weigel noted, its usage exploded in that year. In 1990 it turned up more than 700 times; in 1991 there were more than 2,500 instances; and in 1992 it appeared more than 2,800 times.[15] Bernstein's *NYT* article prompted exposés of PC in the *Wall Street Journal*, *Newsweek*, *New York Magazine*, *Time*, and other influential American outlets. In those articles, journalists used 'political correctness' — with only a thin veneer of irony — to describe a radical creed, a new philosophy around which professors and activists and other intellectual types were rallying.

'PC is, strictly speaking, a totalitarian philosophy,' explained *Newsweek* on 24 December 1990. 'No aspect of university life is too obscure to come under its scrutiny.'[16]

By mid-1991, when the first president Bush addressed a commencement ceremony at the University of Michigan, the old, ironic meaning of PC had largely vanished. For Bush, 'political correctness' was no joking matter but a:

> movement [that] replaces old prejudice with new ones. It declares certain topics off-limits, certain expression off-limits, even certain gestures off-limits. What began as a crusade for civility has soured into a cause of conflict and even censorship. Disputants treat sheer force — getting their foes punished or expelled, for instance — as a substitute for the power of ideas. Throughout history, attempts to micromanage casual conversation have only

incited distrust. They've invited people to look for an insult in every word, gesture, action. And in their own Orwellian way, crusades that demand correct behavior crush diversity in the name of diversity.[17]

Bush's intervention illustrated how and why the new coinage — the redefined 'political correctness' — made such a difference.

The Reaganite opposition to campus radicalism stemmed from old-fashioned Red-baiting. The president's hostility to liberal professors and their protesting students was akin to his derision of Robert Mapplethorpe's photography and the other manifestations of the 'obscenity' that conservatives wanted to ban. Whatever sophistication Bloom brought to the education wars, the argument was still deeply and obviously reactionary — an overt attempt to roll back the legacy of the 1960s and the social movements.

But by the 1990s that rhetoric was tired, precisely because of what those movements had achieved. The diverse reading lists so reviled by Bloom and others reflected a genuine shift in the sensibilities of Americans, the result of decades of activism. Reagan, after all, had championed South African apartheid — but, in 1991, Nelson Mandela was free and almost universally recognised as a hero.

That was why the discovery — or perhaps construction — of 'political correctness' mattered. It allowed conservatives on campus to make the old arguments against equal-opportunity statutes, anti-discrimination codes, attacks on the literary canon, and inclusive language. But it also enabled them to position themselves not as opponents of racial or gender equity, but as advocates of equality. By opposing PC, they said, they weren't being sexist or racist; on the contrary, they were battling a new, authoritarian doctrine espoused by (in George Bush's words) the 'political extremists roam[ing] the land, abusing the privilege of free speech, setting citizens against one another on the basis of their class or race'.

That recalibration rested on a particular conjunction, as Bush made clear. The students were, he told them, graduating at a 'historic moment', with their commencement coinciding 'with this nation's commencement into a world freed from cold war conflict and thrust into an era of cooperation and economic competition'.

For Bush, the West's triumph over the Soviet Union demonstrated the virtues of the market. That victory proved that 'our free enterprise system' could be trusted to deliver equality, since 'no system of development ever has nurtured virtue as completely and rigorously as ours'. Indeed, any attempt to improve on freedom ('say, by picking winners and losers in the economic market') was destined not only to fail, but also to oppress, since 'no conclave of experts, no matter how brilliant, can match the sheer ingenuity of a market that collects and distributes the wisdom of millions of people, all pursuing their destinies in different ways'.

In the Reagan era, the fight against the campus left had been pitched as a battle against African Americans, feminists, gays, and other advocates of inclusion. Bush now flipped the script entirely. For him, the struggle against political correctness was akin to the struggle against the Soviet Union, a crusade for the economic liberty that would, in and of itself, free women, African Americans, and other minorities.

This rhetorical identification of anti-PC with freedom rather than with old-fashioned bigotry was crucial, allowing 'political correctness' to creep into the vocabulary of those who wouldn't have traditionally associated themselves with the right.

But to appreciate just how the war against political correctness spread so widely, it is also necessary to understand the history of the left.

CHAPTER TWO

Three kinds of leftism

The campaign against political correctness took aim at what were presented as the excesses of the great social movements associated with the New Left, such as feminism, the gay and lesbian rights movements, and the struggle against racism.

But the history of these social movements was not as straightforward as this presentation suggests. Rather than an uncomplicated progression, the movements — and the left as a whole — developed through phases associated with distinct tendencies, in ways that became very important for the right's struggle against political correctness. In a sense, the emergence of the modern left could be understood less as a simple evolution and more as a series of ruptures, a process marked by the clash between distinct, and often antagonistic, sets of ideas.

The great revolts of the sixties emerged from a period of social stability and political quiescence. In the United States, an upsurge of industrial action after World War II had been beaten back before the Cold War marginalised both the unions and the Old Left. Buffeted by anti-communism, the activists of the 1950s and the early 1960s were, for the most part, committed to what might be called 'palliationist politics', in which a minority of courageous, middle-class activists spoke and acted on behalf of the oppressed, who weren't expected to take part themselves. Palliationist politics generally involved an embrace of respectability, a commitment to lobbying mainstream politicians for limited reforms, and a general sense that change would be wrought by well-meaning and well-educated people working to assist a largely passive constituency.

For instance, the most important early political organisations for gay men and lesbians in the US were (respectively) the Mattachine Society and the Daughters of Bilitis. Though its members were committed and brave, the Mattachine Society was assiduously non-confrontational, even secretive, and liberal rather than radical (despite the communist convictions of some of its leaders). Its mostly middle-class members just wanted, as Lillian Faderman put it, 'to be allowed to live just like any other citizen and not to be told they were different from their fellow Americans'.[1] The Daughters of Bilitis were similar. Again, the very existence of the group was courageous; again, its mission was much defined by respectability, with its members emphasising their conventional clothing and appearance as they sought to integrate lesbianism into the mainstream.[2]

The Montgomery bus boycott of 1955–56, a key struggle of the early civil-rights movement, signalled a shift in

American politics, one that opened up space for wider dissent after the scarifying experience of McCarthyism. On the campuses, the fight against segregation led to the formation of the Student Non-Violent Co-ordinating Committee, while Students for a Democratic Society emerged as a radical offshoot from the Social Democratic League for Industrial Democracy. The escalation of America's intervention in Vietnam in 1964 spurred a renewed antiwar movement, and the mass protests that followed provided a unifying focus for activists of all sorts. The Berkeley protests popularised civil disobedience among white students; riots rocked the black ghettos every summer from 1964 to 1968; and the Mexican and Chicano members of the United Farmworkers Union under Cesar Chavez launched a boycott and strike of grape growers.[3]

In his compendious account of the 1960s, the activist-turned-historian Todd Gitlin gave a sense of the new mood, describing how, in the spring of 1969 alone, major demonstrations took place in something like 300 colleges and universities, with many of the protests involving occupations and other militant gestures. The progress of 'the movement', as it was invariably described, featured every day in the mainstream press, as well as in a burgeoning number of alternative newspapers, radical magazines, and independent radio programs, all of them discussing 'arrests, trials, police hassles and brutalities, demonstrations against the war, demonstrations of blacks and then Hispanics and other people of colour and their white allies, demonstrations by GIs against the war, crackdowns by the military'. By July of that year, Gitlin noted, 'the *Los Angeles Free Press* sold 95,000 copies a week, the *Berkeley Barb* 85,000, *The East Village Other* 65,000 — all up from 5,000 or fewer in 1965'.[4]

The prevailing tendency might be described as 'direct politics': a focus on mass action, on grassroots mobilisation, on participation and self-organisation by workers, students, and the oppressed. Mario Savio's reference to the ordinary individual preventing the machine of politics from functioning captured the flavour perfectly: rather than depending on respectable saviours, the free-speech demonstrators urged ordinary people to put their own bodies on the line.

The distinction between palliationist and direct politics could be seen most clearly from a comparison between the earlier forms of gay and lesbian activism and the iconic riot that took place after a police raid on the Stonewall Inn in New York in 1969. State violence against gays and lesbians was, of course, nothing new. But Stonewall was different because ordinary people resisted, with chants of 'Gay Power' and 'We Want Freedom'.[5]

'When did you ever see a fag fight back?' asked one of the participants rhetorically. 'Now, times were a-changin'. Tuesday night was the last night for bullshit ... Predominantly, the theme [was], "this shit has got to stop!"'

Stonewall gave rise to gay liberation, a movement that, symptomatically, took its name from black liberation and women's liberation, both of which had been inspired by the national liberation struggle in Vietnam. Where palliationist politics insisted on the distinction between particular interests, direct politics drew connections between issues.

In his brief account of Stonewall, Fred Wasserman noted, 'The early gay liberation activists — and some of the rioters themselves — drew on the militant tactics and radical rhetoric of the New Left; the counterculture; and the black, women's, student, and antiwar movements, in which many of them had been (and continued to be) involved.'[6]

The members of the Mattachine Society and the Daughters of Bilitis tended, for obvious reasons, to preserve their anonymity. Activists in gay liberation, by contrast, openly proclaimed their sexuality. An earlier generation of gays and lesbians merely sought tolerance; those radicalised by Stonewall demanded revolution — or at least profound structural change.

To identify the later 1960s with direct politics and the 1950s with palliationist politics does not, of course, imply that all — or even most — activists in those decades shared the same ideas or advocated the same tactics. Obviously, they did not. Nevertheless, the distinction between the two types of politics captures something about the prevailing tendency, the political centre of gravity.

The small groups of radicals active in the 1950s were, for instance, often forced to adapt to the respectable mood of the times, just as, during the late 1960s, liberals found themselves embracing the tactics and ideas of direct politics: accepting the importance of demonstrations, embracing the need for profound structural change, and insisting on mobilising from below. Direct politics might not have been universally embraced even in 1969, but for a time it became a kind of common sense, giving the period its distinctive flavour.

The spectre of direct politics haunted both the so-called education wars in the late 1980s and the debates about political correctness a few years later.

Bloom, for instance, openly blamed the calamitous state of American education on the 1960s, a decade he dubbed an 'unmitigated disaster' for the universities. He — and others — repeatedly cited the 1969 student occupation of Cornell by armed black militants, an event that led the administration to introduce 'Black Studies' (an almost primal wound for the American right). Yet though Bloom sounded as if he were decrying the protesters' use of violence, this wasn't his argument at all. For Bloom, the problem with the Cornell occupiers wasn't so much their guns as their demands — in essence, their insistence that a university curriculum should be relevant to the people.

Because he saw philosophy as necessarily detached from society, any call that the university reflect the community was, in and of itself, an assault on philosophers. Therein lay his problems with the 1960s — the activists insisted that the curriculum take into account the changing status of African Americans, women, and other excluded groups, and by so doing challenged the autonomy and objectivity of liberal education. Bloom put it like this:

> The university [after the 1960s] had abandoned all claim to study or inform about value — undermining the sense of the value of what it taught, while turning over the decision about values to the folk, the *Zeitgeist*, the relevant. Whether it be Nuremberg or Woodstock, the principle is the same.[7]

It was an extraordinary passage, a comparison of protesters to Nazis, not on the basis of their authoritarianism but because of their tolerance. As Christopher Hitchens quipped, for Bloom, 'the American mind was closed because it had become so goddamned open'.[8]

Bloom's view of the 1950s as 'one of the great periods of the American university' slid over the systemic exclusions of that decade, a time in which the few African-American students able to enrol in southern universities faced physical violence merely to attend class. Yet he presented his argument as a defence of tolerance in the face of intimidation, claiming that, after the 1960s, it became 'almost impossible to question the radical orthodoxy without risking vilification, classroom disruption, loss of confidence and respect'.

Yet by the time he was writing, the direct politics of the 1960s were no longer ascendant. Todd Gitlin noted that, as far back as the mid-1970s, a once-widespread commitment to revolutionary change had given way to 'the practical pursuit of reforms', with many former firebrands becoming what he called 'crisp professional lobbyists' or devoted to winning local office, usually as Democrats. The sense of a unified movement had given way to distinct interest groups, as 'all were compelled to play by the political rules in an unfavourable political climate: to formulate programs, at last, and push them across in a time of tax revolt and shrinking revenues'.[9] Gitlin's account captured what might be described as a third shift: a general move among activists from direct politics to 'delegated politics'.

As the radicalism of the 1960s waned, many former

activists were able to obtain relatively prestigious positions that pertained in some way to their activism, simply because the movements themselves had changed the culture, particularly in higher education. If the paradigmatic figure of the 1960s radical was the demonstrator, the period of the late 1970s might be associated with a leftism embedded in various professional settings. The creation of Black Studies, women's studies, and, eventually, queer studies required lecturers with knowledge of those fields, and so a whole layer of radicals made their way into new academic disciplines. Elsewhere, the social movements gave rise to new non-governmental organisations (NGOs), health services, consultancies, and businesses, all of which required new personnel with distinctive skills and experiences.

Those who retained a commitment to the ideas of the New Left under such circumstances found protests and demonstrations harder to organise. Many became accustomed to making arguments on behalf of a constituency that they no longer mobilised. In the new climate, progressives moderated, for understandable reasons, their slogans, and tempered their rhetoric according to the prevailing mood. The rhetoric of liberation no longer possessed the same force without crowds on the streets, and thus gave way to more achievable, practical demands.

Crucially for the development of anti-PC, the former student protesters who had moved into academia now concentrated on reforming the university. They'd once hoped to change the whole world, but with America moving to the right, making a progressive haven within higher education — or even a single department — became a more realistic goal, particularly since their new professional status gave them access to mechanisms for instigating reforms. Increasingly, leftists who'd once attacked the structures of the university now saw those structures as useful political tools.

Again, this was a general tendency, not a universal law. In some places and for some campaigns, direct politics continued to prevail. Nowhere was the dominance of delegated politics ever total. Nevertheless, at the most general level, a shift in the strategies and sensibilities of activists could be detected, with delegated politics becoming more influential and direct politics declining accordingly.

That was the context for the right's discovery of anti-political correctness: an American higher-education system in which delegated politics was ascendant. The new curricula that the anti-PC crusaders hated so much — the rejection of the traditional white, male, and European canon, the sensitivity to exclusion, the desire for social relevance — had all been popularised by a mass movement that no longer existed. Bloom might have scoffed at Black Studies. But, contrary to what he suggested, such courses were not implemented to assuage an unrepresentative minority, but rather reflected a widespread sentiment among the African-American population. In 1972, for instance, 30,000 people marched in Washington DC in support of the inaugural African Liberation Day, with marches taking place the next year in thirty different cities.[10]

But by the early 1990s, mobilisations on this scale were

unthinkable. The response to the right's attack on progressive curricula accordingly came not from the masses on the streets but from professors at the university, which gave the debate a quite different dynamic.

More than anything, anti-PC took hold because it was able to present the campus left — and later the left as a whole — as censorious and oppressive, a minority using bureaucratic measures to enforce progressive ideas.

Obviously, this involved considerable hyperbole and not a little overt dishonesty. *New York Magazine* illustrated John Taylor's 1991 feature 'Are You Politically Correct?' with pictures of the Hitler Youth and Maoist Red Guards, even though, for the most part, the article discussed what would now be seen as fairly unexceptional attempts to combat racism and sexism.[11]

Likewise, Jerry Adler's *Newsweek* article 'Thought Police' described a student protest against professor Vincent Sarich of the University of California, a controversial figure who'd told students that women possessed smaller brains than men, that race made a difference in academic ability, and that homosexuals preferred to work with female bosses. Did a brief disruption of Sarich's class in protest against his claim that affirmative action discriminated against whites constitute censorship? No, not really. In fact, with a slightly different framing, the protest might have been understood as an exercise in free speech by students who, in an earlier era, would have been compelled to endure a bigoted authority figure in obedient silence.

Again and again, widely circulated examples of campus

'political correctness' rested on misrepresentations or outright deception. '[A] relatively small number of instances,' explained D. Charles Whitney and Ellen Wartella in their study of early media coverage of PC, 'virtually all of them from a small number of elite institutions (and virtually all of them major research universities), have been used to characterize intellectual and political life on thousands of American campuses.'[12] Nevertheless, the nature of delegated politics made the charges of the anti-PC campaigners seem credible.

A comparison of two different actions (on two different continents) against campus homophobia provides a useful illustration.

The first — a textbook example of direct politics — emerged from gay liberation in Australia. On 26 May 1973, Jeremy Fisher — a resident of Robert Menzies College at Macquarie University — tried to commit suicide after struggling to come to terms with his sexuality. When he was taken to hospital, the administration discovered leaflets revealing Fisher's affiliation with gay radicalism. Dr Alan Cole, the master of the college, subsequently informed Fisher that he needed to seek professional help to repress his sexual orientation — and that until he got it, he would be excluded from the institution.

The student union — dominated by activists committed to direct politics — organised a demonstration in support of Fisher, and the staff association pledged its solidarity. Most importantly, the activists approached the Builders Labourers Federation, whose members were currently working on the college. A meeting of unionists on campus voted unanimously to support the campaign, slapping a black ban on the site. Fisher later recalled his discussions with the BLF leadership:

[O]ne day in the Students' Council basement, Bob Pringle, part of the union's leadership, asked me: 'Why do you want to go back into that place?'

'I don't,' I said.

'But we're out on strike to put you back,' he said, a hint of anger in his eyes.

'I thought because I'd been kicked out for being gay,' I answered.

Bob looked at me for a moment, directly into my eyes. All sorts of thoughts whirled in my head. Was he going to withdraw the BLF's support? Did he think I'd tricked him? Did he want to hit me? Then he said: 'I guess you're right. It's the principle of the thing. They shouldn't pick on a bloke because of his sexuality.'[13]

The college eventually bowed to the pressure generated by an intense media campaign, and offered to take Fisher back, though for obvious reasons he never returned.

The second example came from America in 1989. That year, a student called Nina Wu was ordered to move off campus by officials at the University of Connecticut, and then banned from dormitories and cafeterias. Allegedly, she'd put on her door a sign detailing people who would, she said, be 'shot on sight' — a list that included 'preppies', 'bimbos',

'men without chest hair', and, some students said, 'homos'
(Wu denied this). As a result, she'd been disciplined under
a newly rewritten 'student behaviour code' that prohibited
'personal slurs or epithets based on race, sex, ethnic origin,
disability, religion or sexual orientation'.[14]

The Wu case became a cause célèbre for the right, and
featured as a vignette in many of the early anti-PC exposés.

A comparison of the two incidents highlights, in some
respects, just how much the left had achieved. A few
decades earlier, homophobia had been official policy in
most universities — but by 1989 even a minor college in
Connecticut accepted Bob Pringle's once-radical argument
about not picking on 'a bloke because of his sexuality'.

Yet even though both the Wu and the Fisher cases
involved a student being disciplined by the university about
homosexuality, the internal dynamics of the two incidents
were very different, in ways that reflected the distinction
between direct and delegated politics.

In the Fisher episode, the administration used its
institutional power to insist that a gay man not express his
sexuality. The direct campaign by Fisher supporters was
unambiguously against homophobia and for free speech. It
depended on mobilising — and thus convincing — students
and workers, who thereafter felt some responsibility for the
outcome.

With the Wu incident, however, the response came
not from a campaign of workers and students, but from a
university administration. No doubt many University of
Connecticut students opposed homophobia. But they were

not personally involved in responding to Wu's sign, and so didn't feel any obligation to defend the administration's harassment policy. It was thus far easier for conservatives to frame Wu's exclusion as a bureaucratic measure imposed by an unrepresentative minority.

That was precisely what Adler did. He wrote that the case illustrated how:

> [A] generation of campus radicals who grew up in the 1960s … no longer talk of taking to the streets … because they now are gaining access to the conventional weapons of campus politics: social pressure, academic perks (including tenure) and — when they have the administration on their side — outright coercion.[15]

The analysis, with its suggestion of a leftist conspiracy, was typical anti-PC hyperbole. For most former activists, the so-called 'long march through the institutions' wasn't a stealth route into power but a desperate effort to find work in a suddenly harsh economic climate. Even at the most progressive institutions, radical academics were a small and often beleaguered minority, while anti-gay slurs continued as a fairly common part of everyday life.

Weigel noted that, even in 2016, almost no one described themselves as 'politically correct'. To use the jargon of classical rhetoric, the term is an 'exonym': a phrase used by speakers to indicate that they don't belong to that which they described. As a result, she insisted:

[T]here was no neat history of political correctness. There have only been campaigns *against* something called 'political correctness'. For 25 years, invoking this vague and ever-shifting enemy has been a favourite tactic of the right.[16]

This was correct. The targets of anti-PC campaigners varied immensely — and often the supposed incidents of PC censorship simply weren't true. It was rare, for instance, to read a journalistic account of political correctness that didn't mention the story of kindergarten children forced by oversensitive teachers to sing 'Baa Baa Rainbow Sheep'. The anecdote circulated for years — despite being based on an incident where children changed the words as a language game entirely unrelated to race.[17]

More recently, the revived anti-PC that coincided with the Trump campaign painted a picture of an American higher-education system dominated by those whom the *New York Times*' David Brooks described as 'student mobbists [who] manage to combine snowflake fragility and lynch mob irrationalism into one perfectly poisonous cocktail'.[18] In a widely cited piece, Jonathan Chait declared that 'the PC movement has assumed a towering presence in the psychic space of politically active people in general and the left in particular'. In *Time*, Cliff Maloney Jr ('the Executive Director at Young Americans for Liberty') said that 'America's college campuses look and feel a lot more like an authoritarian dictatorship than they do the academic hubs of the modern free world'.[19]

Again, much of this was either exaggerated or dishonest.

As Nathan J. Robinson (and many others) argued in reply, the anti-PC polemicists extrapolated from a few high-profile incidents at elite universities to draw conclusions about the 17 million students enrolled in tuition (in precisely the fashion Whitney and Wartella had complained about three decades earlier). Again and again, the anti-PCers elided the distinction between censorship (a speaker silenced) and debate (a speaker criticised). They presented as edicts speech codes intended as guidelines; they confused student protests with state bans.[20]

Most of all, they ignored the extensive campaigns by conservatives — often aided and abetted by university administrations — to discipline, censure, and sack progressive students or academics. Glenn Greenwald, for instance, documented in exhaustive detail the various well-funded initiatives 'devoted to outlawing or otherwise punishing criticisms of Israel', while activists like David Horowitz, media personalities like Bill O'Reilly, and various well-funded conservative student bodies had run longstanding and often successful drives to dismiss academics they regarded as disloyal.[21] If free speech was under threat on the modern campus, the threat came from the right as much as or more than from the left.

In some ways, though, the hypocrisy of anti-PC merely illustrated how the shift from direct to delegated politics had enabled the right to forge such a powerful weapon. From its inception, opposition to political correctness had been, in Weigel's words, a campaign against 'an impossibly slippery concept', one that presented itself as an apolitical defence of freedom, but that always and only attacked the left. That rhetorical ambiguity gave anti-PC a tremendous flexibility, allowing it to adapt as the priorities of the right changed.

But irrespective of its target, the discourse of anti-PC retained the same structure, always implying that unrepresentative elitists were enforcing their views on fair-minded ordinary people. Such rhetoric was effective, because, as Michael Walzer suggested, by the early 1990s many in the left really had come to rely on victories won 'in the courts, the media, the schools, the civil service — and not in the central arenas of democratic politics'.[22]

Anti-PC targeted, in a sense, a style of activism, rather than any particular argument or ideology — a style fundamentally associated with the top-down character of delegated politics. That was why so many people were prepared to believe spurious stories about teachers censoring 'Baa Baa Black Sheep': they'd come to believe that was the kind of thing that progressives might do.

CHAPTER THREE

Battlers and elites

The fundamental class distinction made by anti-PC campaigners — the contrast between, on the one hand, the sound common sense of working-class battlers and, on the other, the censoriousness of the progressive elites — eventually became so commonplace that many people simply accepted it as a factual description of how society worked.

This was even more remarkable given that throughout most of the 20th century a quite different theory of class prevailed, one derived (however distantly) from various socialist thinkers — and, most importantly, Karl Marx.

Class was about the relationship that prevailed between different groups of people involved in creating social wealth. In particular, it pertained to how people accessed the so-called means of production: the resources, tools, and institutions they required for their labour.

For most of human history, the land itself served as the primary means of production. Capitalism only became possible when the mass dispossession of the peasantry from their fields created a substantial group — a class — who had no way to survive other than by selling their ability to labour. Such was the basis of the working class, differentiated from both the big capitalists, who owned or controlled factories, offices, mines, hospitals, and other means of production, and the little capitalists (or middle class), who were self-employed as farmers, contractors, lawyers, doctors, shopkeepers, or in other small enterprises.

Marx didn't argue that workers were the most oppressed people in society. On the contrary, he stressed that peasants and the unemployed were generally far worse off than wage labourers. Nor did he insist that workers were invariably radical or were devoid of backward prejudices. Instead, he simply pointed out that because humanity depended on labour, they wielded, at least potentially, tremendous power — a power that, in certain circumstances, could transform the world.

On this basis, the left — and indeed most people in the first half of the 20th century — traditionally identified the working class as the key driver of progressive politics.

The understanding of class associated with anti-PC was quite different.

Though the battler/elite distinction evolved from many sources, the version most often articulated today originated from an important group of conservative American theorists.

What was known as 'new-class theory' arose in debates about the nature of the Soviet Union in the late 1930s and early 1940s. Iconoclastic socialists, appalled at the brutality of Soviet society, identified the importance of a managerial layer in running Stalinist Russia. Initially, new-class theory sought to recuperate the socialist idea from association with Stalin's repression by suggesting that the bureaucrats had warped an originally liberatory project. By the end of World War II, however, many of these dissident American leftists were moving to the right. As neo-conservatives, they then drew on that old analysis to explain, and condemn, the social ferment in America in the 1960s.

They recognised that the postwar boom had created a massive expansion in white-collar work: a substantial new layer of jobs associated with the growth of the public service, the expansion of higher education, and the increasing importance of information technology. Many commentators — both at the time and since — understood what was happening as a 'middle-classing' of the West: a social shift that made the blue-collar working class (and hence class analysis in general) less important. Extrapolating from their assessments of how the Soviet Union worked, the neocons concluded that they were witnessing the rise of a new ruling layer, an intellectual elite comparable to the bureaucrats who governed the Stalinist states of Eastern Europe.

The distinctive outlook of the New Left reflected, the neocons said, this novel phenomenon: a so-called new elite of intellectuals imposing on mainstream, decent America its politics, its attachment to the counterculture, its unconventional sexual morality, and its liberal ideas about drugs.[1]

Irving Kristol, the neocon pioneer, identified what he called the 'new class' with 'a goodly proportion of those college-educated people whose skills and vocations proliferate in a "post industrial" society.' He listed, by way of example, scientists, teachers, communication workers, lawyers, and doctors in the public sector, staff in the upper levels of the government bureaucracy, and so on.

In reality, as Barbara Ehrenreich pointed out, college-educated people — or, at least, university academics — were not necessarily supportive of the student revolt. Most professors were politically conservative, with even ostensibly progressive academics such as Eugene Genovese denouncing the student rebels for their 'nihilistic perversions'.[2]

Furthermore, while the expansion of white-collar work after World War II did create a new middle class, it also created a massive layer of white-collar workers. In retrospect, this was the more significant development: the 'proletarianisation' of occupations that were once prestigious, with the logic of the factory spreading to various kinds of intellectual labour. Office staff, teachers, nurses, IT workers: all were subjected to a regimentation once exclusively applied to blue-collar workers in ways that made class more rather than less relevant.

But Kristol and his co-thinkers were not interested in an empirical study of class relationships. The neocons might have associated the 'new class' with particular occupations (such as in education and the public service), but they were more concerned to identify the 'elite' by its ideas rather than its social position. For Kristol, what mattered most about the new class was its hostility to traditional values. The new class was cosmopolitan; it was internationalist; it was enthusiastic about feminism, multiculturalism, and the avant-garde — and it formed, he thought, a kind of fifth column, promoting exotic attitudes quite different from those held intuitively by decent, everyday people.

In their leftist phase, the neocons had been disillusioned by their inability to mobilise working people. In their rightist phase, they accepted as a given that workers were innately, inexorably conservative. It might even be said that, for them and their political descendants, conservatism became constitutive of class.

In 1965, William F. Buckley Jr famously declared: 'I would rather be governed by the first two thousand people in the Boston telephone directory than by the two thousand people on the faculty of Harvard University.'[3] Random suburbanites would, he implied, be far more loyal and sensible than the effete radicals running the campuses.

In other words, the argument always pertained as much to the social conservativism of the masses as to the radicalism of the 'elites'. It depended on the assumption that ordinary people were traditionalists, repelled by the exotic notions expounded by the 'new class'. Or, more exactly, it defined ordinariness by conservatism — and then defined elitism by radicalism.

Of course, even in America, the notion that real workers believed the ideas that the neocons attributed to them was always a fantasy, particularly in the 1960s. In reality, as Ehrenreich pointed out, a revolt of American blue-collar workers did take place during that period, but it did not express right-wing or traditionalist values. On the contrary, 'the late sixties saw the most severe strike wave since shortly after World War II, and by the early seventies the new militancy had swept up autoworkers, rubber workers, steel workers, teamsters, city workers, hospital workers, farmworkers, tugboat crewmen, grave diggers, and postal employees'. The strikers did not embrace the 'racial backlash' that conservative intellectuals attributed to them, with 'black and white workers ... marching, picketing, and organising together in a spirit of class solidarity that had not been seen since the thirties'.

On average, American workers were more opposed to the conflict in Vietnam than were members of the middle class. White workers were less racist than their middle-class counterparts — a study from 1966 suggested that 'the higher one's class of origin or class of destination the more likely that one prefers to exclude Negroes from one's neighbourhood'.[4] Furthermore, workers were often sympathetic to the very counterculture that new-class theory insisted they opposed: smoking dope, growing their hair, and listening to rock music. Ehrenreich described some of the student radicals she knew deciding to 'join the working class' by dressing as squares ... only to discover, when they arrived in the factory, that their longhaired co-workers believed them to be narcotic agents.

Nevertheless, America did not experience an equivalent to the enormous general strikes that rocked France in 1968. Much of the union leadership in the US had come to power during the Cold War, and as such formed a deeply conservative bureaucratic layer within the labour movement. In particular, the building and construction unions were dominated by Catholic anti-communism. In one notorious incident in 1970, right-wing leaders organised 200 building workers to physically attack students protesting the Kent State shootings and US involvement in Vietnam and Cambodia.

The apparent conservatism of the 'hard hats' gave some credence to the neocons' contrast between effete, disloyal intellectuals and manly patriots working in construction — as Ehrenreich said, in the corrupt union leaders of the Catholic right, the middle-class neocons eventually discovered 'a working class more suited to their mood: dumb, reactionary and bigoted'.[5]

Nevertheless, it would be many years before new-class theory really came into its own. The form in which it was expressed became known as 'culture war'. The phrase derived from the German term *Kulturkampf*, coined to describe struggles between religious and secular views in late-19th-century Prussia. The modern usage dated from the 1992 Republican National Convention and the address given there by the American social commentator and activist Patrick Buchanan.

Buchanan had worked as a speechwriter for Richard Nixon and as communications director for Ronald Reagan. But he'd also built a successful and high-profile career as a broadcaster and pundit. In the election of 1992, he stood for the Republican nomination, seeking to unseat the by-then deeply unpopular incumbent, George Bush.

The Buchanan campaign was an explicit assault on the kind of ideas Bush had expressed to the students at the University of Michigan. Where Bush enthused about open markets, Buchanan denounced globalisation and the New World Order. Bush thought free enterprise would bring equality to oppressed groups; Buchanan warned that white America was being destroyed by multiculturalism and homosexuality.

His was, in other words, a challenge to Bush's free-market orientation on the basis of an older, nativist social conservatism — and though he didn't win the nomination, he polled enough votes to alert the Bush team to a substantial constituency on their right. Buchanan was asked to address the national convention and to pull his supporters behind president Bush, the endorsed Republican candidate.

It did not go well. In his speech, Buchanan stressed the importance of the looming contest against Bill Clinton — and, he added pointedly, Hillary Clinton as well. The election would establish what Americans stood for. There was, he said, a religious war taking place:

> It is a cultural war, as critical to the kind of nation we shall be as the Cold War itself. For this war is for the soul of America. And in that struggle for the soul of America, Clinton & Clinton are on the other side, and George Bush is on our side.[6]

The cultural war would, Buchanan said, be fought over 'the amoral idea that gay and lesbian couples should have the same standing in law as married men and women', over the 'right-to-life and for voluntary prayer in the public schools', over control over 'the raw sewage of pornography that so terribly pollutes our popular culture', over opposition to 'environmental extremists who put birds and rats and insects ahead of families, workers, and jobs'.

The Bush wing of the Republicans was appalled, with the president's aides concluding that they'd let 'the brimstone quotient' get out of hand.[7] Bush was, after all, running against Bill Clinton — and though Clinton shared Bush's enthusiasm for the free-market policies that would later be known as 'neoliberalism', he was far more youthful and modern, and clearly comfortable when discussing racism, women's rights, and other social issues.

In any case, many Republican neoliberals genuinely disliked Buchanan's ideas about culture. As market fundamentalists, they were more interested in Adam Smith's invisible hand than the Christian right's invisible god. They didn't care about school prayer, and they weren't invested in abortion; they worried that America First nativism might impede the open trade they advocated. They wanted to spread the influence of the market, not fight about porn.

It was only when Bush lost the election that 'the war for the soul of America' became more attractive to Republicans. Culture war came into its own as a strategy adopted by the right against Clinton and, later, deployed in support of the second George Bush.

In some respects, Buchanan's speech, with its insistence that Republicans fight on the terrain of 'values', merely updated an old conservative approach. Nixon had, after all, pioneered the so-called 'southern strategy', by which he undercut white support for Democrats in the South with the careful deployment of coded racism. Buchanan struck a similar tone, urging Republicans to 'take back' their culture block by block, just as American troops had done when suppressing the mostly black Los Angeles rioters.

Yet, like Bush at the University of Michigan, Buchanan also recognised the difference made by the Cold War. Where Bush thought that the old politics of left and right could be replaced by the struggle for freedom, Buchanan saw the potential for fresh allegiances based on symbolism, history, religion, and morality.

For him, culture war offered a strategy, in the new post–Cold War environment, to align the right with at least some sections of the working class. When, for instance, Buchanan referred to the '25 million unborn children destroyed since Roe V Wade', the idea was to convince voters to no longer think of themselves as socialists or unionists, or Democrats or even workers, but as Christians — and thus to vote with social conservatives against feminists, liberals, and other progressives.

He'd sketched out how this might work by discussing the 'tough, hearty men' facing hardships at the James River Paper Mill in New Hampshire.

'My friends,' Buchanan explained, 'these people are our people. They don't read Adam Smith or Edmund Burke, but they come from the same schoolyards and the same playgrounds and towns as we came from ... We need to let them know we know how bad they're hurting. They don't expect miracles of us, but they need to know we care.'

How might Republicans show they cared? Buchanan offered the example of the Californian lumber town of Hayfork, where jobs were at risk because, he said, 'a federal judge has set aside nine million acres for the habitat of the spotted owl'.[8]

In reality, America wasn't shedding millions of industrial jobs during the recession of 1992 because of a meddling judiciary. Small-town factories were closing down because the American economy had been opened up, a policy to which both parties were committed. Yet environmentally minded judges (whose intervention represented the most delegated form of leftism one could imagine) were easy for small-town factory workers to dislike. Rhetoric against them could — in theory, at least — tap into the simmering unease produced by economic restructuring, directing it safely against the supposed perfidy of urban elitists.

Such a strategy might enable right-wing politicians committed to neoliberal reforms to launch skirmishes about patriotism, morality, sexuality, ethnicity, and similar topics, knowing that the ensuing debate would draw what remained of the left away from economics and inequality, and onto the relatively safe (for the right) terrain of culture. The social anxiety fostered by unpopular market policies could thus be displaced into an attack on condescending academics, or inner-city activists, or uppity minorities, or other examples of delegated leftism. With these 'elites' portrayed as opposing the 'common sense' of ordinary people, progressives could be made to bear the brunt of the rage and tension produced by economic reform, which could then continue unimpeded.

Indeed, an alliance between the neoliberal right and social and religious conservatives might even establish a virtuous circle, in which neoliberalism fuelled culture war, culture war harvested votes for social conservatism, and those votes enabled more neoliberalism. If unemployed factory workers (laid off because of free-trade deals), became incensed about a meddling judiciary, they might vote for anti-environmentalist Republicans, who'd then have a mandate to introduce more free trade.

In his *What's the Matter with America?*, Thomas Frank identified what he called 'the backlash' as a key strategy for the American right: a way of mobilising ordinary people to vote for the rapacious capitalists of the Republican Party. For him, culture war functioned as a kind of bait and switch, a method by which demagogues of the right convinced ordinary people to vote against their own interests:

> The trick never ages; the illusion never wears off. Vote to stop abortion; receive a rollback in capital gains taxes. Vote to make our country strong again, receive deindustrialisation. Vote to screw those politically correct college professors; receive electricity deregulation. Vote to get government off our backs; receive conglomeration and monopoly everywhere from media to meat packing. Vote to strike a blow against elitism; receive a social order in which wealth is more concentrated than ever before in our lifetimes, in which workers have been stripped of power and CEOs are rewarded in a manner beyond imagining.[9]

This, then, was the logic of culture war.

Like the discourse of anti-PC, it was predicated on two related factors. Corey Robin claimed that 'all great counterrevolutionary theories' necessarily cast 'the people' as 'actors without roles, an audience that believes it is on stage'.[10] Culture warriors were best able to position themselves as representing working people against the progressive elite in circumstances of relative social peace, since, almost by definition, mass struggles mobilised workers, who were then much less likely to accept that a conservative politician or pundit spoke on their behalf. Conversely, culture war required activists engaged in delegated politics to be cast as villains — like anti-PC, it depended on identifying a perceived or real gap between progressives (such as those liberal judges agitating for the spotted owl) and the rest of society (the unemployed lumber workers).

In this respect, culture war and anti-PC were variants of the same phenomenon: a deflection of social and class tensions into a different realm. In other respects, though, they retained the stamp of the different circumstances from which they emerged. As a product of the education wars, anti-PC presented itself as a liberal or perhaps libertarian response to censorship and authoritarianism. Culture war, by contrast, was more obviously conservative, explicitly tapping into traditional fears and prejudices.

This was what made them work so well together, as the Australian experience would demonstrate.

CHAPTER FOUR

The Australian way

A study of American newspaper references to 'political correctness' indicated that the original outbreak of anti-PC reached its zenith in that country in 1993. In Australia, however, the peak came slightly later. The archives of the *Sydney Morning Herald* showed the phrase 'political correctness' being used 20 times in 1991, 89 times in 1992, and 227 times the following year, before a crescendo during the 1996 election and its immediate aftermath.[1]

This delay correlated with a shift in anti-PC rhetoric as it moved away from the American university wars. The Australian education system was, after all, very different from its US counterpart, and some of the specific issues central to the US debate (racialised entry quotas, for instance) simply didn't apply.

For this reason, the local campaign against PC was, from the start, entwined with new-class theory and culture war.

In Australia, the centrality of the labour movement to

the direct politics of the New Left posed an obvious problem for the adoption of new-class theories. For instance, as well as backing Jeremy Fisher, the NSW Builders Labourers Federation ran environmental campaigns to save Sydney's parks and buildings (with its famous 'Green Bans' thereafter giving the colour its political connotations), and played an important role in the movement against South African apartheid. The historian Verity Burgmann noted:

> [I]n the 1960s and the 1970s, the interests of the working class and the concerns of the working class and the concerns of the new social movements were seen to be complementary … [T]here was a general expectation that the new social struggles that had developed would combine with working-class organisations and lead to significant social transformation.[2]

As a result, it was initially difficult for conservatives to paint workers as enthusiastic defenders of the status quo, innately hostile to progressive ideas. In 1975, satirist Barry Humphries collaborated with Ross Fitzgerald to publish a sketch in *Quadrant* that depicted a radical schoolteacher called Craig Steppenwolf refusing to teach Shakespeare and instead promoting sexual promiscuity, 'guerrilla basket weaving', and the works of 'Professor Jackie Jacko, a starving Aboriginal grants recipient'.[3] In this vignette of a radical teacher imposing a crazy agenda on his sensible students, the contours of modern culture war could be discerned, but only in embryonic form.

Over the next years, a rhetoric of 'elites' oppressing 'battlers' steadily percolated through the Australian right.

In 1983, *Quadrant* editor Robert Manne, then a leading conservative intellectual, denounced 'the so-called "new class" of university graduates', who, he said, 'were now present throughout many of the key institutions of our society', places where 'their hatreds — America, Capitalism, Moral Puritanism, Anti-Communism — were expressed rancorously and consensually'.[4] Again, the same notion: the left as a malign, disloyal force surreptitiously imposing its agenda on ordinary people.

These early formulations were expressed by right-wing intellectuals for right-wing intellectuals in small-circulation conservative journals.[5] The theory really came into the broader consciousness when it entwined with racial anxieties.

On Australia Day 1986, historian Geoffrey Blainey spurred a nasty debate about multiculturalism. 'Our current emphasis on granting special rights to all kinds of minorities,' he said, 'especially ethnic minorities, is threatening to disperse this nation into many tribes.'[6]

The resulting controversy drew in John Howard, in his first incarnation as federal Liberal Party leader. Howard pushed back against Labor's approach to Indigenous affairs by arguing that 'guilt wasn't hereditary' and that white Australians shouldn't feel guilty about past injustices. For good measure, he also suggested that the rate of Asian immigration should be 'slowed down a little'.[7]

In 1988, Howard helped the Coalition develop its policy document 'Future Directions', which argued that Labor had been pandering to 'special interests', and bemoaned ordinary Australians being made to feel guilty 'for wrongs committed generations ago'. The advertising guru John Singleton promoted 'Future Directions' with a song called 'Son, You're Australian'. Its lyrics ran, in part:

> Never mind the fancy dancers
> Plain-thinking men know their right from wrong
> Don't deal with silver tongues and chancers
> Keep your vision clear and hold it strong.
> I watched as things began to change around me
> The fancy dancers got to have their say
> They changed the vision, spurned the wisdom
> And made Australia change to suit their way.
> It's time we cleansed the muddy waters
> And do the things we know must be done
> So that we teach our sons and daughters
> What it means to be a true Australian.[8]

Here, in a well-funded advertising campaign for a major political party, was the classic culture-war opposition, with the 'plain-thinking men' who understood right and wrong pitted against the silver-tongued 'fancy dancers' who were changing the nation to suit themselves. What was more, Howard's rhetoric made clear that the transformation being wrought by the 'new-class elites' of the left pertained to Asian immigration and reparations for Indigenous people — two issues on which he calculated he could rouse popular indignation.

Though the Australian right drew directly and explicitly on American neocon writings, the local version of new-class theory also repurposed certain ideas associated with the Australian left, such as the contrast made in the 1890s by the radical nationalist *Bulletin* magazine between manly, patriotic bushmen and the weedy, insipid clerks of the metropolis.

Yet the Old Left had understood class as fundamentally material, depending, first and foremost, on social relationships involved in the process of value production. Neo-conservative new-class theory, by contrast, emphasised culture, ideas, and values. Even though they used a similar vocabulary, the two ways of understanding society were conceptually very different.

Two comparatively recent iterations of the theory provided a good illustration of how the 'new class' idea differed from a material understanding of social antagonisms.

In 2003, conservative commentator Professor David Flint published a book about the monarchy called *The Twilight of the Elites*.[9] One might have thought that such a volume with such a title would be a treatise about the decline of the aristocracy. But it was nothing of the sort. In the usual 'new class' fashion, Flint identified elitism with progressive ideas such as Republicanism — and so presented the defenders of a hereditary monarchy as … anti-elitists.

In the more recent *The Lucky Culture and the Rise of an Australian Ruling Class*, former *Weekend Australian* editor Nick Cater devoted hundreds of pages to an excoriation of elitism. Again, because his understanding of elitism bore no relationship to material conditions, he could suggest that activities enjoyed by wealthy and privileged people were, in fact, anti-elitist so long as they were undertaken with a certain dinkum elan. Thus Cater described a performance by violinist Richard Tognetti:

> This is not a musical masterclass but hot, sweaty manual labour; by the end one senses it is not so much applause that Tognetti craves as an ice cold Victoria Bitter ... That is not a bow in Tognetti's hand but a blade, for he does not play his Guarneri del Gesu, he shears it. This is music as Tom Roberts would have painted it; cotton sleeves rolled up, dirt under the fingernails, a clay pipe in the back pocket; there will be no interval in tonight's performance, just a twenty-minute smoko.[10]

It was a deeply silly argument, a presentation that used the tropes of class for claims that stripped the term of all vestiges of its usual meaning. Not surprisingly, such arguments could only really get a hearing in circumstances in which the left — and the intellectual traditions associated with it — were in decline.

In Australia, the New Left developed according to the same tripartite structure apparent in the United States, as a brief outline of activism by women and then by gays and lesbians illustrates.

The Australian labour movement suffered a heavy defeat during the 1949 coal dispute. Throughout the 1950s and the early 1960s, the unions, and the workers they organised, remained relatively quiescent. The long economic boom convinced many that capitalism had entered a new phase in which the cyclical crises of the past would no longer occur. In the resulting atmosphere of political stability and social conservatism, advocating for the oppressed required considerable courage.

In his book *Living Out Loud*, Graham Willett described the first phases of gay and lesbian activism as coinciding with 'the emergence of a new liberal current in Australian political life'.[11] A small number of brave reformers insisted that sexual behaviour was a private matter and that homosexual acts between consenting adults behind closed doors should not be regulated by the state.

The early activists didn't regard themselves as fundamentally changing society so much as bringing about modest reforms. Radical change did not seem on the agenda; the cautious approach of delegated politics made sense to most people. Groups such as the ACT Homosexual Law Reform Society were dominated by liberals from the traditional middle class. They were oriented to politicians, to lawyers, to university students, and to progressive clergymen, using the avenues of liberal democracy to plead for greater toleration: basically, for the right to participate like ordinary citizens.

In her history of the Australian women's movement, *Getting Equal*, Marilyn Lake discussed a similar orientation adopted by feminist activists of the time. They, too, focused on citizenship rights; they, too, prioritised methods associated with palliationist politics, such as lobbying and petitioning politicians for limited reforms.

In 1967, the so-called Penal Powers dispute signalled a new phase of heightened union mobilisation. Over the next years, class antagonisms sharpened. In 1968, more than one million strike days were lost; by 1974, the figure had climbed to four million.

Industrial action on such a scale changed the culture. It meant that ordinary people experienced an unprecedented degree of agency in that portion of their life where they were accustomed to feel powerlessness. The boundaries of possibility shifted, in ways that had previously seemed unimaginable.

In this context, gay activists in Australia enthusiastically welcomed news of the Stonewall riots. Militants adopted the rhetoric and strategies of direct politics as older, more conservative organisations faded away or split, and gay liberation became dominant.

A similar current wedded to direct politics set the pace in the women's movement.

'[W]omen's liberationists,' wrote Lake, 'hungered for 'revolution', for the overthrow of existing social and political structures. They aimed at political and personal transformation, not the acquisition of personal power. There was no desire to enter parliament, and little interest in the conventional politics and the agendas of the major parties.'[12]

Of course, the historical relationship between unionism and women's liberation was by no means simple. But, as in America, direct politics encouraged activists to draw links between their own struggles and those of others. The Glebe women's liberation group, for instance, prepared a leaflet for the 1970 anti-Vietnam moratorium explaining: 'Just as the people of South-East Asia are fighting for the right to govern their country, the Women's Liberation movement asserts that women must fight the pressures in our society which prevent us from determining our own lives.'

In 1975, the sacking of Gough Whitlam — and the defeat of the campaign to reinstall him — opened up a period of relative union quiescence, with the Fraser administration presiding over a right-wing backlash.

The feminist writer and activist Anne Summers outlined the effect on the women's movement of the decline in working-class struggle. 'The optimism and energy that radical groups exuded during the early years of the Whitlam Government … gradually dissipated,' she said. 'Many feminists were fully engaged in running the many services activities … Others had temporarily dropped out of politics, exhausted from setting up these centres, lobbying for funds.'[13]

The mobilisations on which direct politics had depended — not just strikes, but rallies, mass meetings, protests, and the like — were becoming harder to organise, as society in general stabilised. Meanwhile, many of the movements — and the activists who led the movements — had established an institutional foothold, which came to seem more and more important, particularly as the movements declined.

Those two pressures helped delegated politics become ascendant within the women's movement.

In the final part of her history, Lake described the emergence of what she dubbed 'state feminism', when, in the 1970s and the 1980s, 'the institutionalisation of feminism reached its apotheosis, with whole programs and complex administrative machinery established by governments — federal and state — to promote the status of women, equal opportunity, non-discrimination and finally affirmative action'.[14]

In the early 1980s, the gay and lesbian movement also shifted from being a purely outsider phenomenon and established a foothold in the mainstream, as a delegated politics centred on the new gay and lesbian organisations became important.

The key moment was probably the heroic mobilisation of the community in the face of the HIV/AIDS crisis, which necessitated the establishment of an infrastructure around health, as well as the creation of representative bodies able to lobby those in power. For the first time, gay and lesbian activists found it possible to make headway inside established political parties and trade unions, as well as inside the universities and in the public service.

The triumph of delegated over direct politics was also fundamentally connected to the election of the Hawke government in 1983.

A former leader of the Australian Council of Trade Unions (ACTU), Bob Hawke campaigned on a promise of industrial and social reconciliation. Central to this was the Accord: an agreement between the ACTU, representatives of big business, and the government. In return for industrial cooperation, labour-movement leaders were offered input into economic policy — a process that paralleled and accentuated the shift to delegated politics adopted by activists in the various social movements.

The Hawke–Keating era brought progressives into the very heart of mainstream politics, with feminists, environmentalists, unionists, and representatives of the various ethnic organisations given prominent positions and widely consulted, in a way that had never happened before. As Jim George and Michael Hutchison put it, Labor insisted that the nation needed to 'establish itself as a modern republic, confront the need for reconciliation between black and white Australians, represent itself proudly and confidently as a multicultural society, celebrate the arts, and redefine itself as a sophisticated modern society in the global marketplace'.[15]

Yet even as Hawke and Keating embraced the delegated politics emerging from the social movements, Labor also pursued what was then called 'economic rationalism' — and what might today be more accurately described as 'social neoliberalism'. The new government promoted free trade, floated the dollar, deregulated the banks and other key industries, embarked on the privatisation of public assets, dismantled tariff protections, introduced various 'user pays' mechanisms to welfare and education, and adopted other measures associated with the programs of Thatcher and Reagan.[16] As the *Australian* newspaper later approvingly said, 'the most radical free-market reforms in Australia's history were effected by a Labor government led by a former trade union chief'.[17]

It was, said the economist Michael Pusey, a 'revolution from above' that 'transformed our political and economic institutions and touched every nerve of our society'.[18]

The reforms meant a significant redistribution of income, largely to the benefit of major corporations, with deregulation disrupting traditional industries such as manufacturing and agriculture, and producing substantial pockets of unemployment — even before the downturn that Paul Keating dubbed the 'recession we had to have'. As Michael Kimmel argued (in a different context), when the achievements of the delegated left took place in the context of rising inequality, it was easy to think the two phenomena were related and 'that the greater class inequality [was] somehow attendant upon, even caused by, greater social equality'.[19]

A stark gulf opened up between economic winners and losers, leaving many (particularly in rural areas) resentful at the people who'd prospered during reforms they'd experienced as intensely traumatic. The depth of that resentment reflected changes in more than merely the economy. Neoliberalism normalised market relationships in every aspect of life, deliberately breaking down traditions, customs, and sentiments deemed economically irrational. As has often been noted, the project required a remaking of subjectivity. It forced the adoption of an entrepreneurial self, in which the individual negotiated daily life by assessing the market risks and rewards in every transaction. Neoliberalism remade each citizen as a corporation of one, affronting deeply held ideas about the nature of humanity.

Such was the soil from which Australian culture war sprouted. The man who most successfully cultivated it was John Howard.

CHAPTER FIVE

Howard and Hanson

Howard had lost the Liberal leadership in 1989, partly because his comments on Asian immigration — like Buchanan's 1992 speech — had sparked outrage in the media, in the public, and throughout the political class.

Howard, however, did not abandon his strategy. Rather, he bided his time — and, when he reclaimed the leadership in 1995, proceeded with more subtlety. He distanced himself from his prior comments about Asian immigration, this time publicly and repeatedly declaring his support for multiculturalism. Immediately prior to the federal election, an obscure Queensland Liberal candidate named Pauline Hanson published derogatory comments about Indigenous people in a local paper — and Howard backed her disendorsement by the party.

But Howard had not changed his heart so much as his method. Just as Bush abandoned Reagan's censorship to attack PC *as* censorship, Howard's references to immigration gave way to denunciations of political correctness for preventing references to immigration. Howard's old rhetoric had been received as part of a deep and continuing divide within conservative ranks, with the Liberal Party split (even after his removal) between reactionaries and modernisers over issues such as Native Title, multiculturalism, and sexual diversity. His new approach provided a basis for unity, since anti-PC could appeal to small-L liberals concerned about freedom of speech. Indeed, as Mark Rolfe argued, the early agitation against political correctness in Australia drew in many intellectuals who (at the time, at least) identified with the left: Frank Moorhouse, David Williamson, Margaret Bateman, Phillip Adams, and others.[1]

Howard still attacked the so-called elites, condemning 'the noisy, self-interested clamour of powerful vested interests with scant regard for the national interest'.[2] But he did so in a way that presented the delegated politics of the social movements as a credible scapegoat for the social anxiety produced by the Hawke–Keating reforms.

In John Howard's first year of leadership, he addressed the question of 'national identity', denouncing Keating for corralling the Australian people into a particular model of patriotism. In the past, he said, the country had been 'less in the grip of stifling orthodoxies like political correctness'.

Then, after the Liberals' landslide electoral win in 1996, the new PM declared a victory over PC. The election would, he said, enable 'people … to speak a little more freely and a little more openly about what they feel'.[3] The implication was that the perfidious elites had reshaped the country — and then deployed political correctness to prevent Australians from objecting.

Howard's old opposition between the new-class elites and the battlers could now gain traction. Multiculturalists, feminists, progressive academics: after thirteen years of activists committed to delegated politics working with Labor's neoliberalism, the idea of an elite reshaping society while they sneered at and belittled ordinary folk and their travails possessed a new plausibility.

The country had, after all, been remade, in ways that many people did not like, with the delegated left often featuring both as the architects and the beneficiaries of that remaking. On this basis, Howard could contrast PC and the liberal elites with 'families battling to get ahead … young Australians battling to get a decent start … older Australians battling to preserve their dignity'.[4]

Of course, Howard and his team might have attacked elites, but they did not oppose neoliberalism. On the contrary, the new government intensified the free-market project that had been initiated by Labor. But where the ALP (at least initially) proceeded in the name of consensus, Howard sought to destroy union power.

This difference necessitated and facilitated the culture war 'virtuous circle'. Social conservatives didn't instinctively enthuse about neoliberalism: the market tended, after all, to break down the family values, national traditions, religious rituals, and so on that they championed. But Howard could draw Christians and traditionalists behind his market agenda because of their horror at Hawke and Keating's support for feminism, for ethnic minorities, for Indigenous rights, and for other socially progressive causes.

Culture war, in other words, helped organise the various shades of the right behind the new administration. At the same time, Howard used anti-PC to exploit and widen the gulf between the delegated left and its traditional supporters.

John Howard was a career politician leading a mainstream political party. When he — and the media that supported him — attacked multiculturalism, feminism, Indigenous reconciliation, and similar policies, the ultimate target was always the ALP. Howard's culture skirmishes presented the Liberal Party as the alternative to the 'new class', in an anti-elitism that targeted his political enemies but not the political structure as a whole.

His version of culture war could be described as 'insider anti-elitism' — and contrasted with a different but related 'outsider anti-elitism'.

The most significant articulation of mid-1990s outsider anti-elitism was, of course, associated with Pauline Hanson. Despite disendorsement from the Liberal Party, she won her seat and then, in her notorious maiden speech, raised the kind of explicit anti-Asian and anti-indigenous rhetoric from which Howard had retreated.

Hanson positioned herself as an outsider, a maverick who identified the new class not merely with party rivals but with bankers, corporations, and politicians as a whole. Her supporters spelled out the implications of this in a bizarre book entitled *Pauline Hanson: the truth on Asian immigration, the Aboriginal question, the gun debate and the future of Australia,* a tract that took her version of culture war to its logical conclusion.

Its author, retired academic George J. Merritt, argued that Australia's elites were promoting 'a new religion of internationalism, of anti-white racialism, multiculturalism, feminism and Asianisation'. The schemes of the new class would, he said, come to a head in 2050, by which time the nation would be ruled by Poona Li Hung, a part-cyborg lesbian of multiracial descent 'felt by the World Government to be a most suitable president'.[5]

In 1996, six weeks after her maiden parliamentary speech, Hanson appeared on the TV current-affairs show *60 Minutes*. When journalist Tracey Curro asked if she was xenophobic, Hanson didn't know what the word meant. Her puzzled reply, 'Please explain,' was widely mocked, even by progressives.

A generation earlier, direct leftists committed to mobilising ordinary people might have been more careful about their attitudes to someone with limited education. But the nature of delegated politics — with its base among well-educated politicos — predisposed many to see the gaffe as evidence of Hanson's unfitness for public life.

For Hanson's supporters, by contrast, the exchange — and the liberal media's response — illustrated the politically correct mindset against which Hanson had been railing. Many of them might not have understood the word 'xenophobia' either, and they took the condescending reaction from the well-educated as representative of a broader disdain for people like them.

By the mid-1990s, as the academic Damien Cahill

explained, the 'new class' had become shorthand 'for a range of right-wing attitudes towards the welfare state, contemporary culture, Australian history and national identity, Aboriginal rights, feminism, environmentalism and multiculturalism'.[6]

The widespread acceptance of the schema depended on the contradictory relationship between insider and outsider anti-elitism. That is, when Hanson's victory, on an explicitly racist platform, sent shockwaves throughout the nation in 1996, Howard refused to join the chorus of condemnation. On the contrary, he discussed the outcome using the language of anti-PC — defending Hanson, and her right to speak, against her politically correct censors.

Howard understood that Hanson's rhetoric made his own culture wars more effective. He didn't need to make the kind of interventions that had cost him the leadership. He could leave the rhetorical bomb-throwing to Hanson — and then watch as the left became embroiled in often esoteric debates about history and national identity.

As for Hanson, Howard's interventions in the history wars — and his deployment of anti-PC — provided her with invaluable political cover in the public arena. No less a figure than the PM was defending her right to speak; no less a figure than the PM was denouncing political correctness and the dreaded 'new class'.

But a full understanding of the relationship between insider and outsider anti-elitism requires a closer look at the audience for culture war.

The rhetoric of culture war presented ordinary workers as being innately hostile to progressive elites. Accordingly, John Howard always spoke as if he represented suburbanites aggrieved at PC idiocy. Yet the Liberal Party remained, by and large, an organisation talking for — and supported by — the privileged and the wealthy.

After thirteen years of Labor's neoliberalism, workers might have grown cynical about the ALP and apathetic about trade unions, but there was little evidence of active working-class support for Howard.

Hansonism was different. As an outsider political formation, it could appeal to a more plebeian demographic. John Howard looked and spoke like a professional politician of the mainstream right; Pauline Hanson, on the other hand, conveyed an image of angry amateurism, like an aggrieved suburbanite who'd somehow stumbled into the parliament.

In the 1990s, commentators often assumed that Hanson's support came primarily from disaffected blue-collar workers. But the confident assertions about One Nation's 'working-class base' also reflected the growing acceptance by journalists of neocon ideas about the bigotry of ordinary people.

In the past, the left had taken for granted the progressive credentials of the working class. Wage labour, by its nature, fostered collectivity and solidarity. Workers toiled, for the most part, alongside others. They couldn't necessarily choose who those others were. Yet they needed unity if they were to win improvements to wages or conditions. There was, then, an imperative for, as the old slogan put it, workers of the world to unite.

This didn't mean that workers couldn't be prejudiced — or, for that matter, sexist or homophobic. If the fundamental competition between nation states necessarily fostered racism, so too did the competition foisted upon working people scrambling for jobs, housing, and resources.

'Workers are not only collective producers with a common interest in taking collective control over social production,' explained political theorists Bob Brenner and Johanna Brenner. 'They are also individual sellers of labor power in conflict with each other over jobs, promotions, etc. This individualistic point of view has a critical advantage in the current period; in the absence of class against class organisation, it seems to provide an alternative strategy for effective action — a sectionalist strategy which pits one layer of workers against another.'[7]

On this sectionalist basis, outsider anti-elitists could — and sometimes did — attract a working-class following. Blue-collar workers voted for One Nation; some even joined the party. But working-class racism tended to take a different form.

The Australian academic Peter Browne looked at racial attitudes towards the end of Howard's term, a period when Australians were generally believed to be deeply invested in anti-immigrant racism. He argued that the popular sentiment — that is, the sentiment amongst working people — varied according to the question being asked. Those polled directly about 'boat people', 'refugees', or 'immigration' expressed strong feelings. But when they were asked which issues shaped their votes, such topics barely registered. Very low numbers nominated 'refugees and asylum seekers' as either the most or second-most important issue, with health, education and tax scoring more highly (in that order).[8]

When working people — far more likely than the very wealthy to live, work, and socialise with those of different ethnicities — embraced racism, they often did so not so much on a deep ideological basis but as a proxy for the material issues that affected their lives directly: assuming, for instance, that immigrants would strain already overloaded services.

The commentators who described Hanson as a figure rallying the working class did so in many cases because they simply assumed that workers were xenophobic and bigoted. But the available research painted a different picture.

Michael Pusey conducted extensive interviews throughout the 1990s and the early 2000s to assess the impact of neoliberalism in Australia. He discussed conversations with the people he called 'battlers' or 'Hansonites', who were a large proportion of his focus groups in an older outer-western Sydney suburb and a significant factor elsewhere. They were, he said, unremittingly hostile to the economic reforms of the late 1980s and early 1990s, and had not recovered from the recession of 1991. They complaining of being stressed, of working long hours in insecure conditions, and of barely managing with their allotted tasks. The 'battlers' were angry, but in a reactive and unfocused fashion. They saw themselves as vulnerable and under siege, and loathed 'politicians, big business, free-loaders, elites and anyone who seems to be making claims on "the system" that appear to give them an unfair advantage in the merciless struggle to stay afloat'.[9]

Neoliberalism was experienced as particularly traumatising by those confronting remorseless competition in situations where they weren't protected by any kind of solidarity. The wageworkers Pusey described were generally employed in declining industries where the working class was fragmenting. They didn't, by and large, belong to unions; they felt themselves on the verge of unemployment. In rural towns and on the suburban fringes of big cities, in particular, older blue-collar workers were still unlikely to support Howard.

They could, however, be convinced to back Hanson.

Yet, overwhelmingly, the people Pusey quoted were not workers at all, even though many of them performed physical labour and conformed to the cultural stereotypes associated with the neocon depiction of the working class. He describes them as typically 'self-employed in their own business, for example, as courier operators, truck drivers, handyman repairers or car cleaners; they are doing virtually the same work as before but as subcontracted providers for often large companies'. In Marxist terms, they belonged to the blue-collar middle class: they were small-business operators desperately trying to keep themselves afloat amid the intensified waves of competition unleashed by industrial reform.

Historically, this was the traditional constituency for populism, a layer of people terrified of big companies (which drove them out of business), but also fearful of falling back into the working class (from which they felt they'd escaped). It was a milieu that could involve low educational levels but not necessarily low income levels, and one that could become anti-business or anti-labour, or a strange mixture of both.

Hanson's culture-war rhetoric resonated with such people by presenting them with an explanation for why they felt so permanently besieged. The anxiety that governed their lives, she implied, came from the nefarious elites who sneered at their work and their values.

Throughout this period, the other conservative parties were competing with the Hansonites for the same constituency, particularly outside the big cities. Murray Goot, for instance, looked at polling related to One Nation between 1996 and 1998, and concluded that 'many of those attracted to One Nation are voters who would otherwise support one or other of the Coalition parties — with the National Party, proportionately, bearing the greater loss'.[10]

But as an outsider anti-elitist, Pauline Hanson could present herself as the natural champion of the rural lower middle class. She came from the same small-business background herself — she'd run a fish-and-chip shop in Ipswich, after all. Her rambling, unpolished addresses often consisted simply of a list of scapegoats (such as Aborigines, Asians, elitists, and bludgers): a presentation that suited her audience's sense that they were being somehow done down by powerful forces all around them. At the same time, One Nation could openly attack the banks, big business, and 'economic rationalism' in a way that Howard and the Nationals simply couldn't.

For a period of several years, Hanson seemed to be the

primary beneficiary of the strange symbiotic relationship between insider and outsider anti-elitism, a relationship that gave new-class theory and anti-PC a prominence that they never subsequently lost. In the 1998 Queensland election, One Nation won 22.7 per cent of the vote — at the time, an astonishing result.

Yet rather than consolidating this success, the party went, almost immediately, into a prolonged internal crisis that saw many of its leading figures leave. Hanson resigned from One Nation in 2002, and was convicted of electoral fraud the following year (in a verdict that was overturned on appeal). Howard, by contrast, continued to lead the Liberals until 2007.

Their contrasting fortunes reveal the different dynamics of the two types of anti-elitism. Howard pursued culture war as the leader of a major party. He pitched his rhetoric to Pusey's small-business 'battlers', but he wasn't dependent upon them in the fashion that Hanson was. The Liberal Party relied far more on big corporations than it did on, say, handyman repairers in far north Queensland. The businessmen and bankers who supported the Liberals wanted Howard to deliver an economic climate conducive to profit-making — and, if culture war helped him do that, they had no objection. But they themselves cared more about profits than exposing the schemes of Poona Li Hung.

As a result, Howard enjoyed, in the 1990s and early 2000s, a stability that was quite lacking in One Nation.

Hanson's proximity to her supporters meant she could tap very effectively into their anxieties. But it also made her reliant on a base with no particular structural coherence. Small-business people were not predisposed to collectivity in the same way that the working class was. An owner-operator or a shopkeeper related to other owner–operators and shopkeepers as competitors, not as allies. That was why, historically, right-wing populist movements depended on strong — even dictatorial — leaders to hold their forces together. A charismatic figurehead could draw together the atomised individuals of the lower middle class in the same way that a magnet could amass iron filings. Yet this attraction depended on success — and as soon as the figurehead faltered, the filings dropped away.

In the Howard era, the insiders successfully exploited anti-elitism to use — and then defeat — the outsiders. A decade later, however, that dynamic would fundamentally change, as outsider anti-elitism moved to centre stage.

CHAPTER SIX

With us or with the terrorists

In the anti-corporate movement of the late 1990s, a particular anecdote circulated widely. It related to Subcommandante Marcos, the charismatic masked leader of the Mexican insurgent group known as the Zapatistas.

The story went that a government official tasked with suppressing the insurrection in the state of Chiapas had spread a rumour about Marcos's sexuality. The leader of the Zapatistas, the official said, was gay.

In macho Mexico, the charge might have been damning. But rather than angrily asserting his heterosexuality, Marcos responded with one of the poetic communiqués for which he'd become famous.

'Yes,' he replied, 'Marcos is gay. Marcos is gay in San Francisco, black in South Africa, an Asian in Europe, a Chicano in San Ysidro, an anarchist in Spain, a Palestinian in Israel, a Mayan Indian in the streets of San Cristóbal, a Jew in Germany, a Gypsy in Poland, a Mohawk in

Quebec, a pacifist in Bosnia, a single woman on the Metro at 10pm, a peasant without land, a gang member in the slums, an unemployed worker, an unhappy student and, of course, a Zapatista in the mountains.'[1]

The quote was repeated widely in countries a long way from Mexico, since Marcos's response captured the optimism, exuberance, and solidarity emerging at the end of the 20th century, during a brief — and now largely forgotten — revival of direct politics.

The anti-corporate movement was wiped so thoroughly from popular consciousness after its defeat that many no longer remember how, for a few years in the late 1990s, a series of huge demonstrations across the world drew together social activists from different causes and different backgrounds collectively demanding massive structural change.

The global justice movement (or GJM, as it was known) emerged most spectacularly during the so-called 'Battle of Seattle' in 1999, a protest against a summit of the World Trade Organisation, where the unity between environmentalists and members of the powerful teamsters' union was famously embodied in a placard reading 'Teamsters and Turtles: together at last'.

Thereafter, demonstrations ricocheted from country to country, in a pattern that recalled the cascading campaigns of the late 1960s. In September 2000, 20,000 people blockaded the World Economic Forum meeting in Melbourne; in July 2001, 200,000 people marched in Genoa against the summit of the World Trade Organisation.[2]

In a sense, the anti-corporate eruption represented a progressive response to the same historical moment that spurred the Republicans' embrace of culture war: the era following the collapse of the Soviet Union. Where neoliberalism's supporters popularised the idea of TINA ('There Is No Alternative'), the protests that followed Seattle raised the slogan 'Another World Is Possible', challenging accepted notions about globalisation, free-market economics, privatisations, and poverty. The actions brought together a diverse group of constituents — climate-change campaigners, Indigenous people, church groups, students, trade unionists, and others — to critique corporate power and the international order.

But the GJM didn't merely take on neoliberalism. It also challenged delegated politics. Rather than working with established political institutions, the GJM described parliament as fundamentally broken, dominated by corporate interests at the expense of the poor. Where delegated politics tinkered at the edges, GJM supporters demanded fundamental and institutional change. If delegated leftists prioritised the efforts of academics, or the heads of NGOs, or sympathetic politicians, the GJM depended on massive mobilisations that were often physically attacked by police and other state agencies.

There were many reasons for the decline of One Nation after 1998, not least the campaign backed by Tony Abbott about Hanson's campaign-financing that eventually culminated in her imprisonment.

But the marginalisation of the outsider anti-elitists also

coincided with the rise of the GJM. The S11 demonstration at Melbourne's Crown Casino in September 2000 raised many of the issues that preoccupied Hanson's supporters, such as the power wielded by banks and other massive financial institutions, the baleful consequences of unregulated free trade, and the anti-human dynamic of the market. But the protest also mobilised constituencies that Hanson demonised, such as Indigenous people, unionists, environmentalists, and others. As such, it entirely destroyed the culture-war frame. The corporate leaders and politicians inside the WEF were, unequivocally, the elite; the tens of thousands of protesters outside were, equally unequivocally, both ordinary and progressive, in a way that left no space for the faux anti-elitism of Pauline Hanson.

In Australia, as elsewhere, this brief glimpse of hope was shattered by terrible events.

In late August 2001, the federal government sent Special Forces soldiers to board the Norwegian freighter MV *Tampa* to prevent it bringing into Australian territory the 433 asylum-seekers who had been rescued by the crew. With an election looming, John Howard famously declared, 'We will decide who comes into this country and the circumstances in which they come,' as his government set in place the architecture of the 'Pacific Solution'.[3] A few weeks later, Islamist suicide terrorists crashed airlines into the Pentagon and the Twin Towers in New York.

Those two events brought culture war very much back to the fore. Howard went to the polls boasting that he was 'scorned by the elites and held in such disdain'. After the

Liberals' emphatic victory, the right-wing commentator Paul Kelly anticipated the culture war to come, spelling out the opportunity that the dominance of the delegated left presented to the right. Howard, he said, was 'going to focus on social policy this term and … smash the post-Whitlam political alliance between the working class and the tertiary-educated left that defines modern Labor … [Howard] senses that the 30-year alliance of the Australian left is collapsing because of its fundamental contradictions.'[4]

Obviously, 9/11 — and the ensuing 'War on Terror' — reshaped the political climate all across the world. The resurgence of militarised nationalism in the immediate wake of the atrocity confronted the GJM with a very different atmosphere. With war, terrorism, and national security dominating the headlines, the anti-corporate movement struggled with complicated political questions for which no immediate answers presented themselves.

Instead of the revived direct politics that many — and not just on the left — had expected, the 2000s unleashed a new militarisation. The Iraq and Afghanistan commitments justified massive expenditure on defence. The emphasis on terrorism brought national security into public life in ways unparalleled since the Great War, while the traditional bipartisan agreement over foreign policy gave way to almost total lockstep between the two major parties. Politicians draped themselves in khaki for photo ops; the funerals for soldiers killed in action were crowded with prominent government and opposition figures. ASIO and other security agencies, politically discredited after the Cold War, received massive injections of funding and political support, while parliament rushed through draconian anti-terror laws.

The War on Terror turbocharged the basic structure of right-wing culture war since, almost by definition, it accentuated the rhetorical gulf between 'battlers' and 'elites'. In times of peace, the old neocon presentation of the 'new class' as being implicitly disloyal might sound overheated. But 9/11 allowed the right to literalise its accusations, normalising a lexicon of appeasement and betrayal.

In wartime, treason wasn't simply a metaphor.

'Either you are with us or you are with the terrorists,' president George Bush explained to a joint session of Congress.[5]

Bush's press secretary, Ari Fleischer, countered criticisms of US bombing campaigns by warning that Americans needed 'to watch what they say, what they do'.[6] Attorney-general Ashcroft used an address to Congress to warn 'critics' that 'your tactics only aid terrorists — for they erode our national unity and diminish our resolve. They give ammunition to America's enemies, and pause to America's friends.'[7]

The journalist David Neiwert described the proliferation of what he called 'eliminationism': a right-wing discourse that posited liberals and the left not as opponents to be defeated, but as enemies to be annihilated.[8] Fox News star Bill O'Reilly, whose 'No Spin Zone' deliberately recalled the 'no-fly zones' imposed by Washington in Iraq, sounded less like a journalist and more like a combatant when he warned that those who opposed the military would 'be considered enemies of the state by me'. Network talking heads across

America produced a stream of eliminationist books, with titles like *Deliver Us from Evil: defeating terrorism, despotism, and liberalism* (Sean Hannity), *The Enemy at Home: the cultural left and its responsibility for 9/11* (Dinesh D'Souza), *The Enemy Within* (Michael Savage) and *Treason: liberal treachery from the Cold War to the War on Terrorism* (Ann Coulter).

The consequences for new-class theory were obvious. If progressives became 'enemies of the state', then, almost by definition, 'culture war' became an actual war — a struggle against traitors literally assisting the enemy. '[T]he rhetorical attacks on liberalism became enmeshed,' Neiwert argued, 'with a virulent strain of jingoism, which at first blamed liberals for the terrorism, then accused them of treason for questioning Bush's war plans'.[9]

By the 2000s, anti-elitism had taken over the media, partly for ideological reasons but also because it worked as a business model. The virtuous circle identified by right-wing politicians and activists neatly suited news organisations. As huge corporations, they benefited from deregulation and other neoliberal policies; as media outlets, they found new audiences with culture-war rage.

In the US, the repeal of the Fairness Doctrine in 1987 had allowed Rush Limbaugh, and others like him, to develop listenerships by pandering to the conspiratorial outsider anti-elitism that burgeoned during the Clinton years. In 1996, Rupert Murdoch hired former Republican strategist Roger Ailes to build a cable network along similar lines. Right from the start, Fox News prioritised issues by which it could foster resentments against progressives, adopting the slogan 'Fair and Balanced' to differentiate itself from the 'liberal media', and then building its anchors into populist figureheads. Although Fox remained very much a mouthpiece for the GOP, the network flirted with outsider anti-elitism, a balancing act facilitated by the influence exerted by a Republican president during a time of war.

The network's success spawned imitations both within the US (where, for instance, CNN developed its own culture-war fulminators) and around the world. In the 2000s, for instance, Murdoch's national broadsheet, the *Australian*, served a very similar role.

On 12 April 2003, a few days after the toppling of Saddam's statue in Baghdad, the editorialist for the *Australian* told the paper's readers that, apart from the Iraq War, 'there is another war of values, and it is the culture war being fought within the West. This is the war between those who feel that on the whole our values and traditions are sound, and those among the intellectuals who argue they are simply a cloak for racism and brute power.'[10]

As Robert Manne argued in a 2011 *Quarterly Essay*, the *Australian*, like Fox News, played the role 'not so much of reporter or interpreter but rather of national enforcer of those values that lie at the heart of the Murdoch empire: market fundamentalism and the beneficence of American global hegemony'.[11]

How, though, did it perform this function? It was, of course, the country's only national newspaper. But the *Australian* was kept afloat by Murdoch, despite losing money year after year. It never achieved mass circulation. Most

Australians didn't see the angry columns in its opinion section. Why did a paper read by so few people matter?

Manne explained that the dominance of its Canberra coverage meant that the *Australian* influenced the more widely circulating tabloids, such as the *Daily Telegraph* and the *Herald Sun*, as well as setting the agenda for outlets such as the ABC. Just as importantly, it was read by those who constituted what Manne called 'the political class' — 'politicians, leading public servants, business people and the most politically engaged citizens' — something that made it 'an active player in both federal and state politics'.

Such observations were correct, and provided a useful description of how culture-war talking points, which are often remarkably obscure, percolate through the media. But Manne's description revealed as much about the weakness of the right's anti-elitism as about its power.

Consider the prelude to war on Iraq.

The elaborate campaign to make the conflict possible has now been well documented. Many of the key figures in George W. Bush's cabinet — including Richard Perle, John Bolton, Paul Wolfowitz, Dick Cheney, and Donald Rumsfeld — belonged to a neoconservative thinktank known as the Project for a New American Century. Throughout the 1990s, PNAC had developed a particular vision of US foreign policy, predicated on the maintenance of imperial supremacy. 'At present,' it argued in 2000, 'the US faces no global rival. America's grand strategy should aim to preserve and extend this advantageous position as far into the future as possible.'[12]

Iraq loomed large in PNAC's thinking, partly because of its location in an oil-rich region, but also because Saddam Hussein's continuing rule after the war over Kuwait encouraged other minor strongmen who might think they, too, could flout America and survive. The neocons saw Iraqi regime change as essential to the US's strategic dominance, weakened by the first Gulf War and the humiliating American withdrawal from Somalia. As far back as 1998, PNAC sent an open letter to president Bill Clinton, urging Saddam's overthrow. As former Treasury secretary Paul O'Neill noted in his memoirs, Bush officials were considering removing Saddam almost as soon as Bush took office.

But 9/11 fundamentally changed the political possibilities, convincing leaders that they could now achieve goals they'd previously thought unrealistic. According to CBS news, Donald Rumsfeld mulled over an attack on Iraq within hours of the catastrophe in New York, even though all the intelligence pointed toward Osama bin Laden. Notes made by one of his aides documented Rumsfeld declaring that he wanted, 'Best info fast. Judge whether good enough hit Saddam Hussein at same time. Not only Osama Bin Laden. Go massive. Sweep it all up. Things related and not.'[13]

Iraq, then, was an example of this sweeping up. It was a war that the Bush clique chose, an invasion only possible after the shock of 9/11.

All 175 Murdoch newspapers backed the conflict with enthusiasm. Later, Murdoch himself would say, 'With our newspapers we have indeed supported Bush's foreign policy. And we remain committed that way.'[14] As Manne argued, the *Australian*'s foreign editor, Greg Sheridan, played a particularly important role in agitating for war, repeating and amplifying all of the talking points emanating from Washington and London.

The *Australian*'s coverage took for granted the basic logic of new-class theory, presenting suburban Australians as innately patriotic and thus seething with hostility towards the peaceniks of the chattering class. In this sense, the articles by Sheridan and his colleagues did indeed set the tone for Murdoch's tabloids, as well as shaping the views of the political class more generally.

Yet, crucially, they did not convince the people.

Most wars, almost by definition, begin with massive public support. Iraq was different. The international day of action against the war on 15 February 2003 mobilised millions of people (some estimates suggested as many as 30 million) in protests in over 60 countries and over 600 cities, with demonstrations held on every continent (thanks to a small contingent of research scientists holding a protest in Antarctica). Something like 400,000 people took to the streets of New York; three million marched in Rome; two million in London; three million in Spain; and so on.

'President Bush appears to be eyeball to eyeball with a tenacious new adversary,' explained the *New York Times*, 'millions of people who flooded the streets of New York and dozens of other world cities to say they are against war based on the evidence at hand.'[15]

Proportionately, Australia hosted some of the biggest demonstrations anywhere. The 300,000 people marching in

Melbourne were, for instance, the most significant rally in the city's history. Despite all the articles by Sheridan and his colleagues, despite the talk of nuclear explosions and WMDs devastating the West, far, far more Australians protested about Iraq than joined the famous Vietnam Moratorium protests.

In this sense, Iraq illustrated not so much Murdoch's power, but his weakness. Yes, culture war raged in the mass-circulation *Daily Telegraph* and *Herald Sun*, in articles where the rhetoric from the *Australian* was reframed in a more popular style. But media critics had long understood that the working-class subscribers to conservative tabloids weren't passive consumers but filtered what they read in various ways. If they bought the *Telegraph* to look over sporting results on the train, that didn't imply an interest in neoconservative foreign policy, nor an enthusiasm for prolonged fulminations against this or that pacifist academic.

Again, despite the claims of the new-class theorists, culture war didn't necessarily resonate with ordinary workers. Its effectiveness in the 2000s depended as much on the further evolution of the delegated left, which developed a kind of smug detachment from — and a contempt towards — its own traditional base.

The ascendancy of delegated politics had been predicated on both a decline in social struggle and the new opportunities emerging for the organisations, infrastructure, and activists of the social movements to play a role in governance. Bob Hawke's 'Consensus' depended on the Accord with the trade union movement, a strategy that gave social weight to the union apparatus. During the thirteen years of Labor in power, NGOs and former activists helped develop and implement policies in relation to multiculturalism, Indigenous affairs, the status of women, and so on, while progressives established an intellectual and organisational foothold within certain sectors of higher education.

But because delegated politics arose from the separation of an upwardly mobile layer from the movement's original base, the form that it initially took was deeply unstable, and contained the seeds of its own decline. The demobilisation of the people who'd helped build organisations led, inexorably, to a decline of the organisations themselves. From the 1980s on, union density steadily thinned — a trend mirrored within the NGOs, which had become increasingly incapable of activating their supporters in the old manner.

Though Labor had initiated the neoliberal turn, the implementation of neoliberal policies hollowed out the organisations upon which Hawke's consensus rested. The acceptance of market relations as the key form of social interaction necessarily eroded structures originally established through collective processes: markets recognised only consumers, not citizens.

Then, when the conservatives came to power, the governmental support given to NGOs and similar bodies vanished, replaced by an overt hostility that continued throughout the Howard years.

On the left, the ideas associated with delegated politics remained dominant. Increasingly, though, they existed without the infrastructure from which they'd emerged and on which, in many ways, they had depended.

Ironically, the massive Iraq protests provide one of the more spectacular illustrations of the left's weaknesses. For, despite the tremendous mobilisations, the invasion proceeded entirely on schedule, with John Howard telling Channel Seven dismissively: 'I don't know that you can measure public opinion just by the number of people who turn up to demonstrations.'[16]

In a previous period, the Moratoriums against the Vietnam War came as the culmination of a long campaign — one with the backing of the mass organisations built by direct politics. This meant that the individual demonstrations represented more than individuals on the street, since the participating groups spoke on behalf of broader constituencies. The existence of those groups gave the anti-war movement a stability such that it couldn't be taken for granted.

By contrast, the rally on 15 February 2003 was co-ordinated by a tiny group of people, most of whom were long-term activists. Few belonged to political groups; fewer still held positions within the trade union movement. The people who attended the vast protests did so, by and large, as individuals rather than in organised contingents — and that rendered the movement innately fragile.

The astonishingly rapid decline of the anti-war movement reflected, in part, the speed with which the coalition captured Baghdad. Quite understandably, many demonstrators couldn't see a point to further protests, given that the war seemed over almost as soon as it began. Yet, even when America's initial success gave way to a bloody stalemate, the demonstrations didn't revive, in part because the organisations that might have brought people back onto the streets had been atrophied by delegated politics.

This was the basis for the ironic, condescending tinge that came over progressive politics at that time — a mode most apparent in the left's evolving attitudes to the masses. The activists in the early years of the social movements often assumed that the population as a whole was indifferent to political change. On that basis, many progressives oriented themselves to the well-educated, assuming that only lawyers or politicians or other professionals would be interested in reforms on matters with which ordinary people didn't concern themselves.

The rise of direct politics depended on a recognition that the masses themselves could (and often would) fight to change society: that, in other words, the people were the motor of history. Conversely, the second phase of delegated politics corresponded with a different notion — a belief by activists that they were acting on behalf of a passive and perhaps indifferent constituency.

The new disdain for that constituency built, in turn, on the logic of delegated politics, at a moment in which that politics was collapsing. The notion that the population couldn't be mobilised became the conviction that the population was the problem — that if people weren't protesting the war, it was because they were idiots, gullible morons from whom nothing better could be expected.

The writer Emmett Rensin noted what he called 'the smug style' in politics in America, the propensity of progressives to identify the masses as stupid and perhaps dangerous.[17] The evolution of delegated politics into smug politics in Australia correlated with the failure of the anti-war movement to revive even as the War on Terror descended into pointless atrocities in Iraq and Afghanistan. Confronted with this failure — the inability to build an alternative to the carnage on the news every night — leftists could easily conclude the problem lay with 'Joe and Jane Sixpack', who were incapable of grasping the reality of the war.

Smug politics provided a context for Manne's description of the *Australian* as mandatory reading for the political class. Many progressives now saw the masses not as a force capable of improving society, but as a foolish and slightly terrifying reservoir of cultural and political backwardness: in essence, a mirror version of the right's culture-war portrayal. The *Australian* could act as a 'national enforcer', not because the battlers were roused against the left, but because activists in the political class, disoriented by the disappearance of their organisational base, had become convinced that they were. As the left lost confidence in the masses, the claims of the *Australian* — and similar institutions — to speak for the majority of the nation became more credible.

CHAPTER SEVEN

Smug politics

In August 2001, the radical writer and filmmaker Michael Moore presented HarperCollins with the manuscript for a scheduled book. It was still being edited when the 9/11 attack occurred. In the newly hyperpatriotic environment, the publisher baulked at releasing a book ridiculing George Bush and the Republican administration with chapters entitled 'Kill Whitey!' and 'A Very American Coup'.

Moore was instructed to revise substantially a work that would, HarperCollins decreed, appear under the more palatable title *Michael Moore: the American*. That extraordinary editorial intervention, which ostensibly came directly from Rupert Murdoch himself, attracted the attention of a group of librarians. The outraged book-lovers publicised Moore's predicament with sufficient vigour to ensure the text's release in its original form.

On the first day of its release, *Stupid White Men* sold all 50,000 copies of its print run — and by its fifth day was on its ninth printing.[1] Quickly, it became a defining statement of opposition to the Bush administration in the early phases of the War on Terror.

Moore had grown up in the union town of Flint, Michigan, and in many respects his book was an excoriation of the new administration for its cruel indifference to blue-collar Americans. But his title also reflected, as the GJM disintegrated, the new hegemony of smug politics.

Stupid White Men echoed a conviction common among progressives as soon as George Bush took power: namely, the man was an idiot. It was not an unreasonable suggestion. president Bush possessed, for instance, an extraordinary ability to mangle the English language.

'Our nation must come together to unite,' he explained at one point.

'Is our children learning?,' he said on another occasion.

'Families,' Bush said, during a third speech, 'is where our nation finds hope, where wings take dream.'[2]

In 2003, the journalist Frank Bruni explained that 'the Bush I knew was part scamp and part bumbler, a timeless fraternity boy and heedless cutup, a weekday gym rat and weekend napster'.[3] The president apparently loved fart jokes, and would let rip in front of new aides, confident that intentional flatulence helped the fresh appointees to settle in. When he received news of the 9/11 terror attacks, Bush didn't, at first, react — video footage that featured heavily in a subsequent Moore documentary showed him placidly continuing to read to schoolchildren from a book entitled *The Pet Goat*, as if he couldn't grasp the magnitude of the catastrophe.

Considerable evidence could thus be adduced for the Bush-was-a-moron theory.

But what followed politically? If Bush was the stupidest of the stupid white men, how had he come to power? Who had voted for him? Most of all, why weren't ordinary people rising up against the dangerous buffoon who ruled them?

Moore's book drew a simple conclusion. '[I]f you live in a country,' he wrote, 'where forty-four million can't read — and perhaps close to another two hundred million can read but usually don't — well, friends, you and I are living in one very scary place.' The moron president remained in power because the American people were themselves moronic. *Stupid White Men* described Bush as the 'idiot leader of an idiot nation', and explained that 'it comes as no surprise to foreigners that Americans, who love to revel in their stupidity, would "elect" a president who rarely reads anything — including his own briefing papers'.[4]

This was smug politics at its most overt, not just in the assessment of Americans as people 'who love to revel in their stupidity', but in its implication that the reader ('you and I') was, like Moore himself, smarter than the ordinary dopes whom the book discussed.

These formulations simply inverted the culture-war themes of the right. The Republican electoral campaign had, after all, contrasted George W. Bush's folksiness with the supposed superciliousness of his opponent, John Kerry, ridiculed as a windsurfing elitist. Bush was the guy with whom voters could have a beer; Kerry was a know-it-all who'd sneer at them in French.

The 9/11 atrocity and the outbreak of the War on Terror facilitated the Republican efforts to build on this image. Bush became a war president — but a war president of a special type. His minders cast him as John Wayne: a hero, to be sure, but also an everyman, whose greatness distilled the values of the heartland.

When Bush (who'd enlisted as a fighter pilot in Texas to evade the Vietnam War) arrived on an aircraft carrier in a flying suit to declare victory in Iraq, the NBC pundit Chris Matthews hosted Watergate felon Gordon Liddy to discuss his appearance.

'You know, he's in his flight suit,' said Liddy. 'He's striding across the deck, and he's wearing his parachute harness ... and it makes the best of his manly characteristic. ... He has just won every woman's vote in the United States of America. You know, all those women who say size doesn't count — they're all liars.'[5]

This grotesque exchange (and many others like it) provided credence to Moore's assessment of American idiocy. Here was a political culture at rock bottom, with sycophantic journalists enthusing about how the president, unlike his effete opponents, possessed a large penis.

Yet Moore's argument that the people themselves were responsible for Bush's antics implicitly reinforced the Republican case. The right equated the president with the American electorate, and distinguished them both from sneering elitists. Moore did exactly the same — except with the polarities reversed. Conservatives insisted the people and their leaders were wise; Moore judged them both moronic.

The first position was, for obvious reasons, far more politically successful than the second.

The decline of the traditional left-wing infrastructure — parties, organisations, NGOs, and the like — that previously might have given progressives a platform meant that left-wing or liberal celebrities took on an especial cultural significance during the Bush years. For many people on the left — especially as the internet became mainstream — politics became a matter of applauding or sharing an intervention by one or another progressive public figure. To cater to this need, a particular style of humour developed, associated with Stephen Colbert, Jon Stewart, and similar figures. Throughout the Bush years, progressives kept up their morale by blogging about the latest sketch in which Stewart cut some Fox News blowhard or another down to size.

Yet such victories were always Pyrrhic, since the ever-present snark of smug politics affirmed the right's new-class theory even as it mocked it.

The academic Jay Rosen identified something he called 'the cult of savviness' within professionalism journalism. By savviness, he meant the quality of being knowing, ironic, perceptive, shrewd, and unsentimental. 'Savviness is what journalists admire in others,' Rosen wrote. 'Savvy is what they themselves dearly wish to be. (And to be unsavvy is far worse than being wrong.)'[6]

The smug politics of the Bush era depended on the progressive embrace of savviness. The *Daily Show*–style gags only worked for a savvy crowd. Such jokes weren't intended to convince anyone. In fact, almost by their nature, they couldn't convince anyone. To get the sketch — which often consisted of little more than a clip of a conservative saying something stupid, followed by the liberal host mugging to the camera in mock amazement — the audience needed to already know and already accept the correct position.

The critic Emmet Penney explained: 'Each monologue, each snide quip about NASCAR nation was meant to affirm the viewers' sense that they felt the right feelings, saw the world the right way, and, most importantly, weren't hateful slobs who refused to floss their only tooth while singin' the songs of that old time religion.'[7]

During the second half of the 20th century, the right had generally lauded the hard sciences, contrasting the authority and certainty of men in white coats against the emotions of peace protesters and environmentalists. But almost immediately after taking office in 2001, the former oil man George Bush had declared he wouldn't implement the Kyoto Protocol on global warming.

Over the course of the decade, climate denialism became more and more central to culture war, with Republican consultant Frank Luntz explaining to his colleagues the necessity of sowing doubt in the science. The right's new-class attacks on elites morphed into a hostility for climate researchers and other experts, who were depicted as disdainful and contemptuous of the American way of life.

Understandably, progressives rallied to defend expertise. Colbert, for instance, satirically coined the term 'truthiness' in 2005 to describe 'the truth we want to exist'. Using his right-wing persona, he explained, 'Well, anybody who knows me knows I'm no fan of dictionaries or reference books. They're elitist. Constantly telling us what is or isn't true. Or what did or didn't happen.'[8]

Yet there was a common slippage in the progressive defence of truth and science, one facilitated by smug politics. It was a thing, after all, to defend scientists for their expertise in their field. But the call to 'listen to the science' often elided the difference between scientific authority and political authority. A climate researcher possessed specialised knowledge about the effects of atmospheric carbon. The response to her knowledge was, however, political — and politics wasn't a hard science.

Within a democracy, all votes were supposed to count equally. There were no 'experts' in the ballot box — and nor should there be. Yet in their (entirely justified) support for science, it became easy for progressives to equate technical expertise with political expertise — to imply that social issues had already been scientifically settled — and that anyone who disagreed was, by definition, an illiterate or a fool. The assertion of political expertise was another ironic mode, a form of compensation for disempowerment. If progressives couldn't influence society, that was the fault of society — or, more exactly, the people who were too stupid and too venal to appreciate the objective correctness of progressive ideas.

Rensin explained: 'What is important, after all, is to signal that you know these things. What is important is to launch links and mockery at those who don't. The Good Facts are enough: Anybody who fails to capitulate to them is part of the Problem, is terminally uncool. No persuasion, only retweets. Eye roll, crying emoji, forward to John Oliver for sick burns.'[9]

The new mode of smug politics was perfectly represented in the 2006 movie *Idiocracy*, a satire that presented the United States of the future as a dystopia dominated by overweight morons who spent their lives masturbating, eating junk food, and watching programs like *Ow! My Balls!*. The film outlined its set-up by explaining that American society had reversed evolution, allowing the foolish to breed while the intelligent remained childless. As a result, progressive and enlightened individuals were swamped by the backwardness of the great unwashed.

Liberals might not have said openly that they regarded ordinary people as so stupid that their procreation threatened civilisation itself. Yet as a satire, *Idiocracy* spelled out the deep elitism embedded in the prevailing critique of conservativism.

The consolatory power of the 'idiot nation' trope was obvious. If voters were slackjawed rubes, well, it couldn't be the fault of progressives that protests were small or that left-wing ideas lacked purchase. Activists committed to smug politics could take comfort knowing that the masses were too dumb to grasp the cogent arguments being presented to them.

But, politically, such rhetoric was disastrous. By dismissing the people as fools, progressives confirmed everything the culture warriors said: they openly embraced the condescending stereotype of the liberal elitist.

Thomas Frank made the point that, despite the new-class

presentation of progressives as elites, most leftists and liberals were not, and had never been, wealthy or powerful. The decline of delegated politics and years of conservative governance excluded many progressives from the influential jobs they might once have expected. This was, in fact, one of the reasons that celebrities and media identities became so important: they possessed a platform that most progressives did not.

Nevertheless, Frank argued, the increasing reliance on celebrities and the media meant that many ordinary people encountered progressive ideas in, say, magazine articles, where, as he put it, 'singers who were big in the seventies express their concern with neatly folded ribbons for this set of victims or that'. In such settings, progressive causes seemed 'a matter of shallow appearances, of fatuous self-righteousness … a politics in which the beautiful and the wellborn tell the unwashed and the beaten down how they should stop being racist or homophobic, how they should be better people'. [10]

If celebrity liberalism represented one of the more obvious manifestations of smug politics, it was far from being the only one. Consider, for instance, the rise of the so-called New Atheism, a phenomenon that played a surprisingly important role in the development of 21st century culture war.

Atheism itself was nothing new, with strands of atheistic thought identifiable even in the ancient world. The New Atheism — associated with a series of best-selling books published in the mid-2000s by Richard Dawkins, Sam

Harris, Christopher Hitchens, and others — didn't involve any particular philosophical innovation, other than perhaps illustrations drawn from recent developments in natural sciences. The novelty of the movement lay less in its ideas than in the context in which those ideas emerged.

In the past, critiques of religion had mostly been advanced by outsiders and radicals. Opposing institutional Christianity was a dangerous activity, exposing writers to all manner of persecution. For that reason, from the late 19th century on, non-belief was particularly associated with the labour movement and the left — so much so that, for many right-wingers, the epithets 'godless' and 'communist' became almost interchangeable.

By the 2000s, the Old Left and its traditions had largely collapsed, and the most prominent advocates of atheism after 9/11 were very much insiders. Men like Dawkins, Harris, Hitchens, and Daniel Dennett were powerful cultural figures, writing at a time when Christianity no longer possessed particular sway within the world of the academy or letters. When a white celebrity atheist took to the stage at a writers' festival, the foolish believers he mocked were not, by and large, in the audience. George Bush and other Republicans spoke about God, but elsewhere — in Australia and England, and the intellectual centres of America — fervent religiosity was found on the fringes on society, not at the centre.

The political consequences were obvious.

For Marx, of course, religion was the 'opium of the people'. Marx didn't mean that religion was simply a trick. Anyone who'd ever experienced severe pain knew that opium did more than merely befuddle, that at times it could be utterly necessary.

This was Marx's point: religion persisted because it played a social role. Yes, the privileged used God to buttress their power, but that was only part of the story. The rest of that famous quotation ran: 'Religion is the sigh of the oppressed creature, the heart of a heartless world, and the soul of soulless conditions ... The abolition of religion as the illusory happiness of the people is the demand for their real happiness. To call on them to give up their illusions about their condition is to call on them to give up a condition that requires illusions. The criticism of religion is, therefore, in embryo, the criticism of that vale of tears of which religion is the halo.'[11]

Marx wrote in response to the atheists of his day, most of whom imagined that God could be abolished simply by cogent argument. Against such people, he insisted that religion arose not from mistaken thinking but from intolerable social conditions. He took it for granted that religion wasn't simply a set of ideas, that it was simultaneously a cultural identity, an aesthetic, a system of morality, an organisational structure, and much else besides. Conceptually, religion might not have been coherent, but that only made it more appealing to those enduring an oppressive and arbitrary social order. For that reason, God could only be overcome by changing the world that made God seem necessary — by, as Marx put it, transforming 'the criticism of Heaven ... into the criticism of Earth'.

The New Atheists did not espouse the social atheism

associated with Marx. On the contrary, they put forward very much a version of the position he'd criticised, the old Enlightenment treatment of religion as a fallacious intellectual system.

This meant, almost by definition, that they regarded believers as idiots. If religion stemmed from intellectual inadequacy (and not, as Marx argued, from particular social conditions), it stood to reason that those with faith were stupider than those without it. Daniel Dennett's infamous suggestion that sceptics refer to each other as 'brights' was not simply a matter of clumsy phrasing, but a symptomatic expression of the elitism implicit in the New Atheist methodology.[12]

The New Atheists paid little attention to the social function of religion. They didn't ask why, so many centuries after the Enlightenment, the churches still found adherents. They already knew the answer — people went to church because they were dumb.

In other words, New Atheism replicated, in slightly different form, the framework of smug politics. It provided a socially acceptable basis for well-educated, and mostly white, liberals to sneer at suburban believers as risible dullards.

An atheism that approached religiosity as 'the sigh of the oppressed creature' might have facilitated an understanding of why Islam mattered so much in the Middle East, a region in which secular nationalism had become associated with dictatorships such as Saddam's. Such an atheism might have concluded that people in the area were far more likely to abandon God if they were able to enjoy peace, freedom, and prosperity. In the absence of those things, religion offered them a way to endure — and, at times, a way to organise.

If, on the other hand, religiosity was approached as a delusion — and nothing but a delusion — then the people of the Middle East should be assessed, by definition, as deeply and dangerously deluded — so much so that intervention by enlightened Westerners might, perhaps, be a regrettable necessity.

Several prominent New Atheists (most notably Christopher Hitchens) took the argument to its logical conclusion, becoming avowed neoconservatives and vocal advocates of Bush's wars. Others repeated rhetoric more usually associated with the Islamophobic right, with, for instance, Richard Dawkins explaining that Islam constituted the 'greatest force for evil today'.[13]

In this respect, the peculiar brand of smug politics represented by New Atheism was particularly destructive. Not only did it reinforce contempt for ordinary people, it also sowed confusion on the left in relation to one of the key controversies of the 2000s.

Almost by definition, war unleashed hatred against the perceived national adversary. The attacks by Osama bin Laden on New York in the name of Islamism — and then the ensuing invasions launched during the War on Terror — focused attention on the figure of 'the Muslim': identified not only as the foe abroad but also, and perhaps especially, as the enemy within.

The ensuing preoccupation with 'Islam' essentialised old Orientalist stereotypes about the East into an all-purpose explanation of the enemy. Most commentators knew almost nothing about the internal diversity of the Islamic world, let alone the specific political, social, and historical contours of Iraq and Afghanistan. Instead, they presented 'the Muslim' as an eternal archetype, a figure innately and forever fanatical, cruel, superstitious, and patriarchal.

When W. E. B. du Bois struggled to understand the categories of prejudice in 20th-century America, he eventually concluded that 'the black man' was defined not by his own traits but by his treatment: he was 'a person who must ride "Jim Crow" in Georgia'.[14] Had he been alive in 2001, du Bois might have suggested that 'the Muslim' was the person who was searched at the airport.

A new vocabulary transformed Australian politics. Hostility to Islam provided a suddenly respectable lexicon with which to voice the traditional opposition to foreigners seeking entry — and to those already here.

In her 1996 address, Pauline Hanson had said nothing whatsoever about Muslims. After 9/11, she effortlessly shifted gear, replacing her denunciations of Asianisation with a new vocabulary about the perils of Muslims. Indeed, in the 2000s it became acceptable to publish, even in mainstream newspapers, almost all the pre-war tropes of anti-Semitism, so long as the articles referred to Muslims and not Jews.

Muslims were disloyal. Muslims didn't assimilate. Muslims followed a strange and violent creed; Muslims were criminals and terrorists. The old and discredited fascist ravings about kosher food funding became the new, and widely voiced, concern about halal certification. Where, in the 1920s, Jew-baiters developed lurid fantasies about cosmopolitan financiers, in the 2000s outsider elitists clung onto Islamophobia, with the same mysterious influence attributed to jihadists that was once associated with the Elders of Zion.

The sudden upsurge of anti-Muslim sentiment posed a major challenge to progressives. The left understood what Hanson's attacks on Asians represented, but the conversation about Islam was disconcertingly different.

Under such circumstances, New Atheism played a particularly destructive role. Right at the moment when outsider anti-elitism made conspiratorial Islamophobia central to its appeal, New Atheists presented an ostensibly progressive argument that also identified Muslims as deluded and possibly dangerous.

Of course, New Atheists were not the cause of Islamophobia, an upsurge of which was probably inevitable after 9/11. But the traditional association of atheism with the left made the debates about Islam particularly pernicious. The emerging activists of the anti-Islamic far right were able to cloak their intellectual and sometimes historical connections with pre-war fascism by insisting that many progressives were also hostile to Muslims.

CHAPTER EIGHT

Why the culture wars didn't end

In 2006, a year before he won office, Australia's new opposition leader, Kevin Rudd, published a long and thoughtful essay in the *Monthly* about John Howard and the culture wars. In particular, he identified the seeming contradiction at work in the culture wars' virtuous circle — the tension between the conservative emphasis on values and the amorality of neoliberalism.

'Whether it is "family values", the notion of "community service" or the emphasis on "tradition" in the history wars,' Rudd wrote, '"traditional conservative values" are being demolished by an unrestrained market capitalism that sweeps all before it.'

For Rudd, this contradiction provided an opportunity for the ALP, a way to do politics differently. Labor, he suggested, could end the culture wars by building a diverse coalition against neoliberalism, spearheading a moderate alliance of those opposed to the disruption engendered by unfettered market forces.

'Given that John Howard's neoliberal experiment has now reached the extreme,' he concluded, 'the time has come to restore the balance in Australian politics. The time has come to recapture the centre.'[1]

Rudd's emphatic victory in 2007 — and then the triumph of Barack Obama over John McCain and arch-culture warrior Sarah Palin in 2008 — proved, in the minds of many commentators, the validity of his critique.

'The culture wars are over,' proclaimed Richard Nile in the *Australian*.[2]

'I doubt the culture wars will have much of a future,' agreed Mark Bahnisch on the ABC blog *Unleashed*.[3]

After Obama's win, the argument emerged internationally. In the *Guardian*, Paul Harris detected 'signs of a fundamental shift away from the so-called "culture wars" that have raged across American public life'.[4]

When Barack Obama announced his candidacy for the presidency in early 2007, he did so in Springfield, Illinois, in front of the old state capitol, the setting for Abraham Lincoln's iconic 'House Divided' oration. In the speech he delivered, Obama declared his opposition to the Bush agenda. He reminded listeners of his unease about the war in Iraq; he voiced his determination to fight climate change; and he denounced the cruelty of the Republican economic agenda.

Like Rudd, Obama emphasised the possibility of social unity over culture-war rupture. He'd learned, he said, the possibility of 'disagree[ing] without being disagreeable

— that it's possible to compromise so long as you know those principles that can never be compromised; and that so long as we're willing to listen to each other, we can assume the best in people instead of the worst'.[5]

A new kind of politics — a moderate, civilised alternative to what Rudd had dubbed the neoliberal 'Brutopia' — seemed possible, in part because, by the end of the Howard and Bush years, anger was growing everywhere against those with genuine power.

Immediately after 9/11, conservatives had used the War on Terror to paint their opponents as effete, if not actually disloyal: a fifth column assisting the jihadis on the cultural front. But by the mid-2000s, that no longer washed. The military interventions championed by Howard and Bush had proved catastrophic. Trillions of dollars had been expended in Iraq and Afghanistan, and, rather than liberating the populace, the deployments had turned both nations into charnel houses. Denunciations of the cultural elite as soft on terror no longer worked in quite the same way when so much of what the conservative leaders had promised turned out to be patently false.

Then came the Global Financial Crisis.

Teachers, social workers, and academics — those familiar stalking horses of the culture war — couldn't be blamed for wrecking the economy, no matter how snooty they were. As the stock market plummeted, the finger of blame pointed inexorably at the financiers and corporate chiefs who'd become fabulously wealthy even as the system over which they presided lurched into the greatest economic slowdown in a generation.

Under these circumstances, culture war no longer seemed credible. Yet the approach articulated by both Rudd and Obama — the formation of a broad, moderate coalition to undo the conservative agenda — contained its own contradictions.

Certainly, the market worked to dissolve the traditions, customs, and values associated with cultural conservatism. Many of the changing mores that affronted right-wing Christians, for instance, stemmed directly from the commodification of sexuality, which, in turn, derived from the neoliberal insistence on the cash register's applicability to every aspect of human behaviour. Pornography — the bête noire of the Christian right — was an obvious result of market theory, the inevitable result of the economic policies promoted by candidates for whom the Christian right had voted.

But Rudd's plan for a pragmatic alliance against the culture warriors failed to grasp how the internal contradiction he recognised had been managed during the Howard years.

In particular, neither Rudd nor Obama recognised the centrality of rage to the culture-war virtuous circle. When Pusey's 'battlers' and 'Hansonites' voted for Howard or One Nation, they did so precisely because they felt the organising principles of their lives coming apart — and were accordingly looking for someone to punish. They voted out of desperation; they voted because they hated and despised the cultural elites they identified (wrongly) as responsible.

Their anger — and its regular venting against carefully

chosen targets — completed the culture-war virtuous circle. By channelling political energy against the liberal elites, the right could ensure the election of pro-market candidates, who would, in turn, lay the ground for further culture-war rage. By simply focussing on contradiction — and not how that contradiction was resolved — Rudd's analysis missed the totality, something that doomed his solution to failure.

Obama's formulation about 'disagreeing without being disagreeable' — a version of Rudd's pragmatic-coalition idea — might have sounded like common sense, but in people who'd lost their houses in the GFC — or who, like those Pusey interviewed, simply found the modern economy unbearably stressful — exhortations to be agreeable were likely only to generate further outrage, particularly when they were couched in the supercilious style of smug politics. Such people didn't want politeness. They wanted redress — and if they couldn't have redress, they'd settle for revenge.

Obama had pledged to undo the Bush agenda; he'd also promised to replace rancour with what Harris described as 'moderation and toleration'. But it wasn't possible to end the wars in Iraq and Afghanistan without tackling the militarists who'd launched them. Guantanamo couldn't be closed without a campaign against the conservatives (and many liberals) who'd made support for arbitrary detention almost a question of principle. Carbon couldn't be reduced without challenging the fossil-fuel corporations and their lobbyists. Most of all, any serious challenge to inequality meant conflict with the corporations who profited from the status quo.

In a different era, a strong peace movement might have built on the hostility to the Iraq war, insisting that the troops come home at once and that the leaders responsible for the debacle be held to account, just as a healthy trade union movement might have capitalised on the anti-corporate sentiment to push for wage increases and wealth distribution.

But with the organisations of the left in disarray, Obama began abandoning or watering down his key promises almost at once. Rather than fanning the hostility against the elites responsible for war and economic chaos, he urged unity and reconciliation, which, ironically, provided the perfect conditions for the revival and intensification of right-wing culture war. If the material elites weren't held to account, an obvious opening existed to shift the blame for America's circumstances to Obama as the leader of the so-called cultural elites.

'I told you yesterday, buckle up your seatbelt, America ... Find the exit closest to you and prepare for a crash-landing because this plane is coming down because the pilot is intentionally steering it into the trees! Most likely, it will happen sometime after Christmas.'[6]

That was Glenn Beck, the Fox News presenter who, perhaps more than anyone else, personified the revived outsider anti-elitism of the Obama era.

On his show, Beck portrayed Obama as a vengeful black militant, a man who, he explained, had 'a deep-seated hatred for white people, or the white culture'.[7]

Racism provided an obvious way to organise hostility against the nation's first black president, and Beck — and others like him — exploited racial tensions to the hilt. But they did so within the familiar new-class framework, using Obama's blackness to signify the broader agenda of the politically correct elite who were white-anting traditional America.

The continuing decomposition of political authority and institutions — as well as the disastrous record of the Bush presidency — had weakened the appeal of the old insider anti-elitism. Symptomatically, while Beck was certainly conservative, he wasn't a traditional GOP operative. A former alcoholic who'd sobered up through a conversion to Mormonism, he'd launched his media career as an apolitical radio personality specialising in stunts and gimmicks — and he put that experience to good use when he transitioned to political commentary.

On a typical episode, Beck drew frenzied chalkboard diagrams to represent the forces arrayed against patriots. He warned viewers that the Federal Emergency Management Agency might herd conservatives into camps; he explained that the UN was seeking to an install a One World government through its Agenda 21 program; and he claimed that environmentalists were praying to the Babylonian god Baal.[8]

Most of all, he mirrored and amplified the anxieties of his viewers, sobbing uncontrollably before making maudlin promises to die for his country. Even as Obama and his supporters sought to dampen the public's rage, Beck (and a growing number of imitators) amplified it. He agreed that a tiny minority had benefited from the disastrous economy; he, too, thought something had gone terribly wrong in Iraq and Afghanistan. But rather than attacking those with real power, Beck blamed the so-called 'cultural elite': the cosmopolitan liberals who, he said, were preparing a politically correct form of totalitarianism.

Outsider anti-elitism resonated in the wake of the GFC, precisely because its extremism suited the mood of the times. When Beck attacked a liberal academic as 'anti-white', he didn't make an old-fashioned conservative argument about the need for a different curriculum. Instead, he implied that the entire educational system had been infiltrated by globalists — and that the PC elite were deceiving Americans about the real state of affairs.

'President Obama, why don't you just set us on fire?' he cried, in another typical monologue. 'For the love of Pete, what are you doing? Do you not hear — do you not hear the cries of people who are saying stop?'[9]

The formation of the so-called Tea Party provided an even starker illustration of the weird dynamic of outsider anti-elitism.

In 2009, Obama launched a program of subsidies intended to help homeowners to avoid foreclosure. In the abstract, such a measure might have resonated with a populism of the left: a movement in support of measures assisting the victims of the downturn. But that wasn't what happened. After the administration had expended billions bailing out Wall Street, the piecemeal subsidies provided to poor — and disproportionately black — householders came too little and too late to inspire a working class still buffeted by the GFC.

The policy did, however, enrage financiers. In particular, the program inspired the CNBC personality Rick Santelli to deliver an impromptu rant broadcast live from the Chicago stock exchange.

'This is America!' he shouted, to cheers from the traders. 'How many of you people want to pay for your neighbor's mortgage?'[10]

Santelli urged listeners to fight back against Obama's 'socialism'. He didn't, however, call for a vote for the Republican Party. Instead, he invoked the Boston Tea Party, the incident in which American revolutionaries dumped British goods into the harbour rather than comply with the authorities. It was time, Santelli said, for a new Tea Party.

Santelli's rant circulated widely, promoted by the *Drudge Report* and various conservative bloggers. The initial Tea Party protests were comparatively small until Fox News threw its weight behind demonstrations scheduled for Tax Day 2009. The movement that ensued was explicitly pro-capitalist and financially backed by big conservative advocacy organisations such as Americans for Prosperity and FreedomWorks (an organisation funded by the billionaire Koch brothers).

Yet, as Theda Skocpol and Vanessa Williamson stressed, the Tea Party couldn't be dismissed as merely an 'astroturf' creation of corporate money. 'This take on the Tea Party as a kabuki dance entirely manipulated from above simply cannot do justice,' they argued, 'to the volunteer engagement of many thousands of men and women who travel to rallies with their homemade signs and, even more remarkably, have formed ongoing, regularly meeting local Tea Party groups.'[11]

The available data suggested that members of the movement were white, relatively wealthy ('comfortably middle-class', as Skocpol and Williamson put it), well educated, and middle-aged or older. Furthermore, they were inspired by the insurgent sentiment invoked by Santelli. A *Washington Post* survey of Tea Party activists in 2010 found that, while 92 per cent said that opposition to Obama helped build the movement, 87 per cent also spoke of dissatisfaction with Republican leaders.

The rank-and-file Tea Partiers were, in other words, nearly as hostile to the establishment right as they were to the Democrats, so much so that they'd go on to threaten a shutdown of the federal government — much to the horror of traditional capitalist lobby groups such as the Business Roundtable and the Chamber of Commerce.

The loose structure of the movement meant that the Tea Party quickly became home to views rather more esoteric than that expressed in Santelli's original pro-market diatribe. Religious conservatives, along with various libertarians and fringe parties of the far right, such as the Oath Keepers and the John Birch Society, recognised the recruitment opportunity. As Neiwart says, the formation of the Tea Party was 'when the paranoid alternative universe of the conspiracist Patriot movement began to meld with the world of Fox-watching conservatives'.[12]

Again, though, outsider anti-elitism might not have proved so successful for the right had the left not been unwittingly reinforcing some of the main culture-war postulates.

In 2010, the comedians Jon Stewart and Stephen Colbert organised a rally of perhaps 100,000 people in the National Mall of Washington, DC.

Between 2002 and 2007, 65 per cent of income growth in the US had gone to the top 1 per cent of the population. The US Census Bureau then recorded that between 2005 and 2009, the median net worth of the lowest fifth of income earners fell 50 per cent, rendering income inequality higher than at any time since the Great Depression.

By 2010, figures showed that the US was a less equal society than the Ivory Coast, Ethiopia, and Pakistan.[13] Some four million Americans survived on food stamps, and 50 million lacked healthcare, while, on 2009 figures, the top 25 hedge-fund managers earned, on average, more than $1 billion each.[14]

Under such circumstances, Stewart and Colbert might have mobilised their fans to call for income redistribution, or higher wages, or an investigation into the financiers responsible for the GFC (many of whom walked away from the economic wreckage with huge bonuses).

But that wasn't what happened. Rather, Stewart advertised his event as a 'rally to restore sanity' — with Colbert, in character as a conservative pundit, hosting a parallel 'March to Keep Fear Alive'. The intervention was intended to counter (and satirise) the hysterical rhetoric emanating from people like Beck and the Tea Party, under the slogan 'Take it down a notch for America'.[15]

In and of itself, the rally was inconsequential — a media stunt by two comedians. But it provided a salutary illustration of a view commonly held by liberals committed to smug politics: the notion that a centrist constituency could be mobilised against culture-war extremism.

In the abstract, the progressive desire to quell social anger with calm and reason might have seemed laudable. Yet in the specific circumstance in which it was held, the rally was at best tone-deaf, and at worst entirely counterproductive. Beck and the Tea Party validated the anger of people terrified by economic uncertainty and pointless wars. To someone who'd lost their house in the financial crash — or who simply felt unable to cope in a system lacking mercy for the weak — the 'Rally to Restore Sanity' entailed wealthy TV personalities mocking their anger as insane and urging them to calm down.

Once again, the smug sensibility prevailing on the left reinforced the central contention of the culture-war right — the claim that liberals saw themselves as better than ordinary people.

Stewart described himself as 'celebrating moderation' at a time when many Americans felt desperate. By contrast, the shrill conspiracy-mongering and ostentatious empathy of Beck and similar culture warriors matched a prevailing sense among Fox News viewers that something had gone terribly wrong in America. The outsider anti-elitism that emerged in that time laid the basis for the emergence of Donald Trump.

In Australia, the situation played out slightly differently.

After Rudd's victory, Robert Manne published an array of liberal intellectuals offering advice to the new PM under the hopeful title *Dear Mr Rudd*: essentially, a programmatic document for a resurgent delegated politics.[16] In response, Janet Albrechtsen snarked that the elites were 'pitching to the wrong man', since 'Rudd was the Labor Party's perfect alternative conservative candidate' — a man who, on almost every issue, had aligned himself with the Howard government.[17]

Both, in a way, were right.

Kevin Rudd's ascent both reflected the institutional crisis within Labor and offered a partial solution to it. Rudd had campaigned on a wave of anti-Howardism, with the union-led campaign against WorkChoices playing an important role in his triumph. The centrality of the ACTU to the election echoed, for many, Hawke's win in 1983. It wasn't outlandish to imagine Rudd reaching out to the intellectuals of the left in a reprise of Hawke-style delegated politics.

Indeed, in early 2008, the PM announced the 'Australia 2020 summit', a gathering of prominent people intended to 'help shape a long-term strategy for the nation's future' that echoed the Hawke government's famous 1983 economic forum. Many in the progressive intelligentsia saw, not without reason, the 2020 summit as evidence that delegated politics was back.

'[T]he rhetoric has shifted and the faces changed,' wrote David Marr. 'These are the early days of the post-Howard era, but it's already possible to grow a little nostalgic for elite bashing. All gone.'[18]

Yet, in another respect, the venture implicitly recognised that the post-Howard era would not be like the pre-Howard era. Hawke brought to his summit the weight of his authority as a former union leader. The meeting itself consisted of powerful organisations representing key constituencies: journalist Katharine Murphy noted that 'newspapers [had] identified Hawke's delegates not by their names but by their associations'. Rudd's forum, by contrast, was purely advisory and, as Murphy said, 'a celebration of rampant individualism'.[19]

Unlike Hawke and Keating, Rudd lacked a background within the labour movement. Rather than building a traditional factional fiefdom, his power within the party depended on his personal popularity. The 2020 summit was, in that respect, a reflection of Rudd's basic approach. By staging the event outside parliament so soon after an election, Rudd posited the assembled celebrities as an alternative to a broken political system, in a gesture to the disaffected constituency of culture war.

At the same time, the whole forum reeked of a contempt for the electorate as a whole. Rather than presenting progressive ideas to the voters, the PM was inviting unelected worthies to dream up innovative policies once the election was safely over. In that sense, it was pure smug politics, predicated on an idea that ordinary people couldn't accept radical notions, and that fresh thinking could emerge only when film stars, university professors, and journalistic high-flyers were encouraged to brainstorm, free of any democratic accountability.

Unsurprisingly, the event was a shambles, devoid of meaningful outcomes and memorable only for the footage of Rudd dandling Cate Blanchett's baby on his knee.

On the one hand, Rudd represented a repudiation of Howard; on the other, he promised continuity with his predecessor, pledging to govern as an economic and social conservative. His personal popularity allowed him to float, for a while, serenely above the contradictions he embodied, even as they manifested themselves within his government as administrative gridlock.

Eventually, though, the contrast between Rudd's huge promises and his unwillingness to engage in the struggles necessary to fulfil them allowed Tony Abbott to reprise Howard-style insider anti-elitism.

Rudd's signature commitment to climate-change action illustrated the process. By positing global warming as the greatest moral challenge of a generation, he implied he'd lead something akin to direct politics: a prolonged campaign involving ordinary Australians in restructuring their society along environmental lines.

Rudd came undone not because, as the Liberals retrospectively insisted, the public didn't care about the issue, but precisely because they did. When, in late April 2010, Rudd walked away from his much-touted 'Carbon Pollution Reduction Scheme', his popularity collapsed, leaving in its wake a growing cynicism about the whole issue. The gulf between rhetoric and reality made the climate seem less like an emergency and more like an affectation, a trendy cause espoused by sanctimonious politicians and celebrities — precisely as Abbott's culture-war campaign insisted.

Julia Gillard's eventual coup against Rudd failed to address any of the underlying issues wracking the government.

A career politician, Gillard lacked Rudd's outsider appeal (as limited and partial as that had been), even as the ALP's traditional base continued its slow disintegration. Gillard's own inclinations come from delegated politics, but, without the mass organisations that made delegated politics viable, she, too, adapted the social and economic conservatism that Rudd had embraced.

Where American outsider anti-elitism drew upon a deep reservoir of racism, Abbott relied on traditional sexism to help revive Howard-style insider anti-elitism. Gillard was, after all, Australia's first female prime minister. It was relatively easy for Abbott — and the various shock-jocks who assisted him — to imply that, as such, Gillard represented an inversion of the natural order and thus a personification of everything going wrong in the country.

Yet the sexist attacks on Gillard were symptoms rather than causes of the problems her government faced: essentially, the same as those that brought down Rudd. Without any clear support base for her program, Gillard could easily be portrayed as an out-of-touch insider installed by the factions, a Canberra elitist obsessing about PC shibboleths such as climate change.

Gillard's eventual downfall, and the astonishing return of Kevin Rudd, showed that instability and culture war were the new norm.

CHAPTER NINE

The nature of identity

In 1937, a former slave from Oklahoma told a story about her childhood. The woman recalled how, immediately after emancipation, she was approached by her old master. He addressed her in the customary way: 'What you doing, nigger?'

The woman had, however, been speaking to the Northern soldiers. She knew what the Civil War meant; she understood the significance of the South's defeat. As a result, she didn't reply in the usual fashion.

'I ain't a nigger,' she said. 'I's a Negro and I'm Miss Liza Mixon.'

The infuriated white man attacked her with his whip.[1]

The story illustrates the centrality of cultural identity to the experience of oppression and resistance.

When Mixon retold the story in her old age, she did so with incredulity at her own naivety. It wasn't that she thought the appellation didn't matter. On the contrary, she knew it mattered so much that she was amazed that, as a child, she'd once been brave enough to insist upon dignified treatment.

Today, any debate about culture wars — indeed, about the contemporary political climate — needed to come to terms with so-called identity politics.

Unfortunately, this was not at all simple, since the term meant both too little and too much. It could be argued that 'identity politics' had been rendered an entirely unintelligible phrase, weighed down by decades of use and abuse, and increasingly used merely as a pejorative.

'Perhaps the strangest thing about identity politics,' commented the American activist Sherry Wolf, 'is that it's a political orphan — nobody wants to claim it as her own.'

But Wolf also argued that despite becoming 'a philosophical punching bag', identity politics 'remains the underlying politics of the left over the last thirty-five years or so'.[2]

The term's ubiquity meant that, for many people, both on the left and the right, 'identity politics' simply denoted opposition to racism, sexism, homophobia, or any other oppression, particularly one focused on language or culture.

Nevertheless, 'identity politics', in the way it was understood today, had a specific history, connected to the strategic shifts on the left — the progression from direct to delegated and then smug politics.

The term seems to have been first employed in 1977 by a group of African-American lesbian feminists organised as the Combahee River Collective. In a justly famous manifesto, they declared that their emphasis on fighting their own oppression was 'embodied in the concept of identity politics. We believe that the most profound and potentially most radical politics come directly out of our own identity, as opposed to working to end somebody else's oppression ...'[3]

The statement reflected a broader interest in identity that developed and percolated throughout the New Left during the direct-politics period. Many of the more influential theorists of the time — from Frantz Fanon to Che Guevara — stressed, in different ways, the necessity for the oppressed to develop a new self-perception, one not marred by the passivity and despair instilled by the oppressor.

Different radical groups employed a technique known as 'consciousness raising', in which participants were urged to discuss their own lives and experiences so as to make public the effects of oppression in realms previously imagined as private.

'It seemed clear,' said Kathie Sarachild, an early activist in women's liberation, 'that knowing how our own lives related to the general condition of women would make us better fighters on behalf of women as a whole.'[4]

The emphasis on identity extended to celebrities who identified with the wider tumult.

In 1967, the boxer previously known as Cassius Clay fought a heavyweight bout against Ernie Terrell. But he did so under a new name, Muhammad Ali.

'Cassius Clay is a slave name,' the fighter insisted. 'I didn't choose it, and I didn't want it. I am Muhammad Ali, a free name — it means beloved of God — and I insist people use it when speaking to me and of me.'

Terrell refused to acknowledge an identity associated with Malcolm X's Nation of Islam. In the pre-fight publicity, he referred to his opponent as 'Clay'.

Throughout all fifteen rounds of the bout that followed, Ali loudly demanded of his outclassed opponent, 'What's my name, fool? What's my name!'

Ali's example illustrated how, in the context of widespread political unrest, identity was a widely seen process as much as a state, an act of self-definition dependent on the recognition of political enemies and friends.

'Identity was something to be stressed,' noted Andrew Hartman, 'it was something to grow into or become. Only by becoming black, or Chicano, or a liberated woman, or an out-of-the-closet homosexual — and only by showing solidarity with those similarly identified — could one hope to overcome the psychological barriers to liberation imposed by discriminatory cultural norms.'[5]

By joining the much-maligned Nation of Islam and changing his name accordingly, Ali aligned himself not only with African-American militancy but with the colonial world in general and the Vietnamese liberation struggle in particular.

'I ain't got no quarrel with them Viet Cong,' he said in February 1966, while training for his fight against Terrell. Later, he was quoted as saying, 'No Viet Cong ever called me nigger.'

Importantly, Ali's new identity was also a repudiation of respectability within the African-American community. The

Nation of Islam frightened whites, but it also appalled many middle-class African Americans, many of whom thought Terrell's resistance to a then exotic-sounding appellation made sense.

Ali established his new sense of self, at least in part by differentiating himself from Terrell, whom he dismissed as 'an Uncle Tom nigger'.

Throughout the 1960s, different political currents developed different strategic orientations to identity. In all the social movements, a version of separatism emerged: a tendency in which activists insisted that people belonging to particular oppressed groups should organise on their own, withdrawing from others who didn't share their experience or identity.

Interestingly, though, when the Combahee River Collective coined the term 'identity politics', they did so explicitly in opposition to 'separatism'. The women wrote:

> Although we are feminists and lesbians, we feel solidarity with progressive Black men and do not advocate the fractionalization that white women who are separatists demand ... We realize that the liberation of all oppressed peoples necessitates the destruction of the political-economic systems of capitalism and imperialism as well as patriarchy. We are socialists because we believe that work must be organized for the collective benefit of those who do the work and create the products, and not for the profit of the bosses ...[6]

In other words, theirs was quite clearly a direct-politics perspective. They were arguing to fight sexism and racism through systemic, radical change, conducted by the masses of ordinary people. More exactly, their manifesto called for the overthrow of capitalism. The assertion of identity — the point for which the document became famous — was intended to be read in that context. They thought that if black women recognised and fought against their oppression as black women, they would necessarily join a direct struggle against other structural injustices.

Yet by 1977, when the statement was published, the direct-politics tendency was receding, with the delegated politics that would dominate the next decades becoming ascendant.

The manifesto took for granted its members' involvement in strikes, demonstrations, protest campaigns, and the like. It also took for granted a broader movement, in reference to which all radical tendencies defined themselves in one way or another. Increasingly, though, that context no longer existed, as the intellectual and organisational centre of the radicalism moved from the streets to the university.

The shift provided an opening for a different understanding of identity, one that related especially (though not exclusively) to the campuses of the 1980s. By then, the structural change (revolution, no less!) that the Combahee River Collective associated with identity politics no longer resonated with an upwardly mobile cohort of former activists now in mid-career. Alex Callinicos explained:

This was the decade when those radicalised in the 1960s and early 1970s began to enter middle age … Most of them had by then come to occupy some professional, managerial or administrative position, to have become members of the new middle class, at a time when the overconsumptionist dynamic of Western capitalism offered this class rising living standards.[7]

In his important essay 'Identity Crisis', Salar Mohandesi described how activists (particularly, though not exclusively, in the universities) 'began to insist that personal experiences created relatively stable identities, that everyone possessed one of these identities, and that politics should be based on the search for that identity and its subsequent naming, defense, and public expression'. In the 1960s, he said, radicals had argued that exploring personal experience could help people identify oppression and spur them to fight against it. Later activists, however, came to argue for a direct and unmediated link between one's identity and one's politics, so much so that identity became 'a political project in itself'.[8]

Advocates of delegated politics presented identity as a fixed category, a basis for political organising. They claimed that race, gender, sexuality, and other 'identities' correlated with particular political ideas, attitudes, and demands that wouldn't, couldn't, and shouldn't be embraced by those without the lived experience of that identity. Where the Combahee River Collective saw liberation coming through collective solidarity, the new version of identity politics held that those outside a certain identity could provide, at best, secondary assistance as so-called 'allies' to the oppressed.

As Mohandesi argued, the argument usually involved an unresolved determinism, with activists implying a simple correspondence between a person's experiences and his or her political attitudes. In practice, however, identity did not work like that, as Stonewall had shown with especial clarity.

The riots in 1969 became so significant because, in the wake of the police raid, men (and some women) who had been ashamed of their sexuality fought back against the NYPD with chants of, 'I'm a faggot and I'm proud of it!'

At one point, the officers — accustomed to brutalising gay men without resistance — found themselves confronted by a chorus line of high-kicking drag queens who were singing:

> We are the Stonewall girls
> We wear our hair in curls
> We have no underwear
> We show our pubic hairs![9]

Afterwards, the poet Allen Ginsberg commented famously that 'the guys [of Stonewall] were so beautiful — they've lost that wounded look that fags all had ten years ago'.[10]

Stonewall illustrated the relationship between direct politics and identity formation. The street resistance by (often) previously apolitical gay men depended on the construction of a new self, even as, by the act of resisting, the men recognised themselves as worthy of the liberation they'd begun to demand.

Ordinary people changed themselves as they changed the society that oppressed them.

Resistance did not derive from identity — at least, not in any simple way. After all, not all the club-goers fought back or applauded the new defiance. Many of the middle-class activists associated with Mattachine Society — men who, for decades, had been some of most visible and courageous advocates of homosexual rights — were, as Wasserman noted, 'incensed at the antics of rioters'.

Their commitment to the palliationist politics developed during the 1950s meant that they saw a resistance led by drag queens and street hustlers as a disaster, a wrongheaded street battle that undid their efforts to normalise homosexuality in the eyes of respectable society.

There was, in other words, nothing inevitable about the liberated identity that emerged from 1969. It stemmed from particular political ideas and a particular kind of resistance: it didn't grow inexorably from day-to-day experience. Asad Haider argued:

A meaningful common interest does not somehow exist by default. We cannot reduce *any* group of people and the multitudes they contain to a single common interest, as though we were reducing a fraction. A common interest is *constituted* by the composition of these multitudes into a group. And this is a process of political practice.[11]

The people instinctively enthused by a battle against the

homophobic cops were younger and often poorer than the Mattachine Society's leaders. In Wasserman's words, they drew on the 'militant tactics and radical rhetoric of the New Left; the counterculture; and the black, women's, student, and antiwar movements'. For them, claiming a new identity as 'liberated homosexuals' was a necessary part of a broader political project — one that they called 'liberation'.

But the perspective that came to be known as 'identity politics' presented identity in a quite different fashion.

By the 1980s, the establishment of women's studies, black studies, queer studies, cultural studies, and similar disciplines had profoundly changed the curriculum of higher education, dramatically increasing knowledge about literature, art and history previously excluded from serious study. At the same time, the context of the academy rendered the delegated left less able to examine the social and political tensions that it subsumed through a static, reified 'identity'.

More precisely, as Verity Burgmann argued, the upwardly mobile trajectory of many campus activists predisposed them to deny that any such tensions existed. Identity politics, she said, allowed its proponents to proclaim 'a community of interest between feminist bureaucrats and female welfare recipients, gay studies academics and working-class homosexuals, ethnic affairs advisers with unemployed immigrants, and so on'.[12] This move was particularly necessary, given the gulf between the radical intellectuals speaking on behalf of the social movements and those movements' original constituency, which was increasingly passive and disengaged.

Of course, not all advocates of identity politics were necessarily in supervisory positions. As Wolf said, identity politics was, by the late 1980s, becoming ubiquitous on the left, embraced as enthusiastically by impoverished student activists as by academics and heads of NGOs.

Nevertheless, the insistence on 'identity' as a concept eliding internal differences led to political projects in which the interests of the more privileged tended to dominate. In particular, identity politics emphasised symbolism, language, and representation, in ways that became crucial during the early debates about political correctness.

In his 1990 article 'Taking Offense' — one of the key early documents of anti–political correctness — Jerry Adler argued that as identity politics became ascendant, 'the search for euphemisms [became] the great intellectual challenge of American university life'.[13]

Like identity, political terminology had become a key preoccupation during the 1960s. In April 1963, Martin Luther King, for instance, wrote an open letter addressed to church leaders in which he complained about the language used to address African Americans. He told his white peers of the deep humiliation felt when, as he put it, 'your first name becomes "nigger," your middle name becomes "boy" (however old you are) and your last name becomes "John," and your wife and mother are never given the respected title "Mrs."'

King penned his letter from inside a Birmingham jail, where he'd been detained after marching against segregation. He'd been arrested violently, thrown into a dark cell, refused a phone call, and denied even a mattress. He'd gathered together scraps of paper to reply to the religious figures who'd publicly opposed his agitation on the basis that African Americans should obey the law of the land and wait patiently for legislative change.

King's remarks on language appeared in this passage:

[W]hen you have seen vicious mobs lynch your mothers and fathers at will and drown your sisters and brothers at whim; when you have seen hate-filled policemen curse, kick and even kill your black brothers and sisters; when you see the vast majority of your twenty million Negro brothers smothering in an airtight cage of poverty in the midst of an affluent society ... when you go forever fighting a degenerating sense of 'nobodiness' then you will understand why we find it difficult to wait.[14]

The 'Letter from a Birmingham jail' illustrated the dialectical relationship that direct politics created between the symbolic and the material. King was pushing for cultural reform — but not merely cultural reform. His opposition to racist language belonged to a program with immense implications for American society, a program about culture but also about violence and law and poverty. He linked slurs like 'boy' to structural injustices, and then demanded mass struggle to fight them.

The shift from direct to delegated politics introduced a different approach.

In a sense, the campus left, during the 1980s and the

1990s, made a virtue out of necessity. It could no longer mobilise the grassroots — and, in many cases, did not want to do so. But if structural change was no longer on the agenda, cultural reform was more viable than previously, given the new resources controlled by the delegated-politics left. Accordingly, for many activists, the symbolic victories that Adler mocked as a 'search for euphemism' became an end in themselves.

Reforms to mandate inclusive language (to take a common example) were important. But they mattered most for those already at the university. The so-called education wars of the 1980s and 1990s no doubt helped make higher education more palatable for students and activists from oppressed groups, through the spread of women's studies, the appointment of queer officers, the enforcement of anti-racist codes, and so on. The fundamental structures of the university — and of the society as a whole — remained, however, little changed by the new lexicon.

The material reforms that King fought for were particularly important to the poorest African Americans. (It was often forgotten that, by the time of his assassination, he was organising in support of a strike by sanitation workers.) By contrast, the campus reforms fought for in the 1980s and 1990s were far more significant for the relatively small number of people already at university than they were for, say, working-class kids who never attended higher education, in a fashion that academic identity politics, with its confidence in a unified 'community of interest', tended to obscure.

In her introduction to a republication of the Combahee

River Collective's work, Keeanga-Yamahtta Taylor stressed that those women weren't defining identity politics as exclusionary. They didn't think that only those experiencing a particular oppression could fight against it. Nor did they envision identity politics as a tool to claim the mantle of 'most oppressed'. They saw it as an analysis that would validate black women's experiences, while simultaneously creating an opportunity for them to become politically active to fight for the issues most important to them.[15]

The discussions of identity facilitated through consciousness-raising were intended, in other words, to enable a new solidarity, a more profound unity in which those who had previously been excluded could find a place. By contrast, in the later understanding of the idea, identities were defined, first and foremost, as expressions of difference, rather than as a mechanism for collectivity. Not surprisingly, as Elaine Graham-Leigh explained, 'There [was] an obvious tendency ... for these groups to splinter in opposition to each other, particularly when they are involved in competition for scarce government resources, most notably in the fracture of political Blackness into Afro-Caribbean, Asian, Arab and so on.'[16]

Graham-Leigh was talking specifically about Britain, but similar schisms happened everywhere, a necessary result of the unresolved determinism Mohandesi noted. If 'identity' was equated with particular political attitudes, any manifestation of political differences among those with the same 'lived experience' became deeply problematic, with the establishment of a new and different identity a constant temptation. The African-American Marxist Adolph Reed thus wrote scathingly of a tendency for activists to present themselves not so much as representing particular political ideas, but rather as what he called 'pure embodiments of collective aspirations'.[17]

Identity politics emerged out of the transition from direct to delegated politics. But its tendency to fragmentation meant that it was well suited to express the smug, individualised politics that prevailed during the 2000s, a period in which the rhetoric of identity both reflected and facilitated a new attitude to the masses.

The hegemony of identity politics during the Obama period played an important role in the left's difficulties in responding to the new outsider anti-elitism.

The swearing-in of America's first African-American president was, inevitably, a moment of intense drama. Within living memory, racist Jim Crow laws had prevented a man of African ancestry not only from standing for office but also from voting. The euphoria about Obama was real and widespread among African-American voters, who'd turned out in record numbers to support him. Many wept as they watched the footage of a black man taking the oath. A CNN poll on inauguration eve showed that 69 per cent of African Americans understood Obama's election as the fulfilment of Martin Luther King's vision. As Jay Z put it, 'Rosa sat so Martin could walk; Martin walked so Obama could run; Obama is running so we all can fly.'[18]

How, though, would Obama make others fly?

Direct politics rested on participation. For activists in that tradition, a symbolic victory mattered first and foremost because of its effect on the mass movement from which symbols emerged. To use Jay Z's example, Rosa Parks' refusal to give up her seat was a moment of great importance because it signalled the beginning of a campaign. The evening after her arrest, activists circulated a flyer throughout the African-American community explaining:

> If we do not do something to stop these arrests, they will continue … We are, therefore, asking every Negro to stay off the buses Monday in protest of the arrest and trial. Don't ride the buses to work, to town, to school, or anywhere on Monday. You can afford to stay out of school for one day if you have no other way to go except by bus. You can also afford to stay out of town for one day. If you work, take a cab, or walk.[19]

Parks was a respected figure in her community. But, as that leaflet stressed, her defiance mattered precisely because the discrimination she faced was commonplace and not anomalous. She sparked a collective protest, one in which thousands of working people took part. In that sense, she was, to use an almost oxymoronic term, a participatory symbol: Parks was inspirational because other could do — and did — what she had done.

Delegated politics, by contrast, stressed representation. Because the project of delegated politics depended on a relatively passive membership, a political achievement by a leading individual entailed that person doing what others couldn't and wouldn't.

Identity politics tended, then, to emphasise the importance of representation: high-profile members of oppressed groups obtaining visible and prominent positions in culture, politics, or the academy.

How, though, did the accomplishments of a minority change conditions for ordinary people? The question became moot as the institutions of delegated politics withered and weakened, leaving the gulf between the representatives and the represented more pronounced than ever.

As far back as 2000, Naomi Klein had bemoaned the new hegemony of identity politics at a time when the world market was spreading inequality across the planet. Klein wrote:

> In this new globalized context the victories of identity politics have amounted to a rearranging of the furniture while the house burned down. Yes, there are more multi-ethnic sitcoms and even more black executives — but whatever cultural enlightenment has followed has not prevented the population in the underclass from exploding or homelessness from reaching crisis levels in many North American urban centres. Sure, women and gays have better role models in the media and pop culture — but the ownership in the culture industries has consolidated so rapidly that, according to William Kennard, the chairman of the U.S. Federal Communications Commission, 'There

are fewer opportunities of entry by minority groups, community groups, small businesses in general.'[20]

Much of the discussion about the racial implications of Obama's victory emphasised the example that he offered young African Americans. His achievement proved, the argument went, that African Americans could accomplish anything. In the past, the man in the White House had been, well, white, and now a black president taught black kids that they, too, could be great.

The implication was that all the oppressed would be equally uplifted. But, as Burgmann argued, an 'emphasis on equality of opportunity all too easily falls prey to neoliberal inflections, for what is demanded, in effect, is an equal opportunity to become unequal".[21]

Obama was not Rosa Parks. He did not emerge from a mass movement that anyone could join. He'd become president through the traditional route: an elite education, a law degree, and then Chicago machine politics.

In that narrow sense, Obama's triumph set a precedent for African-American leadership, showing aspiring politicians from minority groups that they, too, could play the game. In politics — and, to a lesser extent, in other professional fields — upwardly mobile people of colour could model themselves on Obama. But by the mid-2000s the African-American population was deeply divided, even in the context of a very divided nation. The richest white families in America possessed a remarkable 74 times more wealth than the average white family. For African Americans, however, that figure was nearly three times higher, with well-off households possessing 200 times more than the average.[22]

In that context, Obama's career was far more relevant (inspirational, even) to some people than to others.

Early in 2007, Michael Toner from the Federal Election Commission warned that the looming election would be the most expensive contest in American history, a campaign in which leading candidates would need to have raised at least $100 million to be taken seriously.[23] He was right. The Obama team eventually spent a record-breaking $750 million to secure victory.[24]

In almost any other context, the suggestion that 'inspiration' would, in and of itself, break down structural barriers would be rejected out of hand as patronising nonsense. Yet liberals often presented Obama's victory as a self-help nostrum, motivating others to pull themselves up by their bootstraps.

The smug tinge to such arguments was not far from the surface. For many, Obama's election, in the face of the racism marshalled against him, showed that African Americans mired in poverty simply hadn't tried hard enough. As Taylor put it, the increasing visibility of a black elite bolstered an argument that 'Black inequality [was] the product of the slackening of Black communities' work ethic and self-sufficiency'.[25]

This was particularly important given the evolution of Obama's presidency. Elected on a wave of revulsion against the military adventures and economic inequality of the Bush administration, Obama quickly showed that he differed from his predecessor more in style than substance.

He campaigned against the foreign interventions of the Bush years and the grotesque human-rights violations that accompanied them. Yet, as Pankaj Mishra noted, only three days after his inauguration Obama was launching drone strikes in Pakistan — a precursor to a strategy that would define his presidency. Obama, Mishra pointed out, ordered more strikes with civilian casualties in his first year than Bush conducted throughout his entire presidency. When he accepted the Nobel Peace Prize, he made a point of announcing that he intended to intensify the war on terror. He massively expanded the US state's surveillance and data-mining programs; he waged a savage campaign against whistleblowers and 'invested his office with the lethal power to execute anyone, even American citizens, anywhere in the world'.

Around the world, the symbolism of the first black president — and the necessary opposition by progressives to the racist attacks on him — blunted the critiques the left should have been making of such policies and practices. Identity politics simply didn't provide an adequate framework or a vocabulary with which to analyse a figure like Obama.

Mishra continued:

Obama occasionally denounced the 'fat cats' of Wall Street, but Wall Street contributed heavily to his campaign, and he entrusted his economic policy to it early in his tenure, bailing out banks and the insurance mega-company AIG with no quid pro quo. African Americans had turned out in record numbers in 2008, demonstrating their love of an ostensible compatriot, but Obama ensured that he would be immune to the charge of loving blacks too much. Colour-blind to the suffering caused by mortgage foreclosures, he scolded African Americans, using the neoliberal idiom of individual responsibility, for their moral failings as fathers, husbands and competitors in the global marketplace.[26]

An older politics might have been more able to critique the divisions within a certain 'identity'. Malcolm X, for instance, warned about the dangers of African-American politicians he called 'sell outs'. But identity politics was predicated on the gulf between the representative and the represented. It was precisely the distance between the history-making leader and his passive, impotent constituency that gave him his symbolic power. In a sense, 'selling out' became conceptually impossible, since the higher a representative figure climbed, the more 'inspirational' he supposedly became.

In 2018, news broke that Obama would earn $1.2 million for delivering speeches to Wall Street firms — taking as much as $400,000 from a single speech.[27] The deal, so symptomatic of the structural ties between the political and financial elite, outraged many progressives, particularly in the wake of an election in which Bernie Sanders had captured the imagination of young voters by denouncing corporate influence.

But the comedian Trevor Noah, the successor to Jon Stewart, defended Obama against those he dubbed 'haters', on a symptomatic basis. Yes, he said, the American political system was broken and needed to change. But it was unfair to expect Obama to lead that change.

'So the first black president must also be the first one to not take money afterwards?' Noah asked. 'No, no, no, no, no, my friend. He can't be the first of everything. Fuck that, and fuck you.'[28]

Noah didn't defend the ex-president's financial deals as an unfortunate necessity. On the contrary, he lauded Obama's ability to cash in ('Make that money, Obama!') as a positive good for black America, a further milestone in his precedent-setting career.

Not all adherents of identity politics took the argument so grotesquely far. But Noah voiced a logic inherent in the politics of representation, which, by definition, celebrated the success of the successful and the power of the powerful.

A similar dynamic manifested itself in Australia during the great symbolic moments of the Labor administrations during the same period. Capitalism depended on the constant availability of labour power to individual capitalists. The economy could not function without a steady supply of people willing and able to work. As David McNally and Sue Ferguson pointed out, 'labor power cannot simply be presumed to exist, but is made available to capital only because of its reproduction in and through a particular set of gendered and sexualized social relations that exist beyond the direct labor/capital relation, in the so-called private sphere.'[29] Specifically, capital relied upon the individual family to nurture, raise, socialise, and educate the next generation of workers. As a result, a particular set of ideas about sexuality, gender roles, occupations, divisions, and similar subjects — the so-called 'family values' that underpinned conventional sexism — played a crucial ideological role. Even more than racism, sexism provided a compelling organisational principle for culture war, since gender roles were so caught up with people's intimate and personal experiences.

As soon as Julia Gillard became the first female prime minister of Australia, she received a barrage of gendered abuse from both the media and the opposition. Senator Bill Heffernan labelled her 'deliberately barren'; Alan Jones told listeners he wanted to put her in a chaff bag and dump her in the ocean; Tony Abbott addressed supporters in front of a sign describing Gillard as 'Bob Brown's bitch' and urging voters to 'Ditch the Witch'.[30]

On 9 October 2012, Abbott attacked Gillard, arguing that unless she sacked the speaker Peter Slipper over crude text messages he'd sent, she was as much of a sexist and a misogynist as anyone.

Gillard rose and delivered an impassioned response. 'I will not be lectured about sexism and misogyny by this man,' she said, pointing at Abbott. 'Not now, not ever.'[31] Footage of the exchange went viral, first in Australia and then internationally. Dubbed 'the misogyny speech', Gillard's words were hailed as groundbreaking by the progressive commentariat.

The academic Barbara Pini labelled the incident 'incredibly significant'. 'That the sexism which is so deeply embedded in the Australian body politic was named,' Pini said, 'may give some women licence to express and seek to counter the sexism they have experienced in their working lives.'[32]

Pini's argument about the prevalence of sexism in Australia was obviously correct. Abbott and his supporters could only target Gillard in the fashion that they did because, for many Australian men, any exercise of agency by a woman represented an alarming transgression deserving swift retribution.

But Pini's formulation illustrated the problem with symbolic politics. The circulation of Gillard's speech may well have sparked broader conversations about sexism, perhaps even encouraging others to stand up against misogyny in their own lives. But, without question, its impact was greatest on professional women who, like Gillard herself, already possessed a degree of social power.

The suggestion that inspiration was, in and of itself, sufficient to alter gender relations for working-class women hid a deep and unconscious elitism: it implied that ordinary women endured sexism because they didn't know any better.

Obviously, that wasn't the case. Because of its association with the family — a basic economic unit — sexism was more than simply a set of prejudices to be shrugged off. It was fundamentally connected with material experiences.

In reality, insofar as female workers remained silent about discrimination and abuse, they did so, in most cases, because they understand the consequences of speaking up. A wealthy, powerful woman could deliver a speech describing a colleague as a misogynist in a way that most women fearful of losing their job could not.

Accordingly, a response to sexism meaningful to working women (who were, after all, the bulk of the population) necessitated direct politics. Without a change to the circumstances in which sexism thrived (in the form, say, of stronger protections against unfair dismissal, or greater bargaining power for employees, or more generous unemployment benefits), exhortations to 'be more like Gillard' would be useless.

In any case, Gillard delivered her misogyny speech on the same day that she helped pass the *Social Security Legislation Amendment (Fair Incentives to Work) Act 2012*, which slashed payments to single parents. The measure — which had the effect of moving large numbers of women to the substantially lower Newstart allowance — had far greater material consequences for gender equality than any prime ministerial oratory.

The critic Anwen Crawford later spoke to one of the people affected by the changes, who was dumbfounded by the left's emphasis on Gillard's rhetoric rather than her actions.

'The focus was on Julia Gillard and what an amazing feminist she was,' the woman said, 'but on the same day she's hurting the most vulnerable women. That was particularly difficult to go through.'[33]

Not surprisingly, the accolades heaped by progressives on Gillard as a feminist champion did not change the attitudes of Australian women to her: by midway through 2013, polls showed that the majority of women disapproved of her performance as prime minister.[34]

Again, the left's emphasis on the misogyny speech was emblematic of a certain kind of politics, one that highlighted symbolic resistance at oppression, even — or perhaps especially — when that symbolism barely affected the most oppressed.

Amory Starr noted how identity politics — a particular way of understanding the world — had become utterly dominant on the left, 'naturalised as a way of understanding how individuals and groups make politics'.[35] More and more progressives began to pin their hopes for social change on wealthy and powerful figures serving as a proxy for the dispossessed: the businesswoman smashing the glass ceiling; the outspoken musician; the feisty television personality; and so on. Indeed, as the structural challenge once implicit in the politics of the social movements faded, it became possible for politicians themselves to embrace identity politics.

By a bitter irony, the left had become incapable of recognising the material divisions within oppressed groups precisely at a time when those divisions had become particularly glaring and particularly important.

CHAPTER TEN

Privilege and inequality

Lost my job in 2006. Sold my home and moved in with my
87-year-old mother.

Worked temporary jobs on and off for over 5 years with little
or no benefits.

Cancer survivor. Need medical care. Can't afford health
insurance.

TOO YOUNG TO RETIRE.

Watching my retirement funds and savings shrink.

Moved to Mexico to get medical care. Rent a room and live
on $250 a month. No car. No phone.

Mom is in the hospital and I wonder if I can afford to come
home.[1]

The post appeared on a Tumblr account entitled 'We are
the 99 percent', in support of the Occupy Wall Street sit-in
at Zuccotti Park in New York City's financial district. For
a brief period in 2011, Occupy offered a tantalising glimpse
of a different kind of a left, a direct-politics alternative to

identity liberalism and the culture-war right.

Despite its eventual global impact, OWS began as a small, ad hoc, and quite confused intervention: basically, a handful of protesters establishing themselves in a park. The initial call-out from *Adbusters* magazine asked president Obama to hold a 'Presidential Commission tasked with ending the influence money has over our representatives', but that demand faded away as the occupation became a local — and then national and eventually international — focus for opposition to the neoliberal order.

By a simple act of civil disobedience in the heart of New York's financial district, Occupy popularised two related ideas.

First, it highlighted the huge contrast in wealth and power between those it called the 'One percent' (the global elite) and those it described as the '99 percent' (essentially everyone else). The Tumblr providing personal accounts was part of that. Another entry read:

> I am 45 years old.
>
> I was laid off twice in 18 months.
>
> The second time 6 months after I got married.
>
> I am 'unemployable' because of layoffs.
>
> I have not worked since November 2008.
>
> We have NO healthcare.
>
> My husband works so that I can go to college to get a degree.
>
> We are also dependent on family to make ends meet.

Each story was different, but the individual anecdotes were united by their common experience of economic disempowerment, implicitly contrasted with the super-rich.

The collectivity inherent in Occupy's analysis naturally facilitated its second simple idea: the possibility of ordinary people acting together to change society fundamentally. The idea of mass occupations spread across America and around the world, seized upon (for a while at least) as an organisational alternative to the collapsing infrastructure of the left. '[I]t has temporarily liberated some of the most expensive real estate in the world,' wrote Mike Davis of the Zuccotti Park action, 'and turned a privatized square into a magnetic public space and a catalyst for protest.'[2]

People who didn't belong to political parties, trade unions, church groups, or community organisations could join an occupation and, by so doing, feel that they were making an immediate difference. By controlling strategically located space, occupiers necessarily rediscovered the central ideas of direct politics. They identified the One Percent as a common enemy, and so raised the prospect of structural social change, even if they struggled to articulate what form that might take. The actions were both collective and participatory. The occupations could only survive if people joined them. By their nature, they posed immediate questions to everyone who was involved. How would the encampment be protected? What attitude should the occupation take to police and the media and politicians? Where would food come from? How should the camp be kept functioning? Such issues were confronted by participatory democracy, via extended meetings in which everyone present argued over what was to be done.

Moreover, Occupy identified a new constituency. By definition, the 99 per cent embraced almost anyone. Irrespective of race or gender or sexual orientation, so long as you weren't among the nation's wealthiest, Occupy addressed you. Obviously, hostility to the super-rich did not, in and of itself, resolve the historic divisions of race, sexuality, gender, and so on within the working class, but it did provide a basis for unity against a common enemy. Surveys showed, for instance, that African Americans tended to be more supportive of Occupy than whites, probably because they — like other oppressed groups — had suffered most because of the GFC.[3]

The collectivity of an occupation, the commitment to a shared goal, created an environment in which overcoming division became of importance to everyone. If the camp divided along racial lines — or if people of colour did not feel comfortable in participating — the protest became markedly less viable. Conversely, insofar as the protesters could find ways to work together, they all became stronger. Again, this didn't resolve the legacy of oppression, and in many places the occupations splintered on racial or other grounds. But the mass meetings at least made it possible to debate the necessity of solidarity among the 99 per cent, in an environment in which all recognised the advantages of unity.

Perhaps inevitably, the Occupy movement did not last long. After a brief period of toleration, the authorities, more or less everywhere, sent in the police to disperse the camps, often with extreme brutality. The inability of the protesters to resist the state caused Occupy to disintegrate almost as quickly as it arose.

Nevertheless, even if for only a few months, Occupy put the question of social privilege and social inequality on the agenda all over the world — something the left had, in recent times, found almost impossible.

In a sense, Occupy represented a road not taken. For the majority of this period, a very different approach to privilege dominated on the activist left.

In a number of important essays written from the late 1980s on, the legal theorist Kimberlé Williams Crenshaw developed the term 'intersectionality' to analyse the relationship between interlocking forms of oppression. 'If an accident happens at an intersection,' Crenshaw wrote, 'it can be caused by cars travelling from any number of directions and, sometimes, from all of them. Similarly, if a black woman is harmed because she is at the intersection, her injury could result from sex discrimination or race discrimination.'[4]

Intersectionality theory was, in some respects, a critique of identity politics.[5] After all, the crudest versions of identity politics suffered from an obvious reductionism, implying that all members of a particular group shared similar experiences that almost automatically gave rise to similar politics. Crenshaw, however, insisted that all women did not share the same interests or histories, and neither did all African Americans. Such identities were, she said, complicated and fragmented, with new identities emerging from the intersection of oppressions.

The argument encouraged a more complex analysis.

Intersectionality theorists emphasised the importance of recognising oppression as an interlocking system. The slogan 'My feminism will be intersectional or it will be bullshit' became, for many, a challenge to white liberal feminists who universalised their own experience.

Yet the popularisation of intersectionality theory took place alongside — and often in conjunction with — another, related idea, with which it became entwined.

In 1988, an American writer named Peggy McIntosh wrote an article entitled 'White Privilege and Male Privilege', which was subsequently circulated in amended form as 'White Privilege: unpacking the invisible knapsack'.[6] McIntosh outlined various manifestations of everyday racism drawn from her own experiences. She described these as:

> an invisible package of unearned assets that I can count on cashing in each day, but about which I was 'meant' to remain oblivious. White privilege is like an invisible weightless knapsack of special provisions, assurances, tools, maps, guides, codebooks, passports, visas, clothes, compass, emergency gear, and blank checks.

Her essay culminated in a list outlining many of the 'daily effects of white privilege' in her own life. She could, she said, 'arrange to be in the company of my race most of the time', if she so desired. She could be confident of finding a house she could afford in an area where she wanted to live — and if she did move, she could be 'pretty sure that my neighbors in such a location will be neutral or pleasant to me'. She could go shopping alone without worrying about being harassed; she could see people of her race represented on the television and in the newspapers.

She suggested that, by compiling similar lists of their own 'unearned assets', which would vary according to their circumstances, activists could overcome their complicity with a repressive order. Over the next decades, McIntosh's argument was widely adopted for pedagogical training, and disseminated through activist groups and NGOs, until 'privilege theory' developed into a kind of common sense on the left.[7]

In some respects, McIntosh's presentation echoed ideas and techniques developed by the New Left. As Asad Haider pointed out, a theory known as 'white-skin privilege' had been developed by the Maoist writers Theodore Allen and Noel Ignatiev in the 1960s, while McIntosh's inventory method recalled the 'consciousness raising' employed widely throughout the New Left.[8]

But McIntosh's work reflected the evolution of delegated and smug politics in the way that it inverted ideas appropriated from direct politics.

The consciousness-raising employed by women's liberation, black radicals, and various Maoist organisations was fundamentally linked to mass action. Sarachild, for instance, explained that the technique mattered to the women's movement because it was 'a method of radical organising tested by other revolutions' that would 'keep ... the movement radical by preventing it from getting sidetracked into single issue reforms and single issue organizing'.[9]

By contrast, McIntosh presented her approach less as a method of radicalisation and more as a form of self-improvement. Her 'privilege checking' didn't unveil reasons to revolt so much as expose personal complicity, with the participant tabulating the invisible benefits attached to their identities as a prelude to individual rectification. Someone wanting to change the world must, it was argued, admit their privilege, listen to those who didn't possess the same advantages, and then educate themselves about the history of oppression. Until that happened, they were part of the problem.

Indeed, by locating privilege in the relationship between individuals, the theory made progressives responsible for each other's oppression. When McIntosh listed her own day-to-day experiences of 'white privilege', she offered her description of racism as if it were an explanation — as if, by enjoying those advantages, she were self-evidently responsible for the disadvantages suffered by her workmates.

But that didn't follow at all. In her second point, she noted that she, unlike her non-white colleagues, could live in a nice neighbourhood. The unaffordability of housing — and the racialised manifestations of that — was not, however, a problem for which she was responsible. In any other context, blame for housing shortages would, quite correctly, be directed at governments and property developers rather than at academics.

In this way, McIntosh's concept of privilege reversed the Allen and Ignatiev formulation. Haider noted that the original presentation of 'white skin privilege' described 'white chauvinism' as 'actually *harmful* to white people', because despite the fact that they were granted some advantages over black people, they ended up 'even more entrenched in their condition of exploitation precisely by accepting these advantages'.[10]

For instance, the classic study of income distribution in American cities in the 1970s by the economist Michael Reich found that in places where the gulf between white and black incomes was high, white employees tended to earn less money than white employees in places where the racial disparity was lower.[11] The 'privilege' they enjoyed might have offered them a sense of superiority, but in material terms it left them worse off — exactly the opposite of what McIntosh suggested.

Ignatiev himself had argued:

> White-skin privileges serve only the bourgeoisie, and precisely for that reason they will not let us escape them, but instead pursue us with them through every hour of our life, no matter where we go. They are poison bait. To suggest that the acceptance of white-skin privilege is in the interests of white workers is equivalent to suggesting that swallowing the worm with the hook in it is in the interests of the fish.[12]

The contrast with McIntosh's metaphor of a knapsack full of provisions could not have been starker. For her, oppression was a zero-sum game, with the victimisation experienced by one person the consequence of the advantages enjoyed by another.

Though McIntosh's original examples emphasised race and gender, a specific focus on whiteness wasn't integral to a methodology applicable to any kind of oppression ('able body privilege', 'class privilege', etc). The array of advantages enjoyed by each person varied according to whom that person was being contrasted with: Person A might enjoy 'white privilege' compared to Person B, but Person B might be the beneficiary of 'male privilege' relative to Person A. Sexuality, age, faith, skin colour, geographical location, mental, and physical health: questions of privilege conferred to all of these, as well as many other categories.

Furthermore, following Crenshaw's argument, the intersection of multiple advantages or disadvantages could be understood as creating new and different privilege and oppressions. In fact, because privilege pertained to individual 'lived experience', its manifestations were, by definition, almost infinite, combining and reassembling depending on the circumstances of specific subjects.

This meant that, if privilege checking was used as a method as a necessary precursor to activism, activism itself became problematic, since there was no end to the unexamined privilege that might be discovered within any given group of protesters. With identities (and thus privilege) combining (at least in theory) almost without limit, solidarity was forever deferred: it was difficult to imagine a circumstance in which someone didn't enjoy an 'unearned advantage' over somebody else. The left's new focus on 'microaggressions' — the subtle, unintended expression of prejudice or discrimination in day-to-day life — reflected this understanding of an oppression resulting from everyday people rather than from specific social or economic structures.

Intersectionality might, then, have been intended as a radical critique of identity politics, but in practice it reinterpreted identity in an even more paralysing fashion. Where earlier versions of identity politics at least held out the possibility of the oppressed acting as a bloc, the new understanding of intersectionality and privilege pushed towards a radical individualism, one that implied a struggle of all against all.

It wasn't, then, surprising that the rise of privilege theory paralleled the normalisation of neoliberalism. McIntosh's actuarial description of privilege as an 'unearned asset' echoed an understanding of society as an aggregation of antagonistic subjects, each assessing their advantages over each other like entrepreneurs in the marketplace.

Because of that, privilege theory offered very little strategic direction. As Phoebe Maltz Bovy quipped, 'I've never quite sorted out by what mechanism awareness of privilege is meant to inspire a desire to shed oneself of it.'[13] One would, in fact, expect the opposite — that an acute awareness of privilege among, say, the super-rich would foster the kind of capitalist class-consciousness shown by the One Percent.

By its nature, privilege checking could only become a widespread practice within a milieu already broadly sympathetic to progressive causes. As such, it was, first and foremost, a method for leftists to negotiate their relationships with each other other, coinciding with a broader despair about collective agency — a trend where, as the organisations and institutions associated with delegated politics weakened, activists shifted their emphasis away from changing the world to positioning themselves within the relatively small circles of remaining progressive influence. As Haider wrote elsewhere, 'If the "personal is political", it is in the sense we are left with no practice of politics outside of the fashioning of our own personal identities, and surveillance of the identities of others.'[14]

That inward turn explained the notoriously unforgiving tenor of 'call-out culture', in which activists (particularly online activists) launched sustained campaigns against other progressives for seemingly minor political infractions.

Left-wing infighting was nothing new, of course. Even so, the call-outs of the mid-2000s were notorious for their intensity, which often varied inversely with the real-world consequences of the offences being chastised. 'At the height of its power,' noted Angela Nagle, 'the hysterical liberal call-out, no matter how minor the transgression, could ruin your life.'[15]

Like the privilege theory that it rested upon, call-out culture both reflected and reinforced the left's isolation. A movement engaged in real-world struggles could assess disagreements in relation to their consequences and judge the contending arguments by their practical results. A mass movement obtaining actual outcomes fostered solidarity, a collective identification against a joint enemy. This didn't necessarily make debates civil or productive, but it did at least provide a framework — and even, perhaps, an organisational structure — within which contested issues might be thrashed out with some measure of fairness.

Call-out culture, on the other hand, emerged out of institutional collapse. Where once it was at least hypothetically feasible for disputes to be adjudicated with some procedural rigour by the community group, political party, or trade union to which activists belonged, the decline of such bodies left social media as the forum of choice, despite its manifest unsuitability.

Not surprisingly, some of the more famous call-outs resulted in grotesque injustices. In 2013, for instance, Justine Sacco, a director of corporate communications at IAC, tweeted about a trip to Africa. 'Hope I don't get AIDS,' she said. 'Just kidding. I'm white!' The tweet — widely read as racist — provoked a massive pile-on, after which Sacco lost her job and became internationally notorious. But in his book *So You've Been Publicly Shamed*, Jon Ronson convincingly argues that Sacco had been misinterpreted — that, in fact, her quip was intended as a parody of the very sentiments later attributed to her.[16]

If call-out culture was a product of the left's separation from ordinary people, it also contributed to that separation. Any movement, campaign, or struggle that sought support from outside the ranks of the already converted needed, by definition, people unfamiliar with the ideas of the left. The traditional approach of direct politics — replicated by Occupy — recognised that new recruits carried all kinds of ideological baggage, some of it good and some of it bad. It also understood that active participation in social-change politics provided conditions in which old prejudices could be more easily shed.

But if an acknowledgement of 'unearned entitlements' was a precondition for progressive politics, activism became the preserve of those already convinced, for they alone were sufficiently woke to recognise their various privileges. Everyday folk (without, say, a background in cultural theory) were not liable to admit immediately their complicity with oppression — and, as a result, it was easy for activists committed to smug politics to conclude that such people were, once again, irredeemably reactionary.

Furthermore, the linguistic reforms achieved on campus and generally accepted within the narrow circles of the left didn't necessarily enjoy currency within wider society. As a result, many working-class people remained unfamiliar with the political lexicon that had become hegemonic amongst progressives, and thus could often find themselves treated as overt enemies.

Call-out culture exacerbated the tendency. If a man with no previous experience of activism uttered a sexist phrase, one response might be to explain patiently the problem with the term, its relationship to institutional oppression, and the importance of overcoming misogyny within a movement that needed maximum unity. But spectacular, performative call-outs were not designed to persuade. They were designed to punish, to make public examples of wrongdoers, in the context of an activism that understood itself as policing the left against the backwardness of the masses.

As the philosopher Wendy Brown argued, 'politicised

identity' thus became 'more likely to punish and reproach ... than to find venues for self-affirming action'.[17]

CHAPTER ELEVEN

Trauma and trigger warnings

The growing conviction on the left that ordinary people were the problem rather than the solution manifested itself in many forms. One significant expression of smug politics involved an emphasis on the need for psychological protection for the oppressed, something that made political struggle — and especially mass political struggle — innately dangerous. This understanding of trauma spurred a variety of phenomena — from trigger warnings to safe spaces — that became entwined with culture war more generally.

To understand these specific issues, it is useful to look at changing notions of trauma, a history itself profoundly shaped by politics.

In his book *Crazy Like Us*, Ethan Watters argued that while terrible events invariably left psychic traces, the forms those took were very different across cultures and throughout history. He discussed, in particular, the after-effects of military combat.

'There is no doubt that soldiers often come back from battle with psychological as well as physical injuries,' Watters wrote, '[and that] the fear and horror of direct combat can clearly damage the psyche of men and women. But the medical records of war veterans show that the manifestation of the injury is always tied up with cultural beliefs contemporaneous to the time.'[1]

Considerable evidence exists that individuals from different cultures react to traumatic experiences in ways that deviate from the standard Western list of expected symptoms. Female Salvadoran refugees speak of a sensation they call *calorias*, a feeling of intense heat in their body, while Cambodian refugees, distressed by their inability to perform the correct rituals for the dead, describe visits by vengeful spirits. A study of war trauma in Afghanistan, by contrast, has recorded reactions described as *asabi*, a type of nervous anger, and *fisha-e-bala*, the sensation of internal pressure.

The current understandings of trauma, including those that shaped political strategies on the left, arose from developments in American society in the 1970s. In his history of military psychiatry, Ben Shephard identified, in particular, the Vietnam War as 'help[ing] to create a new "consciousness of trauma" in Western society'.[2]

Ironically, the US went into Vietnam confident that it could protect its soldiers from the psychological symptoms experienced in previous conflicts. Unlike, say, the men of the Great War, American troops in Vietnam weren't expected to endure prolonged bombardments in trenches, but were rotated through relatively short tours, with the so-called

Salmon program placing a psychologist in every combat battalion.

For a while, psychological injuries remained very, very low — well below rates in Korea and World War II. As late as 1970, an American medical researcher argued that 'psychiatric casualties need never again become a major cause of attrition in the United States military in a combat zone'. Yet a subsequent study revealed that by 1988, 479,000 veterans were suffering from post-traumatic stress disorder (PTSD).

Though it was rarely acknowledged, the direct-politics campaign against the Vietnam War in America also resonated deeply within the military itself — including in Vietnam. In 1969, 1,300 active-duty GIs put their names to a huge anti-war message in the *New York Times* one week before the Moratorium rally in Washington — an extraordinary statement by serving soldiers. The ideals of the counterculture, the demands of the peace movement, and the struggle for black liberation: they all found their way to Vietnam.

In 1971, Marine Colonel Robert D. Heinl Jr wrote:

By every conceivable indicator, our army that remains in Vietnam is in a state approaching collapse, with individual units avoiding or having refused combat, murdering their officers and non-commissioned officers ... Sedition, coupled with disaffection from within the ranks, and externally fomented with an audacity and intensity previously inconceivable, infest the Armed Services.[3]

One Department of Defense study in 1972 found that 51 per cent of all troops in Vietnam engaged in 'some form of protest'. Perhaps 500 different underground GI papers were established, with names such as *Harass the Brass*, *All Hands Abandon Ship*, *The Fatigue Press*, and *Star Spangled Bummer*.

When they returned home, many of the ex-soldiers engaged in those protests remained dedicated to stopping the conflict. One of the groups in which they organised was Vietnam Veterans Against the War, founded in 1967. VVAW employed its own version of 'consciousness raising' via special 'rap groups' for veterans, in which ex-soldiers spoke about their attitudes to the military, their changing ideas about masculinity, and their thoughts on politics. At a university meeting discussing both the massacre at My Lai and the shootings at Kent State, VVAW members encountered a New York psychoanalyst called Chaim Shatan, who offered to organise professional volunteers to attend the rap sessions.

In 1972, Shatan wrote for the *New York Times* about what he'd heard from the raps. Soldiers might, he explained, seem fine when they returned to America. But between nine and thirty months later, they experienced 'growing apathy, cynicism, alienation, depression, mistrust and expectation of betrayal, as well as an inability to concentrate, insomnia, nightmares, restlessness, uprootedness and impatience with jobs or study'.[4] He coined the phrase 'post-Vietnam syndrome', on the basis that no standard diagnostic label adequately covered the men's symptoms.

This was the genesis of today's post-traumatic stress disorder, though it wasn't until 1980 that the modern term made its way into the third edition of the authoritative *Diagnostic and Statistical Manual of Mental Disorders.*

By the mid-1980s, government-funded Vet Centers were treating about 150,000 people a year, with another 28,000 visiting Veteran Administration hospitals. Subsequent conflicts — particularly the two wars in Iraq and the occupation of Afghanistan — added immensely to those numbers. In 2003, about 190,000 US veterans sought help for PTSD — and by 2014 the number had risen to 540,000. That year, a study for the Institute of Medicine explained: 'Demands for post-traumatic stress disorder services among service members and veterans are at unprecedented levels and are climbing.'[5]

Because *DSM III* described a response to severe stressors rather than a specific reaction to battle, PTSD could also be applied to non-combat experiences. The 1988 study concluded that something like a million former Vietnam soldiers had suffered PTSD at one time or another — even though only 300,000 had seen action. Away from conflict zones altogether, PTSD was identified in civilian life, with the US Department of Veterans Affairs listing 'natural disasters, serious accidents, assault or abuse, or even sudden and major emotional losses' as potential causes.

Throughout the 1990s, discussions of PTSD in relation to high-profile disasters spread the concept further. A particular understanding of trauma — and traumatic reactions — permeated the culture, eventually becoming entwined with ideas about oppression.

The oft-ridiculed notion of 'safe spaces' provided a

good example. Today, anti-PC campaigners often discuss campus 'safe spaces' as if they are self-evidently ridiculous. Chris Patten, the chancellor of Oxford University, recently described the very idea as 'fundamentally offensive', an attempt by students to stifle free speech by insulating themselves from opinions that might challenge them.[6]

'A university is not a "safe space",' tweeted New Atheist leader Richard Dawkins. 'If you need a safe space, leave, go home, hug your teddy & suck your thumb until ready for university.'[7]

In reality, safe spaces seemed to have been first employed (the history's somewhat contested) in the mid-1960s to designate gay and lesbian bars. The concept wasn't about 'hugging your teddy'. On the contrary, the spaces were 'safe' because they offered shelter from the police at a time when being outed meant public shaming, violence, and arrest. Later, the term made its way into the women's movement. In this context, it designated somewhere that women could talk about their experiences: again, not to insulate themselves from other opinions, but to become empowered to embrace activism.

The association between safe spaces and trauma came considerably later, more or less in parallel with the rise of an associated phenomenon: 'trigger warnings'. In the late 1990s, writers on disccussion threads on LiveJournal and on *Ms Magazine* began to preface conversations about eating disorders or rape with an introductory comment. They were motivated by the growing popular awareness of PTSD. By then, many people knew that a veteran might suffer combat flashbacks after, say, hearing a car backfire — and that someone traumatised by sexual assault might react similarly if confronted by descriptions of sexual violence.

The practice migrated to feminist blogs such as Shakesville, before reaching a wider audience with the advent of Twitter, Tumblr, and Facebook. Trigger warnings manifested themselves on American campuses in the 2010s — with, for instance, Ohio's Oberlin College circulating a guide intended to advise academics about the use of 'triggering' material in 2012.[8]

As this potted history might suggest, right from the start the warnings functioned in different ways for different people. For some, they were almost a matter of etiquette, akin to the notifications offered by TV stations before the screening of disturbing content. In that sense, much of the furore about trigger warnings (like so much about culture war generally), amounted to an enormous beat-up — outraged conservatives might have been equally offended had a lecturer presented sexually explicit material without any notice.

Nevertheless, for at least some activists, trigger warnings did constitute a political strategy. Almost as soon as PTSD was identified, feminists had noted that the stress-response patterns of rape victims were consistent with its diagnostic criteria. A study by the US National Comorbidity Survey Replication found that, among adult men, the lifetime prevalence of PTSD was 3.6 per cent — and the prevalence for women was 9.7 per cent. In Canada, the General Social Survey of 2014 revealed that women were twice as likely as men to experience being sexually assaulted, beaten, choked, or threatened with a gun or a knife. Other results suggested that individuals identifying themselves as 'gay, lesbian or bisexual' were victimised within intimate partnerships at rates that were double those reported within heterosexual relationships, while indigenous women were over than three times more likely to experience abuse at the hands of intimate partners.[9]

As Holly Taylor explained, '[I]ndividuals and groups who are members of marginalized, racialized, and other minority groups are statistically more likely to be abused, assaulted, under-resourced and unsupported, all factors that correlate strongly with higher instances of posttraumatic stress disorder among these populations.'

For some activists, a demand for trigger warnings (and, on occasion, for the provision of safe spaces) was an attempt to redress or mitigate the consequences of oppression so that people from marginalised backgrounds could participate on campus. That was why universities were more likely to offer notices relating to sexual violence than, say, combat experience: they were primarily focused on mitigating the trauma associated with sexism and racism.

As a form of delegated politics, trigger warnings depended on a progressive administration or student union: by definition, they could not function without a coercive body enforcing a policy for potentially harmful content. This meant, of course, that they became prime fodder for anti-PC campaigners. It was easy to present trigger warnings as politically correct censorship — not so much because they involved banning content (they usually didn't), but because they relied on an external authority.

That also limited their applicability. In a liberal-arts college such as Oberlin, the administration might embrace the practice. But because the enthusiasm for trigger warnings coincided with the decline of the left's institutional influence, the applicability of the strategy was radically limited. Trigger warnings could only be offered in controlled (and increasingly rare) circumstances, in which the oppressed or their allies could depend on the state (or a semi-state authority) for assistance.

In lieu of this, the sensibility behind trigger warnings and safe spaces merged into the broader progressive suspicion about, and disdain for, mass action. Most of the time, the left could not actually provide either safe spaces or trigger warnings. But the concepts circulated because they corresponded to a broader understanding of the relationship between oppression and trauma, one that reinforced the already prevailing sense that mass politics was innately dangerous unless tightly controlled.

In many ways, the practicality of trigger warnings, safe spaces, and similar measures mattered less than the argument underpinning them. If, as many psychologists said, oppression caused a trauma that could be further inflamed by hateful words or conduct, almost any mass campaign became deeply problematic. Public resistance to oppression invariably spurred pushback by bigots. If that pushback was psychologically damaging for the oppressed, how, in good conscience, could progressives support a grassroots direct-politics campaign that would risk injuring the very people it was supposed to benefit? The conventional argument from trauma thus justified a conviction that progressive politics rested on a carefully schooled elite, people knowledgeable enough to discuss oppression without risking psychological damage for the oppressed.

Yet there were other ways to think about the effects of oppression — ways far less compatible with the assumptions of smug politics. Indeed, the history of PTSD hinted at a deeper debate about the nature of trauma and the effects of politics.

Chaim Shatam had never intended to establish a general diagnosis for trauma, or even for war. On the contrary, he had sought to differentiate the experience of Vietnam from other conflicts. The veterans he heard were suffering, he said, because of their sense of being 'duped and manipulated' by the military and by their country:

> [T]hey have been scapegoats. Many vets feel victimized, initially by inadequate V.A. treatment and paltry G.I. benefits. But soon their gripes encompass society at large: they feel deceived, used and betrayed. When they see senior officers exonerated for war atrocities without trial, they speak bitterly about the High Command's impunity.[10]

As Watters argued, in Shatan's original formulation, 'it was the moral ambiguity of the Vietnam War and the deceitfulness of the US government and military, not the trauma of battle, that damaged the psyche of the soldier'.[11]

Precisely because of this, members of VVAW understood direct politics as central to their recovery. One of them, a man called Arthur Egendorf, explained: 'The vets who came to the early rap groups brought with them, as an overwhelming residue from the war, a deep demoralisation and loss of trust in their leaders, in the cause, and in the person they were before going in.'[12]

In 1971, VVAW organised a 'medal turn in' ceremony in Washington, in which veterans publicly discarded ribbons and other honours. VVAW organiser Jack Smith described running that event as 'probably the most powerful moment of my life'; Bill Crandell, another vet, described it as 'enormously cathartic'.

The VVAW's 'rap groups' — like the direct-politics practice of 'consciousness-raising' more generally — were intended to help veterans understand their sufferings in political terms: to allow them to connect their experiences with the war as a whole and thus to salve their psychic wounds in the struggle against it.

There was considerable evidence to suggest that, in fact, the anti-war movement did offer, for many, a different kind of meaning. But when American troops withdrew from Vietnam in 1973, the movement rapidly declined — as did, within a few years, the direct-politics left more generally. As a result, the solidarity and purpose many veterans had found in campaigning against the war disappeared.

Yet throughout the 1970s, conservatives remained suspicious of returning soldiers. Vietnam veterans were associated in the public mind with protests and the counterculture, and right-wingers were reluctant to fund programs for them. A depoliticised, psychological explanation for soldiers' anguish mattered because it legitimised arguments for state support. If the veterans' behaviour could be explained as a consequence of their suffering, they could be presented as deserving beneficiaries of social security. They weren't rebellious — they were sick.

By 1980, with the social divisions opened by the anti-war movement largely papered over, 'post-Vietnam syndrome' became 'post-traumatic stress disorder', a condition the American Psychiatric Association included in its *Diagnostic and Statistical Manual* (DSM III) that year. PTSD removed the political specificity that had marked post-Vietnam syndrome. Rather than Vietnam being anomalous, PTSD made it exemplary: the most recent instance of a trauma that could be found in every war since the dawn of time.

That was not to imply that the diagnosis was in some way fake or that it wasn't useful for many veterans. But, as Shephard and others insisted, the scripts by which people understood extreme experiences varied according to circumstances. The particular historical and cultural moment in which post-Vietnam syndrome (a condition associated with the political betrayals of one particular war) became PTSD (a universal disorder) was one in which the tremendous economic, social, and political ferment of the late 1960s and the early 1970s was giving way to a new stability. The new form of the diagnosis reflected the new hegemony of delegated politics, a model of activism in which it made more sense to focus on the soldiers' suffering than on their agency.

The emphasis in the new diagnosis, argued Shephard, 'was on the timelessness of PTSD and the hopelessness of the patient ... The patients were just passive victims of PTSD whose symptoms [could] be measured.'[13]

Watters put it like this:

[A]s it evolved into its modern clinical form, PTSD left behind ... quests for social meaning in tragedy. In doing so, it has set adrift those struggling in the aftermath of trauma. In contrast to those angry but socially engaged Vietnam War veterans, the personal accounts of current-day soldiers returning from Afghanistan and Iraq often seem pigeonholed into a PTSD diagnosis that is tied to a particularly modern style of lonely hyperintrospection.[14]

The popularisation of trauma in the 1980s and 1990s thus paralleled the more general ascendancy of delegated politics over direct politics, and then the later rise of smug politics. A vocabulary developed in therapeutic practice that provided a more general script for a new kind of activism. With progressives already accustomed to working with state or semi-state bodies, the paternalist relationship that PTSD mandated between veterans and the various departments managing their affairs became a kind of common sense.

'In a momentous shift,' said Derek Summerfield, 'contemporary Western culture now emphasises not resilience but vulnerability. We've invited people to see a widening range of experiences as liable to make them ill ...

We are presenting just one version of human nature — one set of ideas about pain and suffering — as being definitive.'[15]

The queer activist Jack Halberstam rightly objected that 'the trigger warning ... gives rise to an understanding of self that makes us vulnerable to paternalistic modes of protection'.[16] But that paternalism was embedded within a politics that had grown up in opposition to the direct-politics perspectives of the VVAW activists. In the era of smug politics, many progressives no longer believed that it was either possible or desirable for the masses to organise themselves. As a result, some version of paternalism became almost inevitable.

Wendy Brown argued:

Politicized identity, premised on exclusion and fueled by the humiliation and suffering imposed by its historically structured impotence in the context of a discourse of sovereign individuals, is as likely to seek generalised political paralysis, to feast on generalized political impotence, as it is to seek its own or collective liberation.[17]

This paralysis, stemming from an understanding of politics as fundamentally dangerous, dominated progressive thought, even as the right became bolder and more confident.

CHAPTER TWELVE

Them and us

Throughout the second decade of the 20th century, the centrifugal forces unleashed by the neoliberal shift continued to pull ordinary people away from traditional sources of authority, leading to an increase in the power of outsider rather than insider anti-elitism.

The evolution of the Tea Party — an organisation named after a key moment in the American revolution — reflected this. The Tea Partiers came together over a shared hostility to liberalism. But, right from the start, they harboured a suspicion of the Republican Party's leaders — and that suspicion continued to build.

Initially, mainstream Republicans had concluded that the anti-establishment rhetoric from the Tea Party — and from the media outlets that serviced them — was tolerable. After all, outsider anti-elitism pushed the political discourse to the right, and motivated activists to campaign for conservative candidates. In this sense, GOP strategists saw the new anti-elitism as a spigot that could be turned on and off. Right-wing politicians assumed that they could attend Tea Party rallies and receive sympathetic coverage from Glenn Beck — and then, once they were safely in office, they could forget the conspiracies and knuckle down to governing in the more or less traditional way.

Yet as the political authority of the mainstream weakened, the virtuous culture-war circle became markedly less stable.

In his 2001 book *Them*, a collection of essays about political and religious extremism, Jon Ronson wrote about meeting the broadcaster Alex Jones during research into the militia movement of the far right. Back then, Jones was 'hollering his powerful apocalyptic vision down an ISDN line from a child's bedroom in his house, with choo-choo train wallpaper and an *Empire Strikes Back* poster pinned to the wall'.[1]

Later, Ronson travelled with Jones to Bohemian Grove in California, where Jones claimed to have seen high-profile politicians performing weird occult ceremonies. 'They were burning a human in effigy in deference to their great owl god,' Jones told Ronson. 'This was a simulated human sacrifice complete with the person begging and pleading for his life. This was bizarre Luciferian garbage.'

Back in 2001, Jones was one of 'them': a fringe figure broadcasting to other extremists.

Fourteen years later, Ronson again met with Jones. By 2015, Jones claimed to be more popular than Rush Limbaugh, with five million daily radio listeners and 80 million video views each month. He told Ronson of a discussion with

Trump, in which The Donald said admiringly, 'You have one of the greatest influences I've ever seen.'[2]

Subsequently, on 2 December 2015, Trump appeared on Jones' program and said publicly: 'Your reputation's amazing. I will not let you down.'

The rise of Jones' *Infowars* empire exemplified a broader phenomenon. The cumulative weight of all that rhetoric about liberal treason, national destruction, and imminent race war had produced a new kind of conservative activist. As David Frum put it, establishment Republicans were kidding themselves when they assumed that the Tea Party was 'a mass movement in favor of the agenda of the *Wall Street Journal* editorial page' — that is, the traditional Republican program.[3] Increasingly, Tea Partiers were listening to people like Jones, rather than conventional political influencers.

In 2008, John McCain, a career politician, had offered a sop to outsider anti-elitists by adopting as his running mate the relatively unknown Sarah Palin, a woman very much shaped by the Fox News/Tea Party milieu. But the unlikely pairing pleased no one. Mainstream pundits were appalled by Palin's folksy incompetence, while outsider anti-elitists blamed the defeat on McCain's refusal to 'let Palin be Palin'.

In 2012, Mitt Romney obtained Tea Party backing and then campaigned more or less as an establishment conservative. In a different era, empty promises to the base about anti-elitism had served politicians like John Howard well. Romney, however, managed neither to motivate populist activists nor to sway undecided voters, and was comprehensively defeated by Obama.

In 2015, the Republican leaders had planned a similar approach. They wanted Jeb Bush as their candidate. He came from an established political dynasty; he was an experienced governor with significant support from big business. On paper, he was ideal. But in the campaign for the Republican nomination, Bush could get almost no traction at all — and neither could any of the other 'serious' options.

Trump's victory — and the constant displays of his distinctive obnoxiousness — obscured the extent to which his main challengers for the Republican nomination also espoused extreme positions, in some cases to the right of Trump himself.

The celebrity surgeon Ben Carson, who enjoyed a brief but unexpected surge of popularity, believed that Darwin's theory of evolution was encouraged by the devil, that Joseph built the Egyptian pyramids to store grain, that Americans were living under the Gestapo, and that homosexuality was a choice '[b]ecause a lot of people who go into prison go into prison straight — and when they come out, they're gay'.[4]

Mike Huckabee, a practising Southern Baptist minister and the author of God, Guns, Grits, and Gravy, explained during one of the debates that 'it's time that we recognise the Supreme Court is not the supreme being, and we change the policy to be pro-life and protect children instead of rip up their body parts and sell them like they're parts to a Buick'.[5]

Rick Santorum denied that climate change was caused by humans, described contraception as 'a license to do things in a sexual realm that is counter to how things are supposed to be',[6] had proposed a full Mexican border wall as far back as 2011, and thought that legalising homosexual acts would legitimise polygamy and incest.

Most importantly, Ted Cruz, the only candidate who came close to defeating Trump, positioned himself as the candidate of the far right. In 2015, Cruz had spoken at a conference headed and organised by Pastor Kevin Swanson, who wanted homosexuals exterminated and who urged his followers to attend same-sex marriages with signs threatening the participants with execution.[7] In the primaries, Cruz endorsed Trump's proposals for Muslim bans and mass deportations — and then denounced Trump as soft on immigration. 'He's advocated allowing folks to come back in and become citizens,' Cruz said. 'I oppose that.'[8]

Cruz was an ideologue, philosophically committed to a particular strand of religious conservatism. Trump, however, was not. Until 2008, he'd most often identified as a Democrat, at one stage proposing that he'd stand for president alongside the famously liberal Oprah Winfrey. Even when he adopted far-right positions on immigration and other issues, he still bucked the conservative consensus on taxation and the reform of social security, while boasting repeatedly (and falsely) that he'd opposed the war in Iraq.

Other politicians understood the Tea Party (and the culture wars more generally) in terms of policy. Trump, whether consciously or not, recognised it, first and foremost, as a revolt, a protest against the status quo. This was why Trump's own idiosyncratic career wasn't the weakness that some of his conservative opponents supposed. His 'New York sensibilities' weren't liabilities but assets, since they differentiated him from all the Bible-thumping ideologues. Even theocratic voters didn't want another theocrat to represent them. Trump was simultaneously sufficiently familiar to be a recognisable culture-war candidate and sufficiently different to be an agent of change.

During, and immediately after, the election, much was made of Trump's supposedly 'white working-class base'. Sharon Smith collated an array of headlines to that effect: articles such as 'How Trump Won: The Revenge of Working Class Whites'; 'The Revenge of the White Man'; 'Revenge of the Forgotten Class'; 'Revenge of the Rural Voter'; 'Why Trump Won: Working-Class Whites'; and so on.[9]

But because most media discussions reflected new-class theory, journalists often assumed that voters who embraced the tropes of culture war belonged to the working class, irrespective of what those people actually did for a living.

If the 'working class' was understood to mean people who sold their labour power for a wage, matters were quite different. The American working class was, after all, increasingly brown rather than white, with American industry dependent on the labour of the very ethnic groups systematically demonised by Trump. Smith said flatly:

People of color will very soon become the majority in the US population, and are already close to 50 per cent among younger generations. Moreover, people of color have always been disproportionately represented within the working class and the poor, due to the economic consequences of racism … Today's working class is multiracial, made up of multiple genders and nationalities, and many people with a variety of disabilities.[10]

In the American context (even more so than in the Australian one), media references to workers were implicitly racialised and geographically specific, with pundits invariably deploying 'working class' as a synonym for older white men from rural areas. Thomas Frank, for instance, wrote a moving account of visiting the town of Marceline in Missouri. Walt Disney, who was born there, once used Marceline as the archetype of small-town USA. Frank described a place in steep decline: a former Democratic stronghold now gripped by unemployment and infrastructural decay. When he sat down with members of the Lions Club in the back room of the Apple Basket Cafe, he discovered most of the men there had voted for Trump:

> Few of them seemed to really support him in the full sense of the word. They were apprehensive about his presidency, they didn't know what to expect from it, but many of them had made the choice anyway … Another described it with a variant on Trump's famous proposition to black voters, which these white people clearly felt applied to them, too: 'Whaddaya got to lose by making a change?'[11]

Yet Frank's description of the town as 'heartlanders' obscured the fact that the men were mostly farmers. Farming involves exhausting physical labour — but it also entails running a small business, generally under intense competition from the giant agricorporations. For this reason, farmers have long provided, both in Australia and the US, a base for right-wing populism, and their support for Trump didn't seem quite as surprising as if they were imagined as archetypical workers.

In any case, while foreign observers judged Clinton as a liberal reformer and, as such, a far more appealing candidate than Trump for voters at the sharp end of deregulated capitalism, the election looked very different for many working-class Americans. Clinton was a representative of the Democratic establishment, with close ties to corporate America. She was a lifetime politician, in the public arena since her husband's presidency in the 1990s. For many people, she was indelibly associated with the structural changes wrought in American society over 30 years. Privatisation of utilities, the systematic rollback of welfare, constant war: voters saw Clinton as representing the status quo rather than any reprieve.

Despite the hope and change promised by Obama, the 2016 election took place in a country that hadn't recovered from the Great Recession. In 2015, the median household income remained lower than it had been in 2007 — which was also lower than its high of 1999. The talk of economic recovery rang particularly hollow in rural areas, where median incomes had continued to sink.

That hardship fed into a widely held sense of decay. American workers, the highest-paid in the world during the post-war boom, had seen their wages steadily decline since the mid-1970s until they'd become the lowest-paid among

OECD countries. A huge proportion held low-wage jobs, far more than in most developed nations.

Yet low-paid workers didn't necessarily vote against Trump. In a system of non-compulsory elections, many simply didn't vote at all. In her book *Hand to Mouth: the truth about being poor in a wealthy world*, Linda Tirado explained that, for many American workers, voting wasn't a priority since they'd never 'been given a whole lot of proof that [their] vote will matter anyway'.[12]

'Upper-income groups were overrepresented in the voting electorate as a whole,' noted Kim Moody, 'and both candidates drew a disproportionate part of their vote from the well-to-do, with Trump a bit more reliant on high-income voters.'[13]

In any case, liberals' own enthusiasm for the Democrats often blinded them to the extent to which Trump pitched his rhetoric to the poor more effectively than Clinton did.

The journalist Christian Parenti wrote of sitting through a large number of Trump speeches and realising that Trump spent much less time discussing immigration, deportations, and walls than he expected. Rather, Trump's rambling addresses tended to circle back, again and again, to the need for jobs. 'A typical Trump speech,' Parenti noted, 'would tee-up with reference to "the wall" but then quickly pivot to economic questions: trade, jobs, descriptions of economic suffering, critiques of deindustrialization.'[14]

By contrast, Clinton infamously announced in West Virginia her desire 'to put a lot of coal miners and coal companies out of business' — a laudable ambition in respect of climate change, but, when presented without any pledge of alternatives for displaced workers, an ominous promise for those already struggling to feed their families. The two-party system forced voters to opt for the least-worst option, and so lower-income Americans who voted Trump weren't necessarily committed to Trumpism as a whole.

The unexpected dynamism of Bernie Sanders' push for the Democratic nomination hinted at how such a constituency might have been mobilised. Sanders' rhetoric touched on themes associated with direct politics. He targeted the massive income gap in the US; he denounced the political weight of corporate power; and he spoke explicitly of the need for a different kind of economic order.

But his eventual defeat merely highlighted the absence of anything similar in the Clinton campaign. Clinton polled around three million more votes than Trump, whose victory was dependant on the vagaries of the electoral system — a mechanism foisted on the American people to assuage former slave states.

Nevertheless, Trump could win on a smaller proportion of the vote than Mitt Romney attracted in 2012 because Clinton performed substantially worse than Obama, and a significant proportion of voters either didn't vote or opted for third-party candidates. Hence Matthew Yglesias's summation of the election: 'If you don't like Trump and never did and find yourself baffled as to how the voters could have possibly disagreed with you, the answer is simple: They didn't. He was able to win not just because of the Electoral College, but because most voters also didn't like his opponent.'[15]

Donald Trump was the least-liked major-party candidate in history — but Hillary Clinton was the second-least-liked Framed like this, the result became less anomalous. Trump triumphed, despite his personal unpopularity, because he was the endorsed Republican candidate fortunate enough to run against a weak Democrat.

But this bald statement of fact doesn't capture the extraordinary flavour of the Trump victory and the way it exemplified the potential of culture war for the right more generally.

Very close to Election Day, a tape of Trump discussing his behaviour towards women surfaced:

> You know I'm automatically attracted to beautiful — I just start kissing them. It's like a magnet. Just kiss. I don't even wait. And when you're a star, they let you do it. You can do anything ... Grab them by the pussy. You can do anything.[16]

Conventional wisdom decreed that the contest was essentially over. In the past, allegations of adultery were assumed to be damaging — perhaps even fatal — for aspirants to the White House. Famously, in 1988, accusations about an affair had forced Gary Hart to drop out of the race for the Democratic nomination. Besides, the conduct about which Trump spoke wasn't just ethically questionable. If he really had done what he claimed, the man running for the most important elected office in the world was a self-confessed criminal. Someone who joked about his propensity for sexual assault could never be president — could he?

The answer to this question revealed itself at the polls. Trump's ability to flout the established norms of American politics was, in many ways, the most striking aspect of the election. 'Time and again, Trump poured gasoline on himself and lit a match,' noted *Politico*'s Michael Kruse and Taylor Gee. 'Time and again, pundits predicted fatal self-immolation. Instead, Trump often rode the ensuing firestorm like an Atlas rocket.'[17]

Though Trump's polling was far less stratospheric than that description suggested, Kruse and Gee were identifying something real: Trump's ability to tap into the culture-war rage felt by a particular constituency and, by so doing, defy the expectations of insider pundits. Conservative columnist David Frum identified Trump's appeal to those he called 'the angriest and most pessimistic people in America' as being to those 'we used to call Middle Americans ... Middle-class and middle-aged; not rich and not poor.' They were, he said, not necessarily super-conservative but they were 'irked when when asked to press 1 for English' because it reminded them of how America had changed. '[T]hey ... feel strongly that life in this country used to be better for people like them — and they want that older country back.'[18]

Frum's description recalled the very similar constituency for anti-elitism in 1990s Australia. Trump was the perfect candidate for such people because he spoke openly — almost obsessively — about decline. 'We got $18 trillion in debt,' he said, launching his run. 'We got nothing but problems … We're dying. We're dying. We need money … We have losers. We have people that don't have it. We have people that are morally corrupt. We have people that are selling this country down the drain … The American dream is dead.'[19]

It was a remarkably bleak perspective — Corey Robin described a 'note of wounded nationalism' as running through Trump's rhetoric — but it suited the grim mood of his core voters.[20] The *Economist*'s reporter noted that Trump's keenest supporters lived in depressed parts of America but weren't necessarily struggling themselves. The description accords with the classic pattern of outsider anti-elitism, in which the cadre for populist movements came from the lower middle class: people fearful of the big end of town but terrified of falling further into the working class. The *Economist* continued:

> At a rally in Delaware, a suburb of Columbus, Ohio, a brief survey revealed a computer programmer, three teachers, a botanist, several small businessmen, and not a single working-class man … At over a dozen Trump rallies, in almost as many states, over the past year, your correspondent has met lawyers, estate agents and a horde of middle-class pensioners — and relatively few blue-collar workers.'[21]

'When I was young, in high school and in college, everybody used to say we never lost a war. America never lost,' Trump told his supporters. 'Now, we never win a war.'[22]

The people most inclined to nod along with such words

were akin to the 'battlers' that Pusey described, people who felt themselves in a situation similar to America itself — always harried, never winning, in an dog-eat-dog society with no pity for losers.

Charlie Post argued that:

The core of Trump's support, like that of Tea Party since 2009, is the older, white, suburban/exurban middle classes. His success among non-college educated whites — he won 52 per cent of all voters without bachelor's degrees — appears to be concentrated among traditional small-business people (construction contractors, small shop keepers, etc) and those supervisors (factory foreman, store and office managers, etc) and semi-professionals (technicians, etc) who do not require a college education. His success among househoulders earning over $75,000 a year reflects the support of the managerial and professional elite of this class … However, the politics of these groups have *radicalised* since the economic crisis of 2008.[23]

Trump's racism gave that radicalisation its structure. His attacks on Muslims and immigrants evoked the vanished, whiter society of the past, and then provided a scapegoat to blame for its disappearance. Racial dog-whistling thus performed a peculiar double move central to his candidacy. On the one hand, for white Tea Partiers, it offered a reassuring reminder of what 'everyone knew'; on the other, it constituted a revolutionary slogan that no one else was prepared to utter.

For instance, Trump launched his presidential bid by attacking Mexican immigrants. 'They're bringing drugs. They're bringing crime. They're rapists,' he said. 'And some, I assume, are good people.'[24]

He made the construction of a border wall — for which, he said, Mexico would pay — a centrepiece of his campaign. The 'big, beautiful wall' was a distinctly Trump-like slogan — the kind of simplistic, offensive idea that had been voiced on Fox for years but not previously adopted by a presidential candidate. Trump's willingness to campaign for it, despite the obvious objections about its cost, cruelty, and purpose, bolstered his appeal to outsider anti-elitists. The more the idea upset insiders, the more Trump's base concluded that at last they'd found a candidate who would not betray them.

At the same time, Trump's anti-immigration campaign built on a long, bipartisan commitment to 'border protection'. As NBC noted in its analysis of the refugee policy, many of Trump's policies were very similar to those implemented by Obama.

'President Barack Obama has often been referred to by immigration groups as the "Deporter in Chief",' explained Serena Marshall. '... According to governmental data, the Obama administration has deported more people than any other president's administration in history. In fact, they have deported more than the sum of all the presidents of the 20th century.'[25]

Even Trump's wall was not without precedent. The legal authorisation for the Trump plan already existed because of the Secure Fence Act of 2006, which legislated for a (smaller) barrier along the southern border. Clinton had voted for that proposal, as had Barack Obama, and so Trump could thus present his agitation against immigrants and refugees as the bold pursuit of a sentiment that was widely held but that remained unimplemented because of the cowardice of elites.[26]

His Islamophobia followed a similar pattern.

Throughout his campaign, Trump pandered to anti-Muslim racism. At one rally, a crowd member said to him, 'We have a problem in this country; it's called Muslims,' before asking him, 'When we can get rid of them?'

Trump responded: 'You know, a lot of people are saying that, and a lot of people are saying that bad things are happening out there. We're going to be looking at that and plenty of other things.'[27]

During the election, he repeatedly pledged to ban 'Muslim immigration', and said he would contemplate closing down mosques and establishing a 'Muslim registry'.

Again, the rhetoric was shocking; again, it appalled much of the commentariat — and, as a result, reinforced Trump's outsider anti-elitist credibility.

Yet Trump's deployment of Islamophobia took place in a certain context. As many Muslims pointed out, president Obama didn't enter a mosque until the end of his two terms in office, despite frequent invitations by Islamic leaders. By contrast, in the immediate wake of 9/11, George Bush made a mosque visit as a deliberate statement. Fifteen years of the War on Terror had changed the tenor of the public discourse on Islam, normalising — almost to the point of invisibility

— low levels of Islamophobia. Trump, of course, made his Islamophobia as visible as possible.

The early history of anti-PC showed why this mattered so much. The campaign against so-called political correctness began as an attack on the campus left. It seized upon the gulf between the activists of delegated politics and their supporters, presenting progressives as imposing their ideas upon ordinary people by force.

By 2016, the discourse of anti-PC was so well established as to be almost taken for granted. To denounce political correctness, Trump didn't need to associate his opponents with state bans. It was quite sufficient merely to hint that they were in some way inhibiting him from saying what needed to be said. This was why Trump's 'gaffes' played so well among his core supporters. He was, they concluded, saying what everyone thought — and he was doing so in defiance of the politically correct censors.

The Clinton campaign's attempt to capitalise on Trump's supposed mistakes merely confirmed that framing. In the second debate, Clinton, quite understandably, attacked Trump's 'grab them by the pussy' remarks. But she did so by contrasting him with traditional politicians.

'You know,' she said, 'with prior Republican nominees for president, I disagreed with them on politics, policies, principles, but I never questioned their fitness to serve. Donald Trump is different.'[28]

She ran through some of the slurs he'd used before concluding, 'So this is who Donald Trump is ... [T]he question our country must answer is that this is not who we are ... I want to send a message ... to the entire world that America already is great, but we are great because we are good, and we will respect one another, and we will work with one another, and we will celebrate our diversity.'

Unwittingly, the passage reinforced almost everything about Trump that appealed to his supporters. They liked him precisely because — as Clinton publicly confirmed — he seemed so different from previous Republican nominees and thus from the status quo. They liked him even more because he echoed their perception of decline, promising to make America great again.

By contrast, Clinton's insistence that America was already great identified her with the status quo. America did not, after all, feel great to many people — and Clinton's inability to grasp this only highlighted the gulf between her life and theirs. As former Clinton adviser Stanley Greenberg complained, 'She ran on continued progress in a change election.'[29]

Her call for 'respect' — again, something that sounded perfectly rational to her supporters — was heard by those sympathetic to Trump as the usual smug political insistence on civility: a PC demand that they should cease complaining.

With his experience as a reality-TV star, Trump understood that by insulting an interviewer, or calling his opponents 'Lyin' Ted' or 'Crooked Hillary', or racially slurring an entire ethnicity, he was producing great content. But he was also manoeuvring his opponents into calling for decorum, at a time when his supporters wanted to scream their rage.

Again, Trump's base was not large. Yet, given the widespread alienation from mainstream politics, a small but vocal layer of activists made a huge difference, particularly as the older Tea Party types were supplemented by the younger, more dynamic enthusiasts of the alt-right, who helped shape the public discourse of Trumpism.

CHAPTER THIRTEEN

The alt-right and appropriation

The term 'alt-right' was popularised by the American white-nationalist leader Richard Spencer, who achieved a degree of international notoriety when, after the 2016 election, he urged his saluting followers to perform a 'Heil Trump'. Stylistically, Spencer differentiated himself from other American fascists. He wasn't a tattooed skinhead; he prided himself on his fashion, his elocution, and his perfectly coiffured hair. Moreover, he harboured intellectual aspirations, completing a masters degree and then enrolling for several years as a PhD student at Duke University.

Spencer's media profile never correlated with his actual political influence, with his racist thinktank the National Policy Institute remaining very much a fringe outfit. Nevertheless, Spencer mattered as one of a number of figures who helped create a sense of radicalism around the 2016 result. He also illustrated, with particular clarity, the growing willingness of the far right to adopt, either explicitly or implicitly, ideas associated with the delegated and smug politics of the left, something that would become very important for Trumpism.

In November 2015, a minor furore erupted when the University of Ottawa's Centre for Students with Disabilities decided to discontinue classes in yoga on the basis that they were culturally appropriative. Yoga, explained a representative of the centre, came from 'cultures that have experienced oppression, cultural genocide and diasporas due to colonialism and Western supremacy', and that made their presentation outside such a context problematic.[1]

Predictably, the students' decision ended up in the media around the world, lambasted by conservatives as another instance of political correctness gone mad. Yet, in the midst of the usual outrage, the Ottawa activists received an endorsement from an unexpected (and no doubt unwelcome) source: Richard Spencer.

The bizarre intervention — an avowed bigot supporting anti-racists — made, on its own terms, a kind of sense, though an explanation requires an extended detour into the politics of 'cultural appropriation'.

Throughout 2014 and 2015, progressive activists had been agitating against attendees at American music festivals wearing so-called 'tribal headdresses'. The semiotics of faux-Indian costumes (invariably based on old-fashioned movie tropes) were obvious — a college student camping out for a festival donned a headdress and painted his face because, consciously or not, he associated Native American culture with the free life of the 'noble savage'.

In this context, the outfits were clearly racist, since they reinforced stereotypes about oppressed people. Yet many activists — and festivals — explained their opposition to the headdresses not by invoking racism, but, like the students at Ottawa, by denouncing 'cultural appropriation'.

As with many ideas associated with identity politics, 'cultural appropriation' meant different things to different people. The legal scholar Susan Scafidi provided the most widely cited gloss. For her, cultural appropriation entailed 'taking intellectual property, traditional knowledge, cultural expressions, or artefacts from someone else's culture without permission. This can include unauthorised use of another culture's dance, dress, music, language, folklore, cuisine, traditional medicine, religious symbols, etc.'[2]

The festival fans were not Indigenous. This meant that, by wearing the costumes, they were using something that was not rightfully theirs, just as the Canadian yoga practitioners were doing with their classes.

The term 'cultural appropriation' spread because it described an obvious (and obviously pernicious) phenomenon, in which art and culture associated with the powerless and the oppressed became the plaything of the wealthy and the privileged, who generally enriched themselves through its use. Jazz, blues, rock, hip-hop: many African-American masters of these genres lived and died in poverty, even as second-rate white imitators grew tremendously wealthy using their material.

Yet the example of popular music also illustrated the difficulty with a simple, one-way model of appropriation.

The theorist Andrew Ross offered many instances of the interpenetration of 'black' and 'white' modes. Ragtime, he says, was 'a "clean" black response to white imitations of the "dirty" black versions of boogie-woogie piano blues', while 'the cakewalk' was a blackface minstrel imitation of 'blacks imitating highfalutin white manners'. The 'moldy figs' were 'white middle-class jazz revivalists' doing their best to sound like 'wizened, old New Orleans musicians who were themselves trying to sound like the real thing for the benefit of their white discoverers'. Dizzy Gillespie mockingly copied the white players who were copying his imitations of white hipsters; Howlin' Wolf got his name from mimicking Jimmie Rodgers, whose yodelling was influenced by African-American blues. When Elvis greased back his hair into a rockabilly quiff, he was, Ross said, 'emulating the black "process" of straightening and curling, itself a black attempt to look "white"'.[3]

Influence, then, went both ways, even if racism ensured that the interactions did not benefit white and black musicians equally. The differing career trajectories of artists from different races could be explained, fairly obviously, by reference to the prejudices of the music industry and of those who consumed its output. So what was at stake in using 'cultural appropriation' rather than 'racism' to describe the treatment of musicians and other art-makers?

Scafidi's definition rested on concepts taken from intellectual property law. They made unlikely foundations for radical theory, given that they presupposed a commodification normally associated with neoliberalism.

Western art had, of course, been bought and sold for profit for centuries. But Scafidi was arguing to apply the same framework to collective forms (folklore, cuisine, or even cultures as a whole), something that in other circumstances the left would instinctively resist.

The problem wasn't merely philosophical. If the idea of 'cultural appropriation' was to inform political practice, activists needed to differentiate legitimate and illegitimate claimants to ownership. But this was not easy. The assertion that white festival attendees should not appropriate native American costumes might have been relatively simple. After this, however, the complexities multiplied. Indigenous communities were, after all, as internally divided as any other population. Who, then, possessed the 'right' to speak for a culture as a whole?

In practice, the argument almost led to white liberals embracing 'authenticity', a deeply problematic (if not implicitly racist) term that obscured the social divisions and complex history of living cultures with an anthropological fetishisation of idealised tradition.

The furore at the University of Ottawa illustrated the difficulties. It wasn't merely that assigning 'ownership' over yoga — something performed in various ways by millions of very different people — made little sense. It was also that the students' assumption about yoga as an 'authentic' representation of traditions on the subcontinent was historically wrong. Modern yoga was, in fact, deeply influenced by the theosophy of the Russian mystic Madame Blavatsky.[4] The very word 'yoga' was, according to *Slate*'s

Michelle Goldberg, repurposed from a totally different context, deliberately chosen to describe a conscious synthesis derived from 'facets of medieval tantric practices [combined] with elements from Indian wrestling exercises, British army calisthenics, and Scandinavian gymnastics'.[5]

The political relationship between colonialism and yoga was, accordingly, much more complex than the students' statement implied. In fact, Indian nationalists saw the spread of their culture as a tool to undercut British rule. To this end, they sent the Hindu monk Swami Vivekananda to America to teach, surmising (correctly) that Western interest in Indian traditions would build support for independence. They weren't, in other words, passive victims but political agents, using yoga's appeal to popularise their struggle.

None of this changed the reality that white people in the imperial centres made more money from yoga than practitioners in India did. But the disparity — a typical manifestation of the colonial relationship — didn't, in the eyes of the nationalists, invalidate yoga's spread. Quite correctly, they recognised that cultural isolation wouldn't bring economic justice. This, they knew, depended on something more material — the political defeat of the British.

Why, then, did the student argument appeal to Spencer?

Spencer enthused about cultural appropriation because he recognised that the development of delegated and smug politics opened opportunities for the right. Unlike other far-right activists, he didn't simply denounce multiculturalism. Instead, he said that he accepted cultural diversity — and that he advocated 'identity politics for white people'.[6]

'So long as we avoid and deny our identities, at a time when every other people is asserting its own, we will have no chance to resist our dispossession, no chance to make our future, no chance to find another horizon,' he declared.[7]

In the wake of 9/11, according to Neil Davidson, outsider anti-elitism had implicitly adopted 'a politics of identity' based on what he called 'that most pernicious of invented categories, the 'white working class'.[8] The original neoconservative presentation of workers as a patriotic, traditionalist counterweight to the effete and disloyal elites came, over time, to function as a right-wing mirror of progressive rhetoric, with pundits and politicians of the right presenting themselves as advocates for a 'working-class' identity (generally defined through an aggregation of cultural clichés pertaining to white, male, rural, blue-collar workers). They claimed authority through lived experience, prefacing their interventions with an invocation of a (real or invented) childhood in a hardscrabble neighbourhood. They demanded speaking rights on the basis of their background; they revelled in a dubious victimhood; and they embraced most of the rhetorical moves associated with a politics they claimed to despise.

As Phoebe Maltz Bovy recognised, conservatives thus drew from the same well that produced left-wing ideas of privilege.[9] Yet, for the most part, they did so without realising how closely they mimicked what they derided, with, for instance, the conservative pundit Bill O'Reilly mocking identity politics — and then unselfconsciously claiming that his Irish–Catholic working-class background gave him an especial insight into the 'real America'.

But Spencer was different. He understood the left's rhetoric, and quite deliberately embraced it. For instance, when he advocated the creation of an ethnostate, a racially segregated homeland for white people similar to Rhodesia or apartheid-era South Africa, he eschewed the oratorical style associated with the Klu Klux Klan (KKK) (which had long put forward a similar demand). Instead, he drew parallels with the Zionist support for Israel as a Jewish ethnostate, and declared he wanted 'a safe space for whites'.[10] His co-thinkers in the European fascist group symptomatically named Generation Identity went so far as to describe their plans for white homelands as 'ethno-pluralism', an idea echoing progressive enthusiasm for an array of diverse but separate identities.

Spencer's identification with the Ottawa students came from a similar place. By presenting yoga as an Indian practice that whites should not access, the students were accepting the existence of an 'authentic' Indian culture. This meant that they were also positing an authentic 'white' culture, and then insisting that whites should stick to that culture. Whether they knew it or not, they thus validated the key assumptions of Spencer's 'identity politics for white people', expressing what he called a nascent form of racial consciousness.

'[T]he reality,' he said, 'is that leftists are engaging in the kind of ideological project that traditionalists should be hard at work on — the formation of 'meta-politics,' consciousness that transcends and precedes any political issue. Put simply, thinking racially — and by that I mean thinking spiritually, historically, and mythologically.'[11] Spencer's enthusiasm for the left's embrace of 'cultural appropriation' reflected his sense of the difference between such ideas and those once held by anti-fascist activists.

The socialists who had led the struggle against fascism after its emergence in the 1920s generally identified themselves as cultural eclectics who were positively enthusiastic about the intermingling of artistic tendencies. In the *Communist Manifesto*, Marx and Engels celebrated the dissolution of national traditions as part of the process that gave their famous slogan, 'Workers of the world, unite' meaning.

'The intellectual creations of individual nations become common property,' they wrote. 'National one-sidedness and narrowmindedness become more and more impossible, and from the numerous national and local literatures, there arises a world literature.'[12]

It was the ideologues of fascism and national socialism, not their opponents, who advocated cultural authenticity. For the far right, protecting the boundaries of their particular culture was an important component of the racial and ethnic pride they valorised.

'All great art is national,' declared Hitler. '... Great musicians, such as Beethoven, Mozart, Bach, created German music that was deeply rooted in the very core of the German spirit and the German mind ... That is equally true of German sculptors, painters, architects.'[13]

The same divisions emerged a generation later when post-war fascists advocated cultural purity in the face of anti-fascists supporting cosmopolitanism. In Britain during the mid–1970s, the National Front declared itself to be protecting the homogeneity of culture against a purported influx of foreigners. For a while, the fascists seemed on the verge of an electoral breakthrough in the UK. They were holding large rallies, and they were winning alarming support among young people and the musicians to whom those young people listened.

In response, leftists formed the Anti-Nazi League to confront the NF with both demonstrations and concerts.[14] The massive multi-racial protests effectively isolated and demoralised the fascists. But they also led to a hybridisation of the music enjoyed by white and black youth. The experience led Bob Marley to sing about a 'punky reggae party' — a fertile collision between musicians 'rejected by society', regardless of their differing traditions.

As Shuja Haider pointed out, 'cultural appropriation' was coined during this time by intellectuals of the so-called Birmingham School to convey precisely the opposite of what the term signifies today.[15] They wanted to celebrate the cultural borrowings through which subaltern groups subverted oppression, the different ways in which (mostly) young people repurposed traditions not their own. In the words of Steel Pulse's singer David Hinds, the ANL and its Rock Against Racism events meant that 'white people started going to gigs with black performers. People started to learn about different languages, dances, foods and cultures.'[16]

From Spencer's perspective, the Ottawa students' stance against yoga was something to be welcomed, simply because it made his job easier. The old Hitlerite argument about a biological Aryan supremacy had been widely discredited. Even claims about the superiority of 'white' culture sounded dubious, given the enthusiasm of most white Americans for cultural forms associated with African Americans. By contrast, the popularisation of 'cultural authenticity' by leftists — in the name of anti-racism, no less — provided a context in which the ideas of the far right could germinate and grow.

Again, Spencer's importance pertained less to his actual influence than what he represented — a genuine fascist embracing key ideas associated with the left. Spencer's personal extremism — his willingness, for instance, to espouse racial nationalism publicly — kept him on the margins of American politics, even during the Trump campaign.

But others were able to adopt a similar approach with far more success.

The unlikely process by which Donald Trump — an old, Republican billionaire — became an icon in a youthful counterculture centred on the far right deserves closer scrutiny, as an example of just what was possible. It's best understood by looking at the evolution of *Breitbart*, the publication that, for a time, became the voice of Trumpism.

Andrew Breitbart — the founder of *Breitbart* — claimed to have begun life as a liberal before embracing the outsider anti-elitism he absorbed from Rush Limbaugh's radio show. Substantially younger than Limbaugh, Breitbart played a role in two early online successes, working with (the then Republican) Ariana Huffington to establish *The Huffington Post* and with Matt Drudge to build *The Drudge Report*. He developed his own profile as a Fox News commentator and Tea Party activist, before founding *Breitbart* in 2007 as a pro-Israel site influenced by (and linked to) European far-right populist movements.

From early on, Breitbart said he was committed to 'the destruction of the old media guard', challenging CNN and the 'liberal media' both stylistically (with a sophisticated understanding of the online space) and politically (with an aggressive outsider anti-elitism).[17]

But it was only after Breitbart's death that his successor, Steve Bannon, declared the site to be 'the platform for the alt-right'. Under Bannon's leadership, *Breitbart* cohered a younger, mostly male audience around a far-right version of identity politics — building, in particular, through a strange intervention into the world of video games.

Bannon, whom Breitbart had once described admiringly as 'the Leni Riefenstahl of the Tea Party movement', had been a naval officer, investment banker. and Hollywood entrepreneur (he acquired the lucrative rights to the sitcom *Seinfeld*).[18] At one stage, however, he had worked for the Hong Kong tech company Internet Gaming Entertainment. The experience, he later explained, exposed him to a gaming culture 'populated by millions of intense young men'. The gamers were socially awkward, but they were also, Bannon concluded, 'smart, focused, relatively wealthy, and highly motivated about issues that mattered to them'. As executive chairman of *Breitbart*, Bannon reoriented his platform to these 'rootless white males'.[19]

He was able to do so because of Gamergate, an intense culture war among video-game players.

In 2014, the ex-boyfriend of a games developer called Zoe Quinn had written a 10,000-word blog post about their breakup, which was understood by gamers congregating on Reddit, 4chan, and other platforms as establishing that Quinn had slept with a journalist from *Kotaku* in order to gain favourable reviews of her work.

In reality, *Kotaku* had never reviewed Quinn's game *Depression Quest*, an idiosyncratic exploration of mental illness. Nevertheless, right-wing gamers, already convinced that feminists were imposing themselves on a supposedly apolitical hobby, became consumed with rage.

'If I ever see you are doing a panel at an event I am going to, I will literally kill you,' read one of the message sent to Quinn. 'You are lower than shit and deserve to be hurt, maimed, killed, and finally, graced with my piss on your rotting corpse a thousand times over.'[20]

Trolls hacked Quinn's social-media accounts. They published her address. They leaked nude photos of her across the internet. They harassed her on her home number. They called her father and other family members. They discussed means by which she might be driven to suicide.

The vitriol directed at Quinn soon extended to the feminist game critic Anita Sarkeesian, developer Brianna Wu, and to many, many others — mostly, though not exclusively, women.

To outsiders, the intensity and scope of Gamergate was difficult to comprehend. Anita Sarkeesian had produced a Youtube series delivering a mild feminist critique of some popular video games. In response, angry men insisted that gaming wasn't sexist — and then threatened to kill her.

Yet the history of computing — and computer gaming — revealed parallels between Gamergate and other manifestations of culture war. Perhaps surprisingly, women had played an important role in the early development of computing. In 1984, 37 per cent of American computer-science graduates were women — a figure that compared favourably with many other professions. Yet, from then on, the percentage dropped precipitously, even as other fields became more female-friendly. By 2016, it was only 18 per cent.

Many of the earliest games were gender-neutral — and some even featured female protagonists. But the industry endured a devastating crash in 1983. The recovery was led by Nintendo, which identified its games as toys, and marketed them overwhelmingly to boys.

NPR journalist Steve Henn suggested, counterintuitively, that the involvement of women also suffered when the first personal computers found their way into American homes: 'This idea that computers are for boys became a narrative. It became the story we told ourselves about the computing revolution. It helped define who geeks were, and it created techie culture.'[21]

Research by Jane Margolis among computer-science students at Carnegie Mellon University in the 1990s established that families were far more likely to purchase computers for sons than daughters, which meant that boys arrived at university with a degree of knowledge and experience that their female counterparts lacked.[22]

Technology — and tech culture — became thoroughly gendered. Yet this gendering was contradictory. The geek milieu of the 1980s and 1990s was unambiguously male, but the geeks themselves were depicted by broader society as feminised: effete, socially awkward loners embracing tech because they couldn't play sport or get girlfriends.

The ubiquity of information technology in the 21st century changed the equation, in several interesting ways. Rather than an idiosyncratic hobby, computing became an everyday activity — and, moreover, for some entrepreneurs, a route to stupendous wealth. The growth of Silicon Valley mainstreamed geek culture, with comic books and sci-fi novels and role-playing games that had once been the preserve of self-identifying nerds reinvented as TV series and Hollywood blockbusters.

The critic Brendan Keogh noted:

Masculine computer culture thus occupies a complex position: a field traditionally inaccessible to those who aren't male or upper middle class, but dominated by those teased and bullied for not being macho, has now obtained a privileged status. The hacker remains an alternative identity to the masculinity of sporting jocks, but it continues to exclude women, even as it has grown in power and influence.[23]

Yet material power and influence was by no means necessarily the majority experience. A tiny number of start-ups became hugely successful, but many tech aficionados remained unemployed or stranded in dead-end jobs. The resulting stew of resentments and entitlements manifested themselves on platforms like 4chan: a repurposed Japanese-style bulletin board created in 2003 by a 15-year-old called Christopher Poole.

Originally pandering to fans of anime, comics, games, and the like, 4chan's inbuilt anonymity encouraged pornography, insider jokes, random arguments, and a distinctive culture. Dale Beran, an early user, suggested the site essentially invented the 'meme', popularised terms such as 'win', 'epic', and 'fail', established conventions for the use of gifs and images in messaging, and so left 'a profound impression on how we as a culture behave and interact'. This impression was a decidedly mixed blessing, given the nature of 4chan, which was 'a bullying and anarchic society of adolescent boys — or at least, men with the mindset of boys — particularly lonely, sex-starved man-boys, who according to their own frequent jokes about the subject, lived in their parents' basement'.[24]

4chan also became synonymous with trolling — online pranks that were sometimes funny, sometimes strange, and often unbelievably cruel (such as the harassment campaign directed at the parents of a child who'd killed himself). Most obviously, trolling reflected aspects of the online experience that, as academic Andrew Jakubowicz put it, enhanced 'the psychological dimensions of anonymity, disengagement, and dis-inhibition'.[25] But the technology didn't emerge in a vacuum. Rather, the internet developed in a dialectical relationship with a neoliberal economic system that it both served and shaped. As a result, 4chan absorbed the peculiar ethics of neoliberalism — in particular, a sense of the individual as entirely responsible for the consequences of his or her actions.

Grieving parents, for instance, attracted 4chan's ire because trolls judged their mourning to be maudlin and phoney. In the online space, as in the marketplace more generally, losers — merely by being losers — deserved whatever they got. If you secretly feared that you might be among their number, the obvious way to protect yourself was by dishing out some spectacular punishment to others.

The 4channers might have been younger and more technologically adept than the traditional constituency of outsider anti-elitism. Yet, like Hanson's 'battlers', basement-dwelling trolls felt themselves alone and subjected to forces they could not defeat. Like the Hansonites, they were deeply nostalgic, not so much for the society of the 1950s as for a tech culture they perceived as being under threat from women.

Not coincidentally, the main 4chan troll factory was called /pol/ (for politically incorrect). For the young men of 4chan, 'political correctness' manifested itself less through the actions of humanities academics and more in the form of games critics slating a title the 4channers particularly liked. But the structure of anti-PC was identical: a rejection of the progressives deemed to be censoring, castigating, or otherwise talking down to ordinary people.

Gamergate brought 4chan's sensibility to a much wider audience. Gaming was, after all, an immensely popular hobby: according to a 2015 study, over 40 per cent of Americans gamed for at least three hours a week. Gamergate might have remained either invisible or incomprehensible to journalists from an older generation, but it resonated widely with those for whom computer games had become the pre-eminent cultural form.

Paradoxically, Gamergate could be understood as a backlash against precisely the popularity that made the whole fracas matter. Just as the middle-class white Trump voters yearned for a vanished American greatness, the male gamers aggrieved at Anita Sarkeesian wanted to protect a version of geekdom they associated with a time that had now passed. Beran noted that 'these are men without jobs, without prospects, and by extension (so they declaimed) without girlfriends … [and] in the one space they feel they can escape the realities of this, the world of the video game, here (to them, it seems) women want to assert their presence and power'.[26]

It was easy, then, to dismiss, as many progressives did, Gamergate as a curious internet psychodrama, an extended tantrum that would inevitably end when male gamers acknowledged a changed world. Yet, like a nostalgia for white Australia, the male yearning for a vanished online space could be weaponised — and the person who recognised this was Milo Yiannopoulos.

Prior to Gamergate, Yiannopoulos was a relatively little-known provocateur working for *Breitbart* who'd previously lambasted gamers as 'unemployed saddos living in their parents' basements'.[27] Nevertheless, he wrote a piece summarising Gamergate as a clash between 'journalists and activists, who care more about gender politics than the video games they are supposed to be reporting on, and gamers, mocked, derided and bullied ... but unbowed'.[28]

Most mainstream publications sympathised (for obvious reasons) with the women being harassed by the Gamergaters. Yiannopoulos, however, correctly concluded that he could attract clicks from the Gamergaters themselves. Later, *Breitbart* editor Alex Marlow subsequently attributed the growth of his publication's younger demographic to the readers who arrived via Gamergate.[29]

But Yiannopoulos was interested in more than mere numbers. Perhaps better than anyone else, he recognised how the Gamergaters were deploying identity politics for the right.

Between August and September 2014, several review sites (*Gamasutra*, *Kotaku*, *Polygon*, and others) published articles arguing that the 'gamer was dead': that, because of the expansion and diversity of the gaming audience, no single idea of a player could be taken for granted. The outpouring of rage in response to this fairly anodyne suggestion lifted (or perhaps sunk) Gamergate to a new level. It also revealed how deeply invested right-wingers were in a 'gamer identity' — and the extent to which they shared ideas with the so-called Social Justice Warriors they derided.

Gamergaters might, and frequently did, denounce identity politics. But they also insisted that that a distinctive gamer culture existed, and was under threat. As their campaign against the SJWs escalated, they began to celebrate that identity. They wrote and published Gamergate songs, stories, and poems. They created the character 'Vivian James' (an auburn-haired woman wearing a headband with the 4chan logo) as a Gamergate mascot. They became obsessed with representation, complaining bitterly about how their 'culture' was portrayed in the media. In a typical post, the gamer behind *The Ralph Retort*, a blog, responded to a Gamergate-themed episode of *Law and Order* by huffing, 'It definitely was offensive as fuck.'[30]

Most of all, they argued that those — like Anita Sarkeesian — who weren't 'real gamers' had no right to speak about gaming. '[S]o many SJWs throw up their arms about cultural appropriation,' one Gamergater wrote, '[but] it seems like they're fine to do it when they believe they should have control of a culture ... They aren't part of the culture, they don't understand the culture and as such they lash out and claim gaming is harmful or promotes toxic behaviour. Many SJWs just don't get not everything is for them.'[31]

This was identity politics — but identity politics repurposed for the far right.

Pitching *Breitbart* to Gamergaters as a sympathetic outlet, Yiannopoulos deliberately appealed to the gamer identity, addressing his readers as if they belonged to a suffering minority.

'If you have ever felt bullied,' he wrote, 'or victimised, or harassed, or marginalised — not by bullshit imaginary concepts like the "patriarchy" but by people who want to stop you expressing yourself and who call you a loser, a manbaby, a shitlord, a privileged cishet white male — then Milo Yiannopoulos is for you.'[32]

The rhetoric reflected the prevalence of identity politics, so ubiquitous as to be taken for granted by the right as well as the left. Yet, unlike an older generation of outsider anti-elitists, the trolls of Gamergate understood — and could exploit — the ideas developed out of the delegated politics of the left.

To counter progressive arguments about representation in gaming, right-wingers launched the #notyourshield, a hashtag under which social-media users allegedly belonging to minorities denounced the left and pledged their support for the status quo. A video-game trope didn't, of course, become any less sexist because a female gamer said she liked it, nor less racist because of approval from a black gamer. Yet the Gamergaters knew that progressives (especially white, male progressives) would struggle to respond to conservative African-American women — which was why they assiduously manufactured sockpuppet accounts on 4chan and the similar 8chan.

A version of this tactic later became a part of Yiannopoulos's own political persona. As he maneouvred himself into position as a spokesperson for gamers, he stressed — as per #notyourshield — that he was gay, of Jewish ancestry, and fond of sleeping with black men.

'We might not look much alike, the average gamer and me,' he wrote. 'But, when you think about it, we're natural

5

ideological bedfellows — and we've both been cast out by the people who ought to have been our defenders ...'

Yiannopoulos was, for a time, the most high-profile exponent of the troll sensibility that gave Trumpism its distinctive sheen. With speaking tours across American universities, he reprised the culture-war skirmishes out of which anti-PC emerged. He sought institutions in which the kind of speech codes that led to Nina Wu's exclusion might be applied to him. Yet where Wu was banned for mocking 'homos', Yiannopoulos announced himself as a 'Dangerous Faggot' — and dared the left to exclude him.

He invited his fans to identify as oppressed, launching the Yiannopoulos Privilege Grant, a college scholarship exclusively for white men. Like many Yiannopoulos initiatives, it came to nothing, with the fund never paying out. But that didn't matter. Like the 4channers, and like a growing number of right-wing provocateurs, Yiannopoulos worried less about outcomes than the lulz — and the best lulz came from the reaction of your targets.

In May 2016, Yiannopoulos wrote enthusiastically about the support for Trump among 4channers and other trolls. '[W]hat begins on /pol/ and leaks out into Twitter,' he said, 'has a way of colouring media coverage and, ultimately, public perception, even among people who don't frequent message boards.'[33]

This was pretty much what happened.

In her book *Kill All Normies*, Angela Nagle made a comparison between the iconography of Obama's first victory and that of Trump's win eight years later.[34] The

2008 campaign was associated with Shepard Fairey's striking 'Hope' poster. Fairey's depiction of Obama was the work of a talented professional designer. Though many progressives adopted it as a personal avatar, the image was very much an official one, endorsed and promulgated by the campaign.

By contrast, the image that defined the Trump election was the Pepe meme — the green frog used to identify the alt-right and, eventually, Trump supporters. Unlike 'Hope', Pepe, a character created by Matt Furie for his *Boy's Club* cartoon, was rendered in a deliberately crude and childlike fashion. Furthermore, the Pepe memes were generated more or less spontaneously by Trump supporters (against the wishes of Furie), not by the Republican campaign itself.

In other words, in 2016, the Republican Party, an organisation not normally considered hip or edgy, had developed a genuine grassroots aesthetic, one that contrasted markedly with the bland, corporate imagery associated with Clinton.

The infrastructure of the Republican Party had not changed appreciably. Nor, indeed, had the voter base — or, at least, not as much as was commonly thought. Yet the election felt particularly shocking because of the vicious troll culture that *Breitbart* and other, similar platforms brought into the mainstream. Later, leaked emails revealed Yiannopoulos and his ghostwriter Allum Bokhari to have been corresponding with representatives of the major elements of the alt-right: the identitarians like Spencer; the strange tech-inspired autodidacts who developed their own anti-liberal theories of 'The Dark Enlightenment'; the white nationalists associated with the American Renaissance; and overt Nazis such as the *Daily Stormer*'s Andrew 'Weev' Auernheimer.[35]

Echoes of those figures resonated throughout the campaign, with Trump and his family circulating 4chan-style material on Twitter and elsewhere. In August 2016, of course, Bannon himself went to work for Trump, an appointment that directly linked the future president with a publication that had promoted the far right and its newly weaponised version of identity politics.

Because both Bannon and Yiannopoulos were later discredited and marginalised, it's easy to forget the cultural impact they had. In many ways, Gamergate should be understood not so much as anomalous but as exemplary, a paradigmatic example of how the far right can use culture war to develop online before bursting into the mainstream. The more recent emergence of the clinical psychologist Jordan Peterson as an alt-right hero followed a very similar pattern, with Peterson building his initial fan base on Reddit, YouTube, and similar platforms by appealing to angry young men who simultaneously embraced and abhorred elements of identity politics. Like more traditional outsider anti-elitists, such figures are liable to collapse as quickly as they rise. There will, however, always be more in the wings.

CHAPTER FOURTEEN

Fascism and democracy

Since World War II, the ideology [Trump] represents has usually lived in dark corners, and we don't even have a name for it anymore. The right name, the correct name, the historically accurate name, is fascism. I don't use that word as an insult only. It is accurate.[1]

That was *Newsweek*'s Jeffrey Tucker in July 2015. Similar warnings appeared in *Slate*, in *Salon*, in the *Daily Beast*, in the *New Republic*, and in many other impeccably mainstream media outlets when Trump spoke casually of registering Muslim Americans and forcibly closing mosques. After the election, footage circulated of Richard Spencer telling Nazi-saluting supporters to 'Heil Trump'. In August 2017, the president responded to the murder of an anti-racist protester at a white supremacist rally in Charlottesville by condemning 'hatred, bigotry and violence on many sides, on many sides' — creating a bizarre equivalency between fascists and those opposed to fascists.[2]

The Nazi publication *The Daily Stormer* openly gloated about Trump's reaction when reporters pressed him to comment on Charlottesville. 'No condemnation at all,' it wrote. 'When asked to condemn, [Trump] just walked out of the room. Really, really good. God bless him.'[3]

As *Slate*'s Jamelle Bouie said, Trump ticked many of the boxes associated with classical fascism. He emphasised strength and he disparaged the weak, while his anti-elitism offered small-business owners and others in the middle class an idealised image of America's vanished greatness.

'Alone and disconnected,' Bouie concluded, 'this rhetoric isn't necessarily fascist. Some of it, in fact, is even anodyne. But together and in the person of Donald Trump, it's clear: The rhetoric of fascism is here. And increasingly, the policies are too. The only thing left is the violence.'[4]

The problem with that argument, though, was that violence was central to classical fascism, not incidental.

'The democrats of *Il Mondo* want to know our program?' Mussolini famously replied to a liberal critic. 'It is to break the bones of the democrats of *Il Mondo*. And the sooner the better.'[5]

Trump might have mocked protesters, but he didn't break their bones. His supporters attended campaign rallies; they didn't form militias. There was, in any case, no reason for them to do so. The traditional function of fascism was to quell, through violence, a left-wing challenge to the capitalist order. Mussolini and Hitler established their bona fides by physically destroying mass socialist and trade union movements, in conditions of political and economic crisis.

Despite the economic polarisation in the US, the American situation in 2016 wasn't comparable. Whatever the lurid stories circulating on *Infowars* and similar sites claimed, capitalism wasn't under threat. The organisations of the American left — including the trade union movement — had never been weaker.

The racism of Trump's Mexican wall and his Muslim ban emboldened, as was intended, racists of all variety. Yet Trump arrived at the White House via the usual route, not at the head of a paramilitary posse.

Neil Davidson used the classic work of the historian Roger Griffin to distinguish fascism's sharp political break with the norms of democracy from the qualitatively different program of the non-fascist far right. He noted that fascism promised to transform the people — to create a 'new man and woman' with new values — while the non-fascist right emphasised the virtues of the people as they already existed.[6]

In other words, fascism spoke of a revolutionary break, a project quite different from the restoration offered by outsider anti-elitism.

Symptomatically, once in power, Trump palpably didn't establish the tyrannical regime associated with fascist transformation. When his Muslim ban faced persistent legal challenges, the courts weren't disbanded. The media continued to function (according to one study, news stories about Trump's first 60 days in office contained about three times more negative assessments than during the same period for Obama), while demonstrations against the Trump agenda proceeded without unusual state repression.

Far from ruling as a dictator, Trump barely exerted the normal authority associated with his office. After the first 100 days of Trump in office, Corey Robin noted that the new president possessed 'no realistic agenda for, or steady interest in, consolidating power'. His promise to be a 'strong leader' was 'a rhetoric, a performance', Robin argued, before concluding: 'Trump has always thought his words were more real than reality. He's always believed his own bullshit. It's time his liberal critics stopped believing it too.'[7]

But the widespread assumption that Trump represented an especial debasement of America's democratic traditions didn't come from nowhere. It reflected a particular understanding of democracy, one that arose from the left's growing disdain for mass politics.[8]

Teasing out the exact meaning of a word like 'democracy' poses a difficult task, not least because almost all political actors today claim to be democrats. But this consensus emerged only recently. Until the 19th century, respectable people used 'democracy' as a term of approbation. For them, it meant mob rule, a society in which the masses oppressed their betters. That was why, during the upheavals that shook Europe in 1848, the insurgent forces were often described 'The Democracy', and why the philosopher Edmund Burke described 'perfect democracy' as 'the most shameless thing in the world'.[9] Even today, *Roget's Thesaurus* hints at an older usage by offering 'democrat' as a synonym for 'commoner'.

But that sense was challenged by a different meaning, one that made 'democracy' more palatable for respectable opinion. The second definition understood democracy not in terms of participation but in terms of representation — a quite different idea.

The debates among the American Founding Fathers illustrated the distinction clearly.

Thomas Jefferson wanted a country run by direct governance based on town meetings — a version of democracy that would, he said, make every man 'a sharer ... a participator in the government of affairs, not merely at an election one day in the year, but every day'. He belonged to a faction, he said, 'who identify themselves with the people, have confidence in them, cherish and consider them as the most honest and safe ... depository of the public interest'.

But Jefferson also identified a rival faction, one whose members 'fear[ed] and distrust[ed] the people'.[10]

Alexander Hamilton belonged to that group. For Hamilton, the masses were 'the Beast', a frightening, animalistic force to be tamed and controlled. Against Jefferson, he insisted that vesting deliberative or judicial powers in the collective body of the people would lead to 'error, confusion and instability'. Instead, he advocated representative democracy, 'where the right of election is well secured and regulated, and the exercise of the legislative executive and judicial authorities is vested in select persons'.

The virtue of a representative scheme was that it dampened the dangerous passions of the multitude. 'Nothing but a permanent body can check the imprudence of democracy,' Hamilton explained. 'Their turbulent and changing disposition requires checks.'[11]

In most countries, a version of the Hamiltonian argument

prevailed. Throughout the developed world, elections — hedged with various checks and restrictions — selected politicians, who duly sat in a parliament for a set period. Such systems were democratic, in that ordinary people voted in elections. But that was all they did. After the votes were counted, the elected representatives governed the country.

Despite the consolidation of parliamentarianism, the argument about the nature of democracy persisted. As Raymond Williams explained in his 1976 book *Keywords*, throughout the 20th century the debate took a new form.[12]

For the direct-politics left, democracy retained something of its original meaning. To take a characteristic formulation, Todd Gitlin described how:

> The New Left style was an extension of a much older small-d democratic tradition. It wanted decisions made by publics, in public, not just announced there. It valued informality, tolerated chaos, scorned order ... Participatory democracy entailed the right of universal assertion. It meant inserting yourself where the social rules said you didn't belong — in fancy meeting halls if you were a sharecropper, off limits and off campus if you were a student.[13]

Gitlin and his comrades valued democratic participation as a means as well as an end. By exerting their will directly (whether through plebiscites, protests, union elections, cooperatives, or elsewhere), the people clarified their ideas and grew in political confidence. The debates and discussions mattered, not merely because of the decisions they delivered, but because the process changed those who took part in it. Direct democracy brought individuals with different experiences and different backgrounds together. By encouraging them to collaborate, it broke down prejudices and suspicion. They became more confident in their abilities and those of the people around them — and that prepared them to take charge of other aspects of their lives.

This was why recent attempts to rebuild a direct-politics social movement (such as the Global Justice Movement and Occupy) developed elaborate mechanisms to involve as many supporters as possible in decision-making.

The delegated-politics left, however, did not share that enthusiasm. On the contrary, because delegated-politics activists saw themselves as acting on behalf of their constituency, they tended to accept the mainstream view of democracy as necessarily representative.

The difference between participatory and representative democracy could seem abstract. In times of social peace — and when the boundary between direct and delegated politics remained fluid — the distinction was often one of degree: enthusiasts for participatory democracy would contest elections, even as they organised protests between polls.

On other occasions, however, the distinction became critical. A major strike depended on workers acting together — an eminently participatory and thus (for some, at least) democratic practice. But for those committed to a strictly representative model, an industrial dispute threatened democracy, since it prevented elected leaders from exercising their mandate.

In 1976, with the direct-politics left still a presence, Williams argued that the 'two conceptions [of democracy] in their extreme forms now confront each other as enemies'.[14]

Much has happened since then. The collapse of the New Left — and the failure of recent protest movements — helped relegate participatory democracy to the fringes of public life, even as the neoliberal turn contributed to a further redefinition of parliament's role. The acceptance of the market as both superhumanly efficient and wise limited, by definition, the space for collective decision-making. Robert McChesney labelled neoliberalism 'the immediate and foremost enemy of genuine participatory democracy', on the basis that the reforms carried out in the 1980s across the Western world deliberately quarantined the economy from democratic pressure.[15] As David Harvey argues, neoliberals 'favour governance by experts and elites'. Typically, they try to insulate institutions such as central banks from political influence, and they have a preference for 'government by executive order and by judicial decision rather than democratic and parliamentary decision making'.[16]

The slow implosion of left organisations affected the consensus among progressives about democratic practice. In the past, officials in trade unions or staff members in major NGOs necessarily accepted at least some role in public life for ordinary people. But the new disdain for the masses associated with smug politics changed that. Activists who saw their country as full of 'stupid white men' — essentially, a dangerous aggregation of reactionary bigots — naturally gravitated to a Hamiltonian position, embracing those restrictive measures necessary to keep 'the Beast' in check.

The ambiguity in the term 'democracy' — its susceptibility to two different, even hostile, meanings — thus helped the left's embrace of smug politics. Those who saw the populace as deluded, racist, and sexist could reassure themselves that their disdain was eminently democratic. They were, they thought, protecting progressive political ideas against 'error, confusion and instability'.

Symptomatically, in 2015, a musical about Alexander Hamilton became a phenomenon, embraced by the icons of progressive America. Barack Obama said the musical reminded him 'of the vital, crazy, kinetic energy that's at the heart of America'; Lena Dunham claimed she wanted 'every kid in America' to see the show, because they would then 'thirst for historical knowledge and then show up to vote'[17]; *Rolling Stone* called *Hamilton* the 'mass-cultural moment [the Obama administration] deserves'.

At first glance, such enthusiasm might have seemed strange. 'Given how Democrats, in particular, embraced the show and Hamilton himself as a paragon of social justice,' wrote Matt Stoller, ' you would think that he had fought to enlarge the democratic rights of all Americans. But Alexander Hamilton … fought — with military force — any model of organizing the American political economy that might promote egalitarian politics.'[18]

In fact, *Hamilton* — and the liberal excitement about it — perfectly illustrated the evolution of delegated politics to smug politics. The historical Hamilton could be rehabilitated as a hero for progressives because, contra Stoller's argument, he didn't oppose 'democracy' so much as *participatory* democracy. The show presented Hamilton as an immigrant entrepreneur, remaking himself in a new country. 'Hey, yo,' he rapped. 'I'm just like my country/I'm young, scrappy and hungry.' The musical linked diversity with an anti-participatory version of representative democracy, replicating more or less exactly the reaction to Trump's victory by progressives committed to smug politics.

The evolution of democratic ideas in relation to Trump was expressed particularly clearly in 2016 in an essay for *New York Magazine* by the idiosyncratic Andrew Sullivan.

For Sullivan, Trump was a neo-fascist demagogue, a racist and an aspiring tyrant who represented 'an extinction-level event' for liberal democracy. But America lacked mechanisms to defend itself from Trump-like candidates because contemporary society destroyed hierarchies. Once upon a time, voting itself had been restricted to the rich and the white. Even when the franchise expanded beyond white property owners, viable candidates still came from a small pool: essentially, only those who had demonstrated their competency in various ways.

Now, though, 'that elitist sorting mechanism' had disintegrated.

Worse still, the rise of the internet gave, Sullivan argued, everyone, including idiots, a platform. As a result: 'We have lost authoritative sources for even a common set of facts. And without such common empirical ground, the emotional component of politics becomes inflamed and reason retreats even further. The more emotive the candidate, the more supporters he or she will get.'[19]

The path had been cleared for Trump, a man bewitching the masses with crass demagoguery so as to establish dictatorial power. Hence Sullivan's conclusion: America needed elites 'to protect democracy from its own destabilising excesses'.

In other words, Trump's rise exposed US politics as insufficiently elitist. Or, as his headline put it, 'democracies end when they are too democratic'.

Sullivan admitted that his argument was 'shocking'. Yet the two meanings of democracy enabled progressives to make the same case, without spelling out the anti-egalitarian implications quite so bluntly. For if 'democracy' was taken to mean representation, it was entirely democratic to prevent the sexist, racist, and homophobic masses from interfering with progressive politicians.

Prior to Trump's election, a version of the argument had been made publicly by progressives in Britain.

In 2016, the Conservative Party implemented a promised plebiscite on membership of the European Union: essentially, a way of settling intractable divisions within the elite about relations with Europe. Most of the political class supported a vote to Remain — and yet the Leave side triumphed. The temptation was to see the result as an electoral manifestation of familiar culture-war stupidity. In the past, anti-elitism ginned up by tabloids had been mostly controllable, and was eventually funnelled back to the mainstream right. Now, though, the main beneficiaries were outsider anti-elitists of various kinds, who agitated strongly for a Leave vote.

Accordingly, many in the political class railed at an outcome understood less as a victory for a particular political perspective than as a kind of category error: an example of what resulted if the ship of state were to be steered by those who seriously believed anti-elitist demagoguery.

'The Brexit has laid bare the political schism of our time,' explained James Traub in *Foreign Policy*. 'It's not about the left versus the right; it's about the sane versus the mindlessly angry.'[20]

For Traub — and many, many others — the vote was a victory for 'the ignorant masses': people too foolish and ill-informed to make reasoned decisions.

Certainly, the Brexit campaign revealed a disturbing level of xenophobia and outright racism, with some Leave activists making the plebiscite a vote on immigration. Nonetheless, despite the tenor of liberal commentary, this wasn't the whole story of the vote. The *Guardian*'s Paul Mason explained some quite reasonable grounds for hostility to the EU project:

> The EU is not — and cannot become — a democracy. Instead, it provides the most hospitable ecosystem in the developed world for rentier monopoly corporations, tax-dodging elites and organised crime. It has an executive so powerful it could crush the left-wing government of Greece; a legislature so weak that it cannot effectively determine laws or control its own civil service. A judiciary that, in the Laval and Viking judgements, subordinated workers' right to strike to an employer's right do business freely.

Its central bank is committed, by treaty, to favour deflation and stagnation over growth. State aid to stricken industries is prohibited. The austerity we deride in Britain as a political choice is, in fact, written into the EU treaty as a non-negotiable obligation. So are the economic principles of the Thatcher era. A Corbyn-led Labour government would have to implement its manifesto in defiance of EU law.[21]

Irrespective of the merits of those particular points, the Leave vote clearly couldn't be reduced to an eruption of irrationalism without doing violence to the complexity of the situation.

The activists of delegated politics had possessed a (sometimes unwarranted) faith in their ability to decide on behalf of the masses, confident that their organisational heft would eventually persuade their traditional constituency to embrace (or at least accept) their choices. But prolonged culture war had shattered that certainty, convincing them that the voters were unmanageable, even dangerous.

They understood Brexit as a grim confirmation of the smug perspective. By conducting a plebiscite, they reasoned, the Conservative Party had urged people to express themselves — and the brutes had duly vomited up their hateful prejudices. The result was a reminder of why consulting the public directly was so dangerous.

'Referendums are alien to our traditions,' said the human-rights lawyer Geoffrey Robertson as he campaigned to overturn the result:

They are inappropriate for complex decision-making, and without careful incorporation in a written constitution, the public expectation aroused by the result can damage our democracy ... Democracy has never meant the tyranny of the simple majority, much less the tyranny of the mob (otherwise, we might still have capital punishment).[22]

The philosopher A. C. Grayling voiced a similar perspective:

[T]here is an excellent reason why most advanced and mature polities do not have systems of 'direct democracy' but instead have systems of representative democracy, in which legislators are not delegates sent by their constituents but agents tasked and empowered to investigate, debate and decide on behalf of their constituents. This reason is that rule by crowd acclamation is a very poor method of government.[23]

Such statements drew upon the old Hamiltonian arguments about democracy as representative rather than participatory. To many progressives, they made intuitive sense, expressing attitudes that had been percolating through the left for some time.

But in the context of massive public alienation, the new progressive consensus provided a huge opportunity for outsider anti-elitists, both in Britain but also in the US, where the Trump campaign watched Brexit closely. Who were these 'agents' that Grayling thought would do such a wonderful job investigating and debating issues around

Europe? The British political class — like its counterparts the world over — was widely discredited by the imposition of austerity, a succession of disastrous wars, and the blatant greed exposed during the scandals over parliamentary entitlements. Ordinary people did not see their leaders as wise and farsighted. They despised them as venal and self-seeking.

Robertson's rhetoric denouncing voters as 'the mob' sounded not only condescending but massively out of touch, a reaction that associated progressives with the elitism of which they'd always been accused. By making such statements, liberals weren't simply condemning the racism manifesting in the No vote, or even the result itself. They were implicitly or explicitly arguing that the public were the problem; that, if given free rein, ordinary people would spew forth their prejudices; and that, as a result, progressive reforms (such as the abolition of capital punishment) could only be achieved despite — even against — the masses.

'It's hard to avoid concluding,' wrote Abi Wilkinson in the *Guardian*, 'that some of my fellow Remainers really do hold vast swaths of the country in contempt.'[24]

In this context, it wasn't so difficult to understand why Trump's mockery of reporters or Yiannopoulos's sexist trolling could be greeted by the Trump base with such glee. Anti-PC had long argued that elites wanted to forcibly impose their dogma on the masses. Much of the time, the proffered examples had been thin: councils employing daffy euphemisms, librarians refusing to circulate Enid Blyton, or whatever. By 2016, however, Trump supporters could point to a proliferation of articles in which liberal journalists explained, more or less openly, that everyday people were dangerous idiots, that they shouldn't be consulted about anything important, and that polls in which they'd expressed their opinions should be nullified.

As a consequence, during the American election, Trump activists and Clinton activists could often, quite literally, not understand each other. Democrat supporters looked at Trump's bluster, his disdain for economic orthodoxy, and the extremist, alt-right figures who clung to his train, and judged him an incompetent who should be excluded from the poll. This was the rationale when, in July 2015, the left-leaning *Huffington Post* editorialised that its Trump coverage would feature under the headline 'entertainment' rather than 'politics'. It explained: 'Trump's campaign is a sideshow. We won't take the bait. If you are interested in what the Donald has to say, you'll find it next to our stories on the Kardashians and *The Bachelorette*.'[25]

Obviously, this was disastrously wrong. Trump's campaign wasn't a sideshow, but one of the biggest stories of the new century. The condescension pervading that editorial was telling. As Lance Selfa noted, the Clinton campaign enjoyed the support of a 'popular front' of most of American business, the media, the political establishment, and liberal activists.[26] The *Huffington Post* therefore seemed to be expressing the sentiment of a broader political class that believed hick voters were incapable of distinguishing reality from reality TV, and as such should somehow be quarantined from serious matters.

At the same time, for many of those committed to smug politics, the accusation that such attitudes were undemocratic sounded bizarre, almost unintelligible. From their perspective, they were defending democracy (which they associated, first and foremost, with representation) in an election in which Donald Trump was manifestly unfit to represent anyone.

The sentiment was captured particularly clearly in a drawing for the *New Yorker* in the wake of the election. In January 2017, the magazine published a cartoon by Will McPhail. It showed the interior of an airliner, with a moustachioed man addressing the other travellers. The caption read: 'These smug pilots have lost touch with regular passengers like us. Who thinks I should fly the plane?' All hands were raised in agreement.[27]

The virality of McPhail's cartoon indicated that the sentiment struck a chord with the many Americans dismayed by the election. Yet the drawing made no reference to any of Trump's specific policies or actions. It wasn't a cartoon about race or gender — it was a cartoon about democracy. More exactly, it presented an explicitly elitist understanding of government, presenting the common sense of the smug-politics left. The drawing depicted society as a jet aeroplane, a complex piece of machinery requiring a highly trained captain and crew for its safe operation. Within that metaphor, the notion that the unqualified passengers might express an opinion seemed so ludicrous as to be comical. Travellers — citizens — should remain in their seats and let the experts do their work. If they didn't, if they interfered with a cockpit they couldn't possibly understand, they'd cause catastrophe and disaster.

Abi Wilkinson noted the praise McPhail received from prominent writers and thinkers associated with mainstream liberalism.

'You nailed it, @NewYorker. Props,' tweeted the *Atlantic*'s Jonathan Merritt.

'This,' said Peter Daou, a former Clinton adviser, as he shared the image on Facebook.

'To me it captured our whole predicament,' wrote the columnist Jill Lawrence in *USA Today*, 'from Brexit to Donald Trump to whatever comes next in the change-or-bust brushfire that is spreading across the globe.'

Such comments weren't, perhaps, surprising from leading Democrats, given their party's commitment to technocratic capitalism. 'That nobody could possibly do a better job than the professionals is a core belief of elite liberalism,' noted Wilkinson.[28] Beltway insiders saw Trump as a crass parvenu, a ghastly reality-show host who'd unfairly beaten far more talented politicians in the race to the White House.

Yet the cartoon, and the enthusiasm it engendered, expressed in embryo the logic of a broader — and quite disastrous — response to Trump. It might, for instance, have been possible for progressives to understand the result in 2016 as a wake-up call, with the victory of such an odious candidate suggesting not only a public discontent with the status quo but a frustration with the normal channels for expressing such discontent.

After all, a few days after Donald Trump's inauguration,

the 'Women's March on Washington' brought some 500,000 people out onto the street — and millions more mobilised in solidarity around the world. The event's title recalled the 1963 'March on Washington for Jobs and Freedom' (the rally at which Martin Luther King gave his famous 'I have a dream' speech), and the scale of the response hinted at a vast potential constituency for a resistance to Trump: one that pushed back against his racism and sexism, and linked that pushback to significant social change.

But this would have been direct politics — and, for liberals committed to smug politics, direct politics was as dangerous as Trump. In early 2017, Thea Riofrancos examined the already extensive literature examining the meaning of Trump's victory for democracy. She curated a selection of typical headlines: 'Is Donald Trump a Threat to Democracy?'; 'An Erosion of Democratic Norms in America'; 'Will Democracy Survive Trump's Populism? Latin America May Tell Us'; 'Trump, Erdogan, Farage: The attractions of populism for politicians, the dangers for democracy'; 'How Stable Are Democracies? Warning Signs Are Flashing Red'; and so on.[29]

Trump certainly threatened democracy in the sense that racism and xenophobia excluded oppressed groups from decision-making. But, as Riofrancos pointed out, that generally wasn't what pundits meant. They objected to Trump on almost exactly the opposite basis. Often, those who labelled Trump a 'fascist' disliked the president's racist, sexist populism as much because it was populist as because it was racist and sexist. Or, more exactly, for many, the three terms went together. Because populism involved the participation of the masses, they saw it as facilitating the racism and sexism that the masses gestated.

'Seen from the fast-shrinking center,' Riofrancos said, 'every populism, right or left, is equally suspect, because each one represents the pathologically unhinged demos that the existing institutional order seeks to moderate, filter, and contain.' Thus, when political researcher David Adler looked at values surveys across Europe and North America, he discovered that centrists were less supportive of civil rights than either the far left or the right.[30]

For mainstream Democrats, Trump was a fascist not because he mobilised an army of goons to beat up opponents, nor because, once in power, he established an authoritarian regime. His 'fascism' pertained to a perception of him challenging the balance by which democratic representatives kept the populace in line. But this meant that mass campaigns resisting Trump were equally suspect — for they, too, threatened to bring the unruly and the uncontrollable into the streets.

The enthusiasm of young people for the Sanders campaign had been seen by the Democratic leadership as a problem rather than an opportunity. Even after Clinton's defeat, mainstream Democrats worried about protests getting out of control and tilting the party too far to the left. Increasingly, they devoted themselves to finding ways to remove Trump without engaging the masses at all.

This was why many liberals focused more on painting Trump as a Russian pawn than they did on organising grassroots opposition to his policies. Space prohibits a full discussion of the supposed Russian involvement in the 2016 election, except to note that the allegations relied heavily on speculation, innuendo, and anonymous sources. In any case, whatever the extent of foreign intervention, it was impossible to deny that Trump had marshalled considerable genuine support.

But for the liberal opponents of Trump who disdained the public, the claim that 'Putin hacked the election' took on an almost talismanic significance, since it suggested an administrative method of deposing the president. If Trump had not been validly elected, he could be removed by court order or impeachment, the traditional mechanisms for maintaining a parliamentary system. The exposure of the supposed Trump–Putin connection offered, liberals thought, a way to bring down the 'fascist' regime and restore normalcy to American politics.

The same logic underpinned a focus on Trump's mental health. Again, the various diagnoses depicting Trump as unhinged, or psychotic, or otherwise cognitively impaired were circulated by liberals who imagined that a diagnosis of insanity would enable the removal of the president and thus somehow turn the clock back to politics as conducted during the Obama years.

Yet more than 61 million Americans voted for Trump. They weren't all Russian agents, or duped by bots or hackers. The removal of a democratically elected president by a court order would be understood, for obvious reasons, by these voters as something very much like a military coup.

Even if it succeeded, deposing Trump bureaucratically would not address the fundamental question: how did such a ghastly figure assemble such supporters — and what could be done to fight them?

Conclusion

We need a post-identity liberalism, and it should draw
from the past successes of pre-identity liberalism. Such
a liberalism would concentrate on widening its base by
appealing to Americans as Americans and emphasizing the
issues that affect a vast majority of them. It would speak to
the nation as a nation of citizens who are in this together
and must help one another. As for narrower issues that are
highly charged symbolically and can drive potential allies
away, especially those touching on sexuality and religion,
such a liberalism would work quietly, sensitively and with
a proper sense of scale.[1]

This was American academic Mark Lilla responding to
Trump's victory (or, more exactly, Clinton's defeat), a
critique that he subsequently expanded into a full-length
book.[2] Versions of the same argument were made repeatedly,
both in Australia and the United States.

Essentially, they insisted that, because culture war

worked so well, progressives needed to minimise the right's opportunities to wage it. This meant avoiding the topics, themes, and arguments that facilitated successful cultural skirmishes, so as to win back the voters who'd deserted to the right.

'America,' said Lilla, paraphrasing Bernie Sanders, 'is sick and tired of hearing about liberals' damn bathrooms.'

In Australia, similar claims arose in 2016 when One Nation brought a certain alt-right flavour to the parliament after winning four Senate places on the basis of Hanson's 'Fed Up' campaign. One of its new senators, Malcolm Roberts, was, after all, a sometime supporter of the conspiratorial 'Sovereign Citizen' movement and the author of a 300,000-word manifesto claiming climate change to be a UN plot.

In a typical piece in the wake of the election, Margo Kingston acknowledged that Hanson's policies were 'misconceived', particularly on race. Nevertheless, Kingston suggested that because Hanson was liked 'by most "ordinary" Australians', her critics — 'the educated, the elites, the right-thinking city folks' — needed to find some common ground. They ought 'to go with her to where her voters are and have a chat'.[3]

Often such arguments explicitly referenced class. Commentators took the critique of economic orthodoxy from outsider anti-elitism as a wake-up call for progressives, who needed to abandon esoteric minority issues and relearn language that resonated with ordinary people.

The Lilla-style responses identified — quite correctly — that, for many on the left, arguments against oppression had become entwined with a hostility to ordinary people in a way that made anti-PC and other culture-war sallies incredibly successful. It was easy to dismiss activists as elitists when those activists wore their disdain for the public almost as a badge of pride.

Yet, from this entirely valid beginning, the arguments sometimes concluded that progressives should tone down their emphasis on oppression: a quite different and much less persuasive suggestion.

For instance, in the name of rejecting 'elitist snobbery', Kingston condemned the Greens for calling Hanson a racist and a bigot. Greens leaders should instead, she said, declare that they 'look[ed] forward to discussing [Hanson's] views with her'.

But Hanson *was* a racist. Kingston's comments reflected a broader unwillingness by many liberals to recognise Islamophobia as a form of bigotry structurally identical to anti-Semitism. One Nation's revival came on the back of Reclaim Australia's anti-Islam rallies throughout the country, events where far-right activists retooled traditional anti-Semitic tropes to denounce Muslims for their food ('halal certification'), clothes (the burka), and their supposed propensity to violence. Had Hanson won election on a platform of old-style Jew-baiting, progressives would have (quite correctly) insisted that such a program be labelled as racist and quarantined from discussion. What were Asian or Indigenous or Muslim Australians to think about progressives who couldn't acknowledge bigotry as bigotry? The strategy implied that ethnic or religious minorities were dispensable — and that the left (always envisaged as white, male, and straight) should cut them loose so as to chat with the prejudiced.

It was a morally unpalatable conclusion. But it was also wrong, predicated on false assumptions. Insofar as anti-PC and culture war found a hearing, they did so because of real anger — the alienation of many people from the status quo. But recognising the sources of culture-war rage was one thing … and accepting the form in which they manifested themselves was quite another.

Though Lilla spoke in the name of a 'post-identity liberalism', his argument actually shared the framework accepted by both the culture-war right and the smug-politics left. His thesis rested, after all, on a presentation of 'ordinary Americans' as a solid bloc defined by traditional values. This was the basis on which he concluded that progressives needed to avoid controversial policies: he assumed that radical ideas pertaining to sexuality or religion would necessarily alienate suburban voters.

But recent Australian experience challenged all of that. In 2004, John Howard devised what, at the time, seemed like a typically cunning culture-war manoeuvre. When two same-sex couples returned home and sought recognition in Australian courts for marriages conducted overseas, Howard identified an opportunity to drive a wedge between the ALP's white-collar and blue-collar supporters: the Liberals duly moved an amendment to the *Marriage Act* to ban non-heterosexual unions.

The ALP recognised that Howard intended a trap. After a brief hesitation, it threw its weight behind his amendment.

'Labor has made clear that we don't support gay marriage,' Nicola Roxon told journalists.[4]

In retrospect, the decision seems utterly wrongheaded. But it's important to recognise that Labor was, in essence, adopting a version of Lilla's argument. Conscious of treating 'highly charged' issues 'sensitively', ALP strategists decided that that equal marriage would alienate the innately conservative suburban voters the party needed.

On this basis, they decided that same-sex rights were dispensable. 'Labor members and community members generally understand,' said Julia Gillard at the time, 'that [the changes to the law] are not worth getting hot under the collar about.'[5] But then something unexpected happened.

Howard, naturally, had proffered the opposition's backing as evidence he'd acted on behalf of all Australians (even though a Newspoll that year actually showed that 38 per cent of respondents supported equality). 'Nobody can say [the amendment] is being used as a wedge,' he declared, 'nobody can say it's a diversion, everybody can say it's a united expression of the national parliament and therefore of the will of the Australian people.'[6]

But the bipartisan parliamentary support for marriage inequality pushed activists committed to same-sex rights away from the mainstream political process. Spurned by both major parties, they set out instead to change public opinion. They staged marches. They held public meetings. They gathered signatures on petitions. They argued everywhere and anywhere about why equality mattered and why homophobia was wrong.

In other words, they embraced, to some extent at least, direct politics — and, as a result, public sentiment shifted. By 2008, the figure supporting reform was 46.9 per cent. In 2011, it had grown to 54 per cent — and thereafter continued to rise.

Before long, the falsity of the old faith in the division between the reactionary masses and the progressive elites became apparent. Every survey showed that the bulk of the population supported equality — an equality blocked not by socially conservative workers, but by recent parliamentary legislation. By the 2010s, most ordinary people regarded the matter as simple: same-sex couples should, they thought, enjoy the same rights as everyone else.

It was, in fact, the politicians, not the people, who remained committed to conservative ideas. An entire generation of MPs had grown up accepting that only elitists cared about matters of sexuality, that working-class people were unshakeably committed to traditional values. Even as the polls shifted, a succession of prime ministers — Rudd, Gillard, and then Abbott — refused to reform the marriage legislation.

It took until 2017 for Malcolm Turnbull to act, staging a version of the marriage plebiscite originally promised by Tony Abbott. The homophobic implications of the survey — why, activists asked, a referendum on this issue and no other? — generated widespread anxiety. The experience of the plebiscite was not a happy one, with counselling organisations reporting a significant rise in the demand for their services.

In any case, many Australian progressives had (like their counterparts in America and Britain) embraced a politics that rejected direct voting as illegitimate and dangerous. Father Rod Bower of the Gosford Anglican Church on the NSW central coast, whose pithy slogans on his church signboard had made him something of a cult figure, expressed a widely held sentiment when he denounced the very idea of a plebiscite because it threatened the 'wide space' that should stand between the 'angry mob' and 'actual decisions'.[7]

Yet, paradoxically, a process devised by Tony Abbott to frustrate the popular will eventually resulted in far more public involvement in the outcome, as the announcement of the plebiscite necessarily broadened the grassroots activism of the equality campaign. With every adult Australian eligible to vote, activists redoubled their efforts, taking the campaign to streets, workplaces, and campuses. The Australian Electoral Commission labelled the resulting surge in enrolments 'extraordinary', as a remarkable 765,000 people added themselves to the electoral roll to participate.[8]

Conceptually, the government's embrace of a plebiscite highlighted the absurdity of the 'reactionary masses/ progressive elites' schema that had dominated Australian politics for so long. Turnbull's recourse to a public vote amounted to an acknowledgement that parliamentary representatives were incapable of leading those they ostensibly represented; it signalled that politicians required the populace to act before they could even undo their own handiwork.

Moreover, the result was a landslide, with the Yes vote

winning comprehensively across the country. The Australian people — widely considered by both the smug-politics left and the culture-war right to be incorrigibly conservative — delivered marriage equality, even as the political class systematically put obstacles in their way.

By the time of Mardi Gras 2018, the leadership of the Liberal Party and the ALP were desperately seeking to associate themselves with the result of the plebiscite, an outcome they'd been entirely unable to deliver through parliament. In the space of a few short years, same-sex marriage had gone from an eccentric, extreme cause to a long-overdue reform and a historic achievement for which politicians wanted to take credit.

In that process, we can see, in embryo, the contours of very different strategy against culture war and those who waged it: a response based on direct politics.

First and foremost, a direct-politics perspective on culture war rejected the notion, held on both the right and the left, that the working class was innately backward or defined by its opposition to progressive ideas and culture. On the contrary, it posited the people — the 'angry mob' — as the solution rather than the problem, insisting that real change came from the bottom up rather than the top down.

That didn't necessitate any romanticisation of the public. Obviously, ordinary people could be racist and sexist and bigoted in all kinds of ways. When Labor MPs supported Howard's amendment to the marriage legislation, they calculated that a majority of their supporters were hostile to same-sex rights — and they may well have been right.

An overt, aggressive homophobia was, after all, part of the traditional masculinity espoused by many working-class men.

But the decision also relied on another notion, a central pillar of the culture wars. Labor's strategy was based on an assessment not only of the public mood, but on the permanence of that mood. New-class theory distinguished itself from older understandings of class in that it didn't start with material relationships, but rather set its parameters by ideas and social attitudes. Conservative values, it insisted, weren't merely particular attitudes that some working-class people might on some occasions hold. Rather, they were what defined you as belonging to the working class. If you were a worker, you talked a certain way, you wore certain clothes, you liked certain sports, and you hated progressive ideas — and if you didn't tick those boxes, you were an elitist.

The schema simply didn't admit the possibility of political change, particularly not in respect of sexuality. Gender roles were, after all, almost constitutive of the new-class division, invariably imagined as an opposition between a staunchly heterosexual working class and the sexually ambiguous sandal-wearing elite.

The plebiscite, however, provided a stunning demonstration of just how quickly the ideas held by ordinary people could evolve. Homosexuality, a crime punishable by death in some states until the middle of the 20th century, had remained illegal in Tasmania until 1997. Yet, in a referendum only 20 years later, Tasmanians opted for Yes at a rate exceeding the national average, with only 36.4 per cent of people voting No.[9]

An earlier generation of activists would have seen nothing surprising in this. Throughout most of the 20th century, the left had taken for granted that social change depended on the mobilisation of ordinary people, invariably fighting against the wealthy and the powerful. The most important social reforms in Australian history — from the eight-hour day to the provisions of the welfare state — were won through agitation conducted by working-class organisations (most obviously, the trade unions). From the early battles for Indigenous rights in the 1930s to the struggles for equal pay in the 1970s, unions played key roles in combating oppression.

But the left had also understood that popular support for progressive ideas didn't come from nowhere — that successful campaigns depended on actively convincing working-class people about the importance of a particular issue.

In an interview in 2000, Jack Mundey, who led the NSW Builders Labourers Federation with Bob Pringle in the early 1970s, discussed the union's efforts to support women's liberation and to back the Gurindji campaign for land rights at Wave Hill in the Northern Territory. He described bringing Vincent Lingiari and Dexter Daniels, the leaders of the Gurindji people, to building sites to speak directly to the men there. Often, he said, it was the first time the white workers had met an Indigenous person.

Likewise, he discussed how the decision to defend Jeremy Fisher necessitated prolonged debate. 'We had people from

the gay movement,' he explained, 'go out and talk about …
the way they were being ignored or the way that they were
being downgraded and insulted.'

It was the commitment, he said, to 'winning … the hearts
and minds of the workers by direct consultation, by talking
to them', that allowed the union to take such progressive
stances.[10]

On one level, Mundey's direct–politics approach sounded
entirely obvious. If you wanted to enlist ordinary people
on the side of change, you needed to persuade them. Yet it
constituted a strategy that is almost entirely missing from
discussions about culture war and political correctness today.

In the interview, he acknowledged that not all building
workers immediately saw the relevance of the union's
campaigns. Some of the men were homophobic; others were
racist or sexist — and Mundey and Pringle did not shout
these individuals down nor excommunicate them, as per an
online 'call–out'.

Nor, however, did they simply agree to disagree, in the
fashion that some liberals advocate today. They didn't meet
racist ideas halfway or nod along with homophobia. On the
contrary, they flatly told the conservative unionists they were
wrong, and then tried to convince them of the importance
of solidarity.

Of course, the BLF's campaigns took place in a very
different era, a time in which all the social movements were
peaking and the trade unions were growing in both strength
and industrial confidence. Nevertheless, the methodology
of direct politics remains relevant today. The success of the

equal-love campaign stemmed, in many ways, from the adoption of similar tactics.

The nature of a plebiscite meant that activists had to address themselves to voters, rather than seek to persuade politicians or the political class. Because the poll wasn't compulsory, they had to persuade people to post their votes, which meant convincing the public to feel an investment in the result. The campaign made same-sex rights immediate and personal, forcing ordinary people to consider the issue in a way that they simply wouldn't if they were watching politicians decide for them. Anecdotal evidence suggested that many older heterosexuals grappled with what equality meant to their sons, daughters, workmates, friends, and relatives — and then voted accordingly.

In Victoria, in particular, the union movement threw itself into the campaign under the slogan 'Equality is union business'. The Victorian Trades Hall organised volunteers to ring potential voters, produced T-shirts, posters, and other resources, and sent substantial contingents to all the rallies. The Construction, Forestry, Mining and Energy Union, the nation's most militant union, hosted workplace meetings to encourage a Yes vote, explaining that unionism was 'built on people finding strength and power in coming together'.[11]

The plebiscite was, of course, an anomalous event, with the government's recourse to direct election the result of a peculiar confluence of circumstances. Nevertheless, it illustrated a broader point: simply, that a basic confidence in ordinary people offered the foundation for a viable alternative to culture war.

In a fascinating article for *Overland*, the activist Joanna Horton described another example, on a much, much smaller scale. She wrote about the work of the Anti-Poverty Network Queensland, a group campaigning in Logan among poor and working-class people to agitate against the cashless welfare card, and for an increase to the pathetically small Newstart allowance:

> Those of us involved with political organising often harbour the belief that we are more politically aware than others; that the 'ordinary people' who exist outside our theoretical and organisational worlds are apathetic, or apolitical, or unenlightened. I have never found this to be particularly true. Like many people, those I met in Logan had lost faith in politics, but they were highly politicised. They had a keen awareness of their subjectivity in relation to the various institutions that structure their lives: Centrelink, the police, the state in all its variously indifferent and punitive manifestations.[12]

But this awareness didn't mean that they necessarily drew progressive conclusions. 'Lived experience' didn't, in and of itself, automatically give rise to particular political positions. Some residents of Logan agreed with left-wing ideas, but, as Horton explained, others were indifferent to the debates dominating the public sphere. When they did express political convictions, some were Islamophobic or otherwise racist. Several voiced their enthusiasm for Pauline Hanson.

Again, the activists didn't dismiss the admirers of Hanson

out of hand; they didn't answer the racist comments with insults. Rather, they used the workers' own circumstances to detach them from the prejudices they'd absorbed.

When, for instance, a welfare recipient complained about 'the Muslims', the activists directed their attention to a common enemy. 'Are the Muslims cutting your Centrelink payments?' they asked. 'Malcolm Turnbull and Tony Abbott and all that lot — are they Muslims? No, and that's who's cutting your payments off!'

Cashless welfare was, after all, initially introduced via the Basics Card, part of the Howard government's Northern Territory Intervention into Indigenous Australia. The Intervention sent military personnel into remote Indigenous townships, a measure that would have been inconceivable in response to sex-abuse allegations in white communities. Anti-Indigenous prejudice helped normalise welfare quarantining before it was extended from Indigenous areas to apply more generally. The people of Logan were thus well positioned to understand racism as a threat to all working people, irrespective of their backgrounds.

'It's in the material conditions of people's lives,' concluded Horton, 'the things they're already experts on, things they don't need to be persuaded to care about … where there is common ground for an ideological left turn.'

The same argument applies in reverse. When discussions shift away from ordinary people's lives, when arguments get fought out in spaces that have little to do with the working-class experience, culture warriors generally succeed in pushing the debate to the right.

In 2011, a number of fair-skinned Indigenous people took legal action against News Ltd columnist Andrew Bolt, using Section 18C of the *Racial Discrimination Act* to seek redress.

Legally, the case was a victory for the complainants. The court found against Bolt, who was then required to append a few sentences to his articles, amending various erroneous claims.

Politically, however, the result was a huge win for Bolt. The finding against him did nothing to diminish his influence. On the contrary, he extracted an extraordinary amount of capital from the case, which became, for years thereafter, a cause célèbre on the right — cited again and again to warn against the censorious, politically correct regime constructed and enforced by the elites.

Now, for anyone seriously concerned about liberty, there were far more serious threats than Section 18C. The *Racial Discrimination Act* does not contain any provisions as draconian as the codes imposed on building workers, who, for example, lost the right of silence when confronted by the Australian Building and Construction Commission. There is nothing in Section 18C comparable to the unprecedented bans on assembly and expression contained in Australian terror laws, or to the restrictions faced by employees working in offshore detention centres.

In any case, the notion that Bolt was somehow censored was preposterous. He was neither imprisoned nor fined. The judge didn't even insist that he apologise. The offending articles remained online, accessible to anyone who cared to read them. All that the judgement required was the correction of a few passages that the columnist had acknowledged as incorrect. The supposedly silenced Bolt continued to promulgate his opinions on his TV program and his radio show, and in his regular articles in the nation's biggest-circulation newspapers.

Nevertheless, if we think about *Eatock v Bolt* in the light of working-class life, we can understand how the anti-PC campaigners extracted such mileage from the case. Many — if not most — working-class people experienced the legal system as both deeply alien and thoroughly hostile. Progressive barristers and well-educated advocates might regard the courtroom fondly, but for those already alienated from the public sphere, a magistrate was, first and foremost, a guy who took your kids away or fined you for growing some weed.

This was the context in which the Bolt case could be so easily sold as 'political correctness gone mad'. Whatever their ethnicity, few working-class people possessed either the funds or the cultural capital necessary to contemplate legal redress for their own experiences of racism. As a result, they couldn't imagine using Section 18C in their own workplaces or schools.

In any case, the defenders of the *Human Rights Act* often spoke of its utility through the vocabulary of smug politics, implicitly presenting the legislation as necessary to hold back the bigotry of the masses. That helped the culture warriors depict Section 18C as a measure not for ordinary people to use, but rather as something to be used against them.

If the right successfully portrayed *Eatock v Bolt* as the PC elite telling everyone else what to do, it was because the description resonated with many people's experiences of both the courts and the left.

In Corey Robin's formulation, culture war transformed the masses into 'actors without roles'. In the rhetoric of the right, the so-called battlers were always seen but never heard. A pundit or politician might thunder against PC madness on behalf of ordinary people, but the people themselves possessed no agency whatsoever. This was why direct politics mattered so much. It brought the masses onto the stage; it allowed them to speak and act on their own behalf, in ways that shattered the culture-war frame.

In this sense, the common accusation that PC resulted from progressives going too far missed the point entirely. The problem was precisely the opposite — charges of political correctness got a hearing when the left hadn't gone far enough.

Take Mark Lilla's dismissal of debates about 'bathrooms' as liable to repel potential allies. In fact, his chosen example was inadvertently apt — a perfect illustration of how his analysis replicated the worst failures of the Clinton campaign.

If, during the US election, debates about toilets became a PC proxy for transgender issues, it was because of the Democrats' commitment to the narrowest version of delegated politics. The grotesque oppression endured by transgender people was, quite obviously, far broader than a lack of access to bathrooms (as humiliating as institutional misgendering could be).

For instance, a recent study by Human Rights Watch involving interviews with more than 350 students and 145 educators in five different US states showed schools to be a profoundly hostile environment for LGBT students.[13] A survey conducted by the LGBT teachers' group, the Gay, Lesbian and Straight Education Network, found that 75 per cent of transgender youth felt unsafe when studying, with a result that many had lower marks than their peers, were more likely to skip school, and were less likely to continue with education.[14]

Working-class Americans might or might not have been sick of hearing about 'damn bathrooms'. But education mattered intensely to ordinary people. If a gender-inclusive anti-bullying program came about through a bold reform of public schools, was it really so difficult to imagine working-class voters signing up to support it? If a campaign against transphobia were presented in such a form, why wouldn't ordinary people draw the connection between the horrendous treatment of trans kids and the shoddy services provided to other students from low-income families?

Research by the National Center for Transgender Equality suggested that as many as one in four transgender people had lost jobs because of bias. Obviously, transgender workers were targeted in specific ways. But workplace discrimination, bullying, and insecurity were endemic throughout America. Again, it wasn't difficult to see how a pledge to make working life less toxic — for transgender people and for everyone — might gain a hearing with working-class voters.

Contrary to what Lilla implied, the Clinton campaign didn't fail because it alienated Americans with its radicalism. As Neil Davidson argued, the problem was not 'that that the Democrats became obsessed with identity at the expense of economics', but rather that their policies did little to stop the oppression of the groups for whom they claimed to be campaigning.[15]

To build a solid constituency for the fight against oppression, progressives needed to up the ante, as issue after issue illustrated.

In 2017, the actor Alyssa Milano promoted the hashtag #MeToo after multiple harassment, assault, and rape allegations emerged against the movie mogul Harvey Weinstein. She wanted, she said, 'to give people a sense of the magnitude of the problem'. The overwhelming response on Twitter and elsewhere demonstrated a profound shift in attitudes to the behaviour of powerful men. Huge numbers of victims publicised their experiences and demanded justice, in a movement that spread from country to country, and from industry to industry.

From the very start, pundits advised #MeToo activists against sounding too radical, warning them that maximalist slogans would alienate ordinary people. Yet this missed the point entirely. What would it take to end sexual harassment in the workplaces of everyday working women? Under what circumstances would, say, migrant cleaners be empowered to fight back against predatory supervisors? What would best equip call-centre operators to deal with the Harvey Weinsteins in their own offices?

In many industries, a culture of abuse grew directly from job insecurity. Short-term contracts and casualisation gave managers tremendous power over the low-paid staff on their payroll. In such circumstances, the fight against sexual harassment could scarcely be separated from a fight for better working conditions — a radical demand, but one with an obvious appeal to the working class as a whole.

Clearly, the traditional justice system had been failing victims of sexual assault. Equally clearly, neither social media nor the traditional press provided an adequate alternative, not simply because cases like the withdrawal of abuse allegations against *Star Trek* actor George Takei highlighted the perils of trial-by-headline, but also because many people didn't possess the kind of media access necessary to generate real action.[16] The 'Me Too' slogan had, after all, been coined more than a decade earlier by Tarana Burke, but in 2006 the impoverished women and girls of colour with whom she'd been concerned hadn't been able to interest mainstream publications in their stories.[17]

Hence the importance of direct politics. In one of the best articles on the question, Stephanie Convery wrote:

> It seems to me that the things we need to be fighting for are ... more about (to use that tired old word) empowerment ... Fighting for empowerment means fighting for things like adequate single-parent payments. Like welfare and public housing. Like strong unions with a focus on workplace safety, job security, and rigorous standards against sexual harassment, to support the victims

of workplace harassment or violence and to ensure proper protocols are in place to investigate, monitor and issue sanctions.[18]

Such slogans were radical — and that was what made them relevant.

In the 1970s, the commitment to direct politics meant an equally overt commitment to major structural change, a recognition that the fight against oppression only became meaningful by altering the social conditions from which that oppression stemmed. Everywhere, radicals demanded 'liberation'.

In the years since, the term has vanished from the political lexicon. 'Liberation' sounds embarrassing and quaint, the legacy of a bygone era. Certainly, the collapse of the Soviet Union and the regimes associated with it have discredited many of the hazier notions associated with the term. No one believes that freedom from oppression might be found in the barracks-room socialism that once prevailed in Eastern Europe.

Nevertheless, a genuine alternative to culture war necessitates the rediscovery of liberation, simply because any serious response to the problems facing ordinary people requires material change and not just symbolic redress. The women's liberationists of the 1970s marched for accessible childcare, equality in the workplace, free contraception, abortion on demand, improved healthcare, shelters for victims of violence, and much else besides. Those demands might not be sufficient to end sexism, but they remain, today as then, entirely necessary to fight the sexism experienced by most women.

Likewise, greater representation of Indigenous people in the media might be a good thing in and of itself. But it wouldn't and couldn't address the structural poverty faced by the great majority of Indigenous Australians, a poverty intimately connected with more than 200 years of dispossession and discrimination. Just as in the 1970s, a real solution to racism in Australia necessitates profound economic change.

In a period like today, an argument for direct politics as the antidote to culture war might seem quixotic, almost demobilising. There are no unions like the BLF active anymore; indeed, strike rates are at all-time lows. Should we not content ourselves with a more realistic slogan than 'liberation'?

There are several answers to this.

First, participatory activism, even on a small scale, offers an alternative to the widespread disenchantment from conventional politics. The experience of taking control of even a minor aspect of your life or circumstances radically changed one's perceptions of political possibilities.

Revisiting Thomas Jefferson's ideas about participatory democracy, Hannah Arendt insisted that 'no one could be called happy or free without participating or having a share in public power'. The conflict between Jefferson and Hamilton, she concluded, went deeper than a mere difference about voting mechanisms. For Arendt, when the personal and the political came together, people experienced 'a feeling of happiness they could acquire nowhere else'.[19]

This is why direct politics matters.

Arendt was discussing the American Revolution. But the same phenomenon — that strange, ecstatic happiness — can be found in much, much smaller manifestations of participatory politics.

The very first gay-rights protest in Australia was a minor picket at Liberal Party headquarters in October 1971 against the ferociously anti-gay Jim Cameron. The activists were understandably terrified, knowing that, by their participation, they were exposing themselves to public ridicule, homophobic assault, and perhaps even arrest.

Afterwards, however, they described how their involvement transformed them. The action gave them, they said, 'an incredible feeling of morale; of comradeship; of feeling that you were actually doing something'. Later, two of the activists found the confidence to hold hands openly as they walked across Martin Place Plaza. Another phoned his parents and came out to them about his sexuality.[20]

The accounts from the first Sydney Mardi Gras in 1978 were remarkably similar. Famously, the marchers were beaten brutally by police — and then publicly shamed by a *Sydney Morning Herald* article that listed their names and addresses, exposing them to recriminations from employers and landlords.

Once again, though, most recalled not terror or fear but a strange joy that stayed with them for years. 'It was a great thing to be in,' remembered participant Kate Harrison many years later. 'I was young, not out for so many years, still having a lot of difficulties with being out as a lesbian. I have no memory as vivid as that night.'[21]

Kate Rowe, another attendee, said something similar: 'Nineteen seventy-eight changed my whole life.'

This transformational aspect of direct politics mattered. Reshaping the world didn't have to be a tedious business, a dreary task that you engaged in out of duty. It didn't have to be traumatic for the oppressed. It could, in fact, be an antidote to the misery of an unjust order.

'Perhaps the best kept political secret of our time,' said Barbara Ehrenreich, 'is that politics, as a democratic undertaking, can be not only "fun," in the entertaining sense, but profoundly uplifting, even ecstatic.'[22]

In an era in which most people despise politicians and parliament, and the grubby manoeuvres with which they were both associated, a politics of fun stands more chance of capturing the imagination than injunctions to be realistic. Obviously, we cannot create mass movements by effort of will; but, even on a small scale, the methods of direct politics make a difference, simply because they're so different from the grey landscape of the status quo. In this sense, the ecstatic, uplifting endeavour that Ehrenreich describes provides a platform with which to undercut the radicalism of the outsider right, offering the alienated and the marginalised a positive cause with which to identify.

But there is another reason for progressives to embrace liberation in the 21st century, expressed in a famous slogan from Paris in 1968. It ran: 'Be realistic, demand the impossible.'

Deep down, everyone knows the severity of the world's problems — and everyone understands that solutions that aren't radical aren't serious.

Today, many public events open with an acknowledgment of the value of Indigenous Australia. We're assured that such ceremonies remind us to think about the necessity of racial justice. No doubt that's true. But it's also true that, in the context of the dire circumstances facing Indigenous Australia, an obsession with symbolism alone can, in fact, discredit the fight against racism. The most recent statistics show that Aboriginal and Torres Strait Islander children are 25 times more likely to be in detention than non–Indigenous children.[23] In this context, if we're not talking about the need for structural change, we're simply not acknowledging reality.

Likewise, we've all seen the government campaigns in which well-meaning celebrities urge us to fight climate change by turning off our lights, or riding to work, or embracing some other entirely symbolic gesture. It's not simply that no one believes them; it's also that they actively foster denialism. Most people, when confronted with a TV personality assuring them that by changing their globes they can save the planet, conclude either that the planet isn't in any danger — or, alternatively, that it's irrevocably doomed.

The architect Daniel Burnham once warned against what he called 'little plans' on the basis that 'they have no magic to stir men's blood'. Certainly, in our current circumstances, a 'realistic', pragmatic program sounds utterly utopian.

The legendary Irish republican and socialist James

Connolly once wrote a poetic broadside against this kind of timidity. It began:

> Some men, faint-hearted, ever seek
> Our programme to retouch,
> And will insist, whene'er they speak
> That we demand too much.

Connolly, later to give his life for his beliefs, had no time for such trimmers. He continued:

> 'Tis passing strange, yet I declare
> Such statements give me mirth,
> For our demands most moderate are,
> We only want the earth.[24]

In 1907, the last line might have seemed like a rhetorical flourish. Today, it's a simple statement of fact.

Acknowledgements

Thank you to Stephanie Convery for her ideas, critiques, and constant encouragement. Thank you to Julia Carlomagno for her early support and to Henry Rosenbloom for his editing. Thank you also to Sam Cummins, Alison Croggon, Jenny Darling (and her anonymous reader), Rjurik Davidson, David Garland, Ben Hillier, Benjamin Laird, Corey Oakley, Sam Wallman, and Jacinda Woodhead. Some of the ideas in this book featured in articles published earlier in *Overland*, *Meanjin*, the *Guardian*, and *Eureka Street* (though the material has been substantially reworked). Thank you to the editors of those publications.

Notes

Introduction

1   Nick Adams, *Retaking America: crushing political correctness*, New York, Simon & Schuster, 2016.

2   Kimberley A. Strassel, *The Intimidation Game: how the left is silencing free speech*, New York, Twelve, 2016; Kirsten Powers, *The Silencing: how the left is killing free speech*, Washington D.C., Regnery Publishing, 2015; Ben Shapiro, *Bullies: how the left's culture of fear and intimidation silences Americans*, New York, Threshold Editions, 2013.

3   James Robertson, 'From Ashfield Pigeons to President Trump's Endorsement: the rise of Nick Adams', *Sydney Morning Herald*, 4 March 2017, <https://www.smh.com.au/national/nsw/from-ashfield-pigeons-to-president-trumps-endorsement-the-rise-of-nick-adams-20170304-guqph0.html>.

4   'Sydney Council Wants to Eradicate Pigeons over Bird Flu', *AM*, 2 November 2005, <http://www.abc.net.au/am/content/2005/s1495770.htm>.

5   Adams, 28.

6   'Megyn Kelly to Donald Trump: 'You've Called Women You Don't like Fat Pigs, Slobs — and Disgusting Animals', *Independent*, 7 August 2015, <https://www.independent.co.uk/news/world/americas/megyn-kelly-to-donald-trump-youve-called-women-you-dont-like-fat-pigs-slobs-and-disgusting-animals-10444690.html>.

7   Adams, viii.

8   Glenn Greenwald, *No Place to Hide: Edward Snowden, the NSA, and the surveillance state*, London, Hamish Hamilton, 2014, 92.

9   Ben Kamisar, 'Carson: 'Political Correctness Is Ruining Our
     Country', *The Hill*, 25 August 2015, <http://thehill.com/blogs/
     ballot-box/presidential-races/254999-carson-political-correctness-
     is-ruining-our-country>; Ryan Lovelace, 'Cruz: "Political
     Correctness Is Killing People"', *Washington Examiner*, 15 December
     2015, <https://www.washingtonexaminer.com/cruz-political-
     correctness-is-killing-people>; Robynn Tysver, 'Fiorina in Iowa:
     "Political correctness is now choking candid conversation"',
     Omaha World Herald, 12 November 2015, <http://www.omaha.
     com/news/politics/fiorina-in-iowa-political-correctness-is-now-
     choking-candid-conversation/article_92d46040-05df-56cc-86b0-
     ffec70132a80.html>.

10   Ben Norton, 'How the Hillary Clinton Campaign Deliberately
     "Elevated" Donald Trump with Its "Pied Piper" Strategy', *Salon*,
     10 November 2016, <https://www.salon.com/2016/11/09/
     the-hillary-clinton-campaign-intentionally-created-donald-trump-
     with-its-pied-piper-strategy/>.

11   Nolan D. McCaskill, 'Trump Accuses Cruz's Father of Helping
     JFK's Assassin', *Politico*, 3 May 2016, <https://www.politico.com/
     blogs/2016-gop-primary-live-updates-and-results/2016/05/
     trump-ted-cruz-father-222730>.

12   'Donald Trump Threatens to Jail Hillary Clinton in Second
     Presidential Debate', *Guardian*, 11 October 2016, <https://
     www.theguardian.com/us-news/2016/oct/10/debate-donald-
     trump-threatens-to-jail-hillary-clinton>; 'Donald Trump
     Criticized for Mocking Disabled Reporter', *Snopes*, 11 January
     2017, <https://www.snopes.com/news/2016/07/28/donald-
     trump-criticized-for-mocking-disabled-reporter/; Libby Nelson,
     '"Grab 'em by the Pussy": how Trump talked about women in
     private is horrifying', *Vox*, 7 October 2016, <https://www.vox.
     com/2016/10/7/13205842/trump-secret-recording-women>.

13   Larry Elliott, 'World's Eight Richest People Have Same Wealth
     as Poorest 50%', *Guardian*, 16 January 2017, <https://www.
     theguardian.com/global-development/2017/jan/16/worlds-eight-
     richest-people-have-same-wealth-as-poorest-50>.

14   Noah Kirsch, 'The 3 Richest Americans Hold More Wealth Than
     Bottom 50% of the Country, Study Finds', *Forbes*, 9 November
     2017, <https://www.forbes.com/sites/noahkirsch/2017/11/09/
     the-3-richest-americans-hold-more-wealth-than-bottom-50-of-
     country-study-finds/>.

15 Kareem Abdul-Jabbar, 'Every GOP Candidate Is Wrong about Political Correctness', *Washington Post*, 22 February 2016, <https://www.washingtonpost.com/>.

16 Jason Wilson, 'The New Patriotism', *Overland*, 225, Summer 2016, <https://overland.org.au/previous-issues/issue-225/feature-jason-wilson/>; Milo Yiannopoulos, 'Milo on how Feminism Hurts Men and Women', *Breitbart*, 7 October 2016, <http://www.breitbart.com/milo/2016/10/07/full-text-milo-feminism-auburn/>.

17 Bari Weiss, 'Meet the Renegades of the Intellectual Dark Web', *New York Times*, 8 May 2018, <https://www.nytimes.com/2018/05/08/opinion/intellectual-dark-web.html>.

18 Jean-Pierre Chigne, 'April 2018 Was the 400th Consecutive Warmer-than-Average Month due to Global Warming', *Tech Times*, 17 May 2018, <http://www.techtimes.com/articles/228022/20180517/april-2018-was-the-400th-consecutive-warmer-than-average-month-due-to-global-warming.htm>.

Chapter One: Inventing PC

1 Moira Weigel, 'Political Correctness: how the right invented a phantom enemy', *Guardian*, 30 November 2016, <https://www.theguardian.com/us-news/2016/nov/30/political-correctness-how-the-right-invented-phantom-enemy-donald-trump>.

2 Clive Hamilton, 'Political Correctness: its origins and the backlash against it', *The Conversation*, 31 August 2015, <http://theconversation.com/political-correctness-its-origins-and-the-backlash-against-it-46862>.

3 'Mario Savio's "Bodies upon the Gears" Speech — 50 Years Later' *Detroit Metro Times*, 1 December 2014, <https://www.metrotimes.com/news-hits/archives/2014/12/01/mario-savios-bodies-upon-the-gears-speech-50-years-later>.

4 See Ellen Schrecker, 'The Roots of the Right-Wing Attack on Higher Education', *Thought & Action*, 26, 2010, 71–82.

5 *Stanford Daily*, Volume 155, Issue 65, 22 May 1969.

6 Adams, *Retaking America*, 43.

7 'Republican Party Platforms: Republican Party platform of 1984', *The American Presidency Project*, <http://www.presidency.ucsb.edu/ws/index.php?pid=25845>.

8 Allan Bloom, *The Closing of the American Mind*, New York, Simon & Schuster, 2008.

9   E. D. Hirsch Jr, *Cultural Literacy: what every American needs to know*, New York, Vintage, 1988; Roger Kimball, *Tenured Radicals: how politics has corrupted our higher education*, ERIC, 1990; Dinesh d'Souza, *Illiberal Education: the politics of race and sex on campus*, New York, Simon & Schuster, 1991.

10   William J. Bennett, *To Reclaim a Legacy: a report on the humanities in higher education*, Washington, National Endowment for the Humanities, 1984, 3.

11   Bloom, *The Closing of the American Mind*, 337.

12   'Ronald Reagan and UC Berkeley People's Park Riots 1969', *Rolling Stone*, 15 May 2017, <https://www.rollingstone.com/culture/news/ronald-reagan-and-uc-berkeley-peoples-park-riots-1969-w482300>.

13   Michael Berube, 'Public Image Limited: political correctness and the media's big lie' in *Debating PC: the controversy over political correctness on college campuses*, New York, Laurel, 1992, 130.

14   Richard Bernstein, 'The Rising Hegemony of the Politically Correct', *New York Times*, 28 October 1990.

15   Weigel, 'Political Correctness'.

16   Jerry Adler, 'Taking Offense: is this the new enlightenment on campus or the new McCarthyism?', *Newsweek*, 24 December 1990.

17   'Excerpts From President's Speech to University of Michigan Graduates', *New York Times*, 5 May 1991, <https://www.nytimes.com/1991/05/05/us/excerpts-from-president-s-speech-to-university-of-michigan-graduates.html>.

Chapter Two: Three kinds of leftism

1   Lillian Faderman, *The Gay Revolution: the story of the struggle*, New York, Simon & Schuster, 2015, 71.

2   See Marcia M. Gallo, 'Daughters of Bilitis', in Marc Stein, *Encyclopedia of Lesbian, Gay, Bisexual, and Transgender History in America*, New York, Charles Scribner's Sons, 2004.

3   For more on this, see Chris Harman, *The Fire Last Time: 1968 and after*, London, Bookmarks, 1988.

4   Todd Gitlin, *The Sixties: years of hope, days of rage*, New York, Bantam, 1993, 343.

5   Fred Wasserman, 'Stonewall Riots', in Stein, *Encyclopedia of Lesbian, Gay, Bisexual, and Transgender History in America*, 155.

6   Wasserman, 'Stonewall Riots', 155.

7   Bloom, *The Closing of the American Mind*, 313.

8   Christopher Hitchens, 'The Egg-Head's Egger-On', *London Review of Books*, 27 April 2000.

9   Gitlin, *The Sixties*, 422.

10 Max Elbaum, *Revolution in the Air: sixties radicals turn to Lenin, Mao and Che*, London, Verso, 2002, 28.

11 John Taylor, 'Are You Politically Correct?', *New York*, 21, 1991, 32–40.

12 D. Charles Whitney and Ellen Wartella, 'Media Coverage of the "Political Correctness" Debate', *Journal of Communication*, 42(2), 1992, 90.

13 Jordan Humphreys, 'Gay Liberation at Macquarie', *Radical History of Macquarie University*, 23 February 2013, <https://radicalhistoryofmacquarieuniversity.wordpress.com/gay-liberation-at-macquarie/>.

14 Nick Ravo, 'Campus Slur Alters a Code Against Bias', *New York Times*, 11 December 1989, <https://www.nytimes.com/1989/12/11/nyregion/campus-slur-alters-a-code-against-bias.html>.

15 Jerry Adler, 'Taking Offense'.

16 Weigel, 'Political Correctness'.

17 'Baa Baa "Rainbow" Sheep', *'Political Correctness Gone Mad' Gone Mad*, 16 October 2011, <https://pcgonemadgonemad.wordpress.com/2011/10/16/hello-world/>.

18 David Brooks, 'Understanding Student Mobbists', *New York Times*, 8 March 2018, <https://www.nytimes.com/2018/03/08/opinion/student-mobs.html>.

19 Jonathan Chait, 'Not a Very P.C. Thing to Say', *NYMag*, 27 January 2015, <http://nymag.com/daily/intelligencer/2015/01/not-a-very-pc-thing-to-say.html>; 'College Campuses Have No Right to Limit Free Speech', *Time*, 13 October 2016, <http://time.com/4530197/college-free-speech-zone/>.

20 Nathan J. Robinson, 'The Stereotypes about College Students and Free Speech Are False', *Current Affairs*, 1 February 2018, <https://www.currentaffairs.org/2018/02/why-do-those-college-students-hate-free-speech-so-much>.

21 Glenn Greenwald, 'The Greatest Threat to Campus Free Speech is Coming from Dianne Feinstein and her Military-Contractor Husband', *The Intercept*, 26 September 2015, <https://theintercept.com/2015/09/25/dianne-feinstein-husband-threaten-univ-calif-demanding-ban-excessive-israel-criticism/>.

22   Quoted in George McKenna, *The Puritan Origins of American Patriotism*, New Haven, Yale University Press, 2007, 233.

Chapter Three: Battlers and elites

1   See Andrew Hartman, *A War for the Soul of America: a history of the culture wars*, Chicago, University of Chicago Press, 2015.
2   Barbara Ehrenreich, *Fear of Falling*, New York, Pantheon, 1989, 269.
3   Quoted in Hartman, *A War for the Soul of America*, 52.
4   Ehrenreich, *Fear of Falling*, 113.
5   Ehrenreich, *Fear of Falling*, 101.
6   Patrick Buchanan, '1992 Republican National Convention Speech', *Patrick J. Buchanan — Official Website*, 17 August 1992, <http://buchanan.org/blog/1992-republican-national-convention-speech-148>.
7   Dave Helling, '1992 Republican convention: "There is a religious war going on"', *The Kansas City Star*, 18 July 2016, <http://www.kansascity.com/news/politics-government/election/article88423762.html>.
8   Buchanan, '1992 Republican National Convention Speech'.
9   Thomas Frank, *What's the Matter with America?: the resistible rise of the American right*, London, Harvill Secker, 2004, 7.
10   Corey Robin, *The Reactionary Mind: conservatism from Edmund Burke to Donald Trump*, Oxford, Oxford University Press, 2017, 97.

Chapter Four: The Australian way

1   See <https://archives.smh.com.au/>.
2   Verity Burgmann, *Power, Profit and Protest. Australian social movements and globalisation*, Sydney, Allen & Unwin, 2003, 16.
3   Barry Humphries and Ross Fitzgerald, 'Craig Steppenwolf: a monologue for the music-hall', *Quadrant* 19(8), 1975, 47.
4   Robert Manne, 'On Being an Editor', *Quadrant*, January/February 1983, 88.
5   See Aubrey Belford, 'The Formation of Right-Wing Anti-Elitist Discourse Amongst Australian Intellectuals: 1972–1988', unpublished honours thesis, 2008.
6   Andrew Markus, *Race: John Howard and the remaking of Australia*, Sydney, Allen & Unwin, 2001, 72.
7   See Markus, *Race*, 86–89.
8   Quoted in Marian Sawer and Barry Hindess, *Us and Them: anti elitism in Australia*, Perth, API Network, 2004, 3.

9   David Flint, *The Twilight of the Elites*, Sydney, Freedom Publishing, 2003.

10 Nick Cater, *The Lucky Culture*, Sydney, HarperCollins Australia, 2013, 283.

11 Graham Willett, *Living out Loud: a history of gay and lesbian activism in Australia*, Sydney, Allen & Unwin, 2000, 20.

12 Marilyn Lake, *Getting Equal: the history of Australian feminism*, Sydney, Allen & Unwin, 1999, 231.

13 Anne Summers, 'Women', in Allan Patience and Brian Head, *From Whitlam to Fraser: reform and reaction in Australian politics*, Melbourne, Oxford University Press, 1979, 98.

14 Lake, *Getting Equal*, 253.

15 Jim George and Michael Hutchison, 'Culture War as Foreign Policy in US and Australia', in Jim George, *The Culture Wars: Australian and American politics in the 21st Century*, Melbourne, Palgrave Macmillan Australia, 2009, 49.

16 See Elizabeth Humphrys and Damien Cahill, 'How Labor Made Neoliberalism', *Critical Sociology*, 43(4-5), 2017, 669–684.

17 'Celebrating Two Decades of Reforming Government', *Australian*, 4 March 2003.

18 Michael Pusey, '25 Years of Neoliberalism in Australia' in Robert Manne and David McKnight (eds), *Goodbye to All That: on the failure of neo-liberalism and the urgency of change*, Melbourne, Black Inc., 2010, 159.

19 Michael Kimmel, *Angry White Men: American masculinity at the end of an era*, London, Hachette, 2017, 281.

Chapter Five: Howard and Hanson

1   Mark Rolfe, 'Free Speech, Political Correctness and the Rhetoric of Social Unity under John Howard', *Just Policy: a journal of Australian social policy*, 15, 1999, 38; Ross Fitzgerald, 'Free Speech: what are its limits', *Overland*, 134, Autumn 1994.

2   John Howard, *The Role of Government: a modern liberal approach: first headland speech*, Melbouren, Menzies Research Centre, 1995.

3   Quoted in Robert Manne, 'The Howard Years: a political interpretation', in Robert Manne (ed.), *The Howard Years*, Melbourne, Black Inc., 2004, 16.

4   Quoted in Tony Stephens, 'Middle Ground of Power', *Sydney Morning Herald*, 9 August 2003, <https://www.smh.com.au/articles/2003/08/08/1060145847972.html>.

5   Pauline Hanson and George J. Merritt, *Pauline Hanson — the Truth: on Asian immigration, the Aboriginal question, the gun debate and the future of Australia*, Parkholme, St. George Publications, 1997, 159.

6   Damien Cahill, 'The Australian Right's New Class Discourse and the Construction of the Political Community', in Raymond Markey (eds), *Labour and Community*, Wollongong, University of Wollongong Press, 53.

7   Quoted in Lance Selfa (ed.), *US Politics in An Age of Uncertainty*, Chicago, Haymarket Books, 2018.

8   Peter Browne, 'Boats and Votes', *Inside Story*, 6 July 2010, <http://insidestory.org.au/boats-and-votes/>.

9   Michael Pusey and Shaun Wilson, *The Experience of Middle Australia: the dark side of economic reform*, Melbourne, Cambridge University Press, 2003, 59.

10   Murray Goot, 'Hanson's Heartland: who's for one nation and why' in Robert Manne (ed.), *Two Nations: the causes and effects of the rise of the One Nation Party in Australia*, Melbourne, Bookman Press, 1998, 55.

Chapter Six: With us or with the terrorists

1   Quoted in Naomi Klein, 'Naomi Klein on the Appeal of Subcomandante Marcos', *Guardian*, 3 March 2001, <http://www.theguardian.com/books/2001/mar/03/politics>.

2   See Elizabeth Humphrys, 'From Offense to Defence: the Australian Global Justice Movement and the impact of 9/11', Masters Thesis, University of Technology Sydney, 2010.

3   John Howard, 'Election Speech, 2001', Museum of Australian Democracy at Old Parliament House, <https://electionspeeches.moadoph.gov.au/speeches/2001-john-howard>.

4   Quoted in David McKnight, *Beyond Right and Left*, 136.

5   George W. Bush, 'President Declares "Freedom at War with Fear"', The White House Archives, 20 September 2001, <https://georgewbush-whitehouse.archives.gov/news/releases/2001/09/20010920-8.html>.

6   Ari Fleischer, 'White House Briefing', *Washington Post*, 26 September 2001, <http://www.washingtonpost.com/wp-srv/nation/specials/attacked/transcripts/fleischertext_092601.html>.

7   'Ashcroft: Critics of New Terror Measures Undermine Effort', *CNN*, 7 December 2001, <http://edition.cnn.com/2001/US/12/06/inv.ashcroft.hearing/>.

8   David Neiwert, *Eliminationists: how hate talk radicalized the American right*, London, Routledge, 2016, 75.

9   Neiwert, *Eliminationists*, 97.

10   Quoted in Geoff Boucher and Matthew Sharpe, *Times Will Suit Them*, Sydney, Allen & Unwin, 2008, 26.

11   Robert Manne, 'Bad News: Murdoch's *Australian* and the shaping of the nation', *Quarterly Essay*, 43, Melbourne, Black Inc., 2011.

12   Quoted in Alex Callinicos, 'The grand strategy of the American empire', *International Socialism*, Winter 2002, <https://www.marxists.org/history/etol/writers/callinicos/2002/xx/strategy.htm>.

13   Julian Borger, 'Blogger Bares Rumsfeld's Post 9/11 Orders', *Guardian*, 24 February 2006, <http://www.theguardian.com/world/2006/feb/24/freedomofinformation.september11>.

14   Manne, 'Bad News', 16.

15   Patrick E. Tyler, 'Threats and Responses: news analysis; a new power in the streets', *New York Times*, 17 February 2003, <https://www.nytimes.com/2003/02/17/world/threats-and-responses-news-analysis-a-new-power-in-the-streets.html>.

16   Matt Wate, Peter Fray, Neil Mercer and Aban Contractor, 'Howard Rejects Global Protests', *Sydney Morning Herald*, 17 February 2003, <https://www.smh.com.au/articles/2003/02/16/1045330468377.html>.

17   Emmett Rensin, 'The Smug Style in American Liberalism', *Vox*, 21 April 2016, <https://www.vox.com/2016/4/21/11451378/smug-american-liberalism>.

Chapter Seven: Smug Politics

1   Michael Byrnes, 'Librarian Makes a Difference for "Stupid White Men" Author Michael Moore', SICE, Indiana University Bloomington, 25 July 2002, <https://www.sice.indiana.edu/news/story.html?ils_id=443>.

2   'Bushism', *Wikipedia*, 2 April 2018, <https://en.wikipedia.org/w/index.php?title=Bushism&oldid=833798423>.

3   Frank Bruni, *Ambling into History: the unlikely odyssey of George W. Bush*, New York, HarperCollins, 2003, 4.

4   Michael Moore, *Stupid White Men*, New York, HarperCollins, 2003, 89.

5   '"You Can't Believe Bush," One Pundit Said. But on "Hardball", They Praised the Full Package', *Daily Howler*, 13 May 2003, <http://www.dailyhowler.com/dh051303.shtml>.

6   Jay Rosen, 'Why Political Coverage Is Broken', keynote address,
    Melbourne Writers Festival, 26 August 2011, <http://pressthink.
    org/2011/08/why-political-coverage-is-broken/>.

7   Emmet Penney, 'Lectureporn: the vulgar art of liberal narcissism', *Paste*,
    26 June 2017, <https://www.pastemagazine.com/articles/2017/06/
    lectureporn-the-vulgar-art-of-liberal-narcissism.html>.

8   *The Colbert Report*, Comedy Central Official Site, accessed 9 April
    2018, <http://www.cc.com/shows/the-colbert-report>.

9   Rensin, 'The Smug Style in American Liberalism'.

10 Frank, *What's the Matter with America?*, 241.

11 Karl Marx, 'A Contribution to the Critique of Hegel's Philosophy
    of Right', <https://www.marxists.org/archive/marx/works/1843/
    critique-hpr/intro.htm>.

12 Daniel C. Dennett, 'The Bright Stuff', *New York Times*, 12 July
    2003, <https://www.nytimes.com/2003/07/12/opinion/the-
    bright-stuff.html>.

13 Andrew Brown, 'Richard Dawkins' Latest Anti-Muslim Twitter
    Spat Lays Bare His Hypocrisy', *Guardian*, 22 April 2013, <http://
    www.theguardian.com/commentisfree/2013/apr/22/richard-
    dawkins-islamophobic>.

14 W. E. B. DuBois, 'The Superior Race', *The Smart Set*, 70(4), 1923,
    <http://www.webdubois.org/dbSuperiorRace.html>.

Chapter Eight: Why the culture wars didn't end

1   Kevin Rudd, 'Howard's Brutopia', *Monthly*, November 2006.

2   Richard Nile, 'End of the culture wars', *Australian*, 28 September
    2009, <http://www.news.com.au/news/end-of-the-culture-wars/
    news-story/afa7216e0dc1aa4ad06ea0a05b022b5c>.

3   Mark Bahnisch, 'Culture war a dead duck', ABC News, 13 November
    2007, <http://www.abc.net.au/news/2007-11-13/38924>.

4   Paul Harris, 'Barack Obama Brings Truce in Culture War',
    Guardian, 12 April 2009, <https://www.theguardian.com/
    world/2009/apr/12/barack-obama-religion-homosexuality>.

5   Barack Obama, 'Illinois Sen. Barack Obama's Announcement
    Speech', 10 February 2007, <http://www.washingtonpost.com/
    wp-dyn/content/article/2007/02/10/AR2007021000879.html>.

6   Christine Schwen, 'Beck, Ailes Lie about Beck's "Slaughtered"
    Comments', *Media Matters for America*, 2 February 2010, <https://
    www.mediamatters.org/blog/2010/02/02/beck-ailes-lie-about-
    becks-slaughtered-comments/159902>.

7   Michael Calderone, 'Fox's Beck: Obama is "a racist"',
     Politico, 28 July 2009, <http://www.politico.com/blogs/
     michaelcalderone/0709/Foxs_Beck_Obama_is_a_racist.html>.

8   Jeffrey Feldman, 'Glenn Beck Recycles X-Files Plot to Spread
     Fear of Obama', *Huffington Post*, 15 April 2009, <https://www.
     huffingtonpost.com/jeffrey-feldman/glenn-beck-recycles-
     x-fil_b_175068.html>; 'What Is Agenda 21? After watching
     this, you may not want to know', *The Blaze*, 19 November
     2012, <https://www.theblaze.com/news/2012/11/19/what-
     is-agenda-21-after-watching-this-you-may-not-want-to-
     know>; 'Glenn Beck: Dangers of Environmental Extremism',
     Fox News, 18 October 2010, <http://www.foxnews.com/
     story/2010/10/18/glenn-beck-dangers-environmental-
     extremism.html>.

9   'Glenn Beck Imitates Obama Pouring Gasoline On "Average
     American" (VIDEO)', *Huffington Post*, 5 September 2009, <https://
     www.huffingtonpost.com.au/entry/glenn-beck-imitates-
     obama_n_185578>.

10   Steven Perlberg, 'Rick Santelli Started The Tea Party With A Rant
     Exactly 5 Years Ago Today — Here's How He Feels About It Now',
     Business Insider, 20 February 2014, <https://www.businessinsider.
     com.au/rick-santelli-tea-party-rant-2014-2>.

11   Theda Skocpol and Vanessa Williamson, *The Tea Party and the
     Remaking of Republican Conservatism,* New York, Oxford University
     Press, 2016, 12.

12   David Neiwert, *Alt-America: the rise of the radical right in the age of
     Trump*, New York, Verso, 2017, 117.

13   Zaid Jilani, 'GRAPH: Income Inequality in U.S. Worse than Ivory
     Coast, Pakistan, Ethiopia', *Think Progress*, 4 May 2011, <https://
     thinkprogress.org/graph-income-inequality-in-u-s-worse-than-
     ivory-coast-pakistan-ethiopia-7fdd35d64caf/>.

14   Jeff Cox, 'Record 46 Million Americans Are on Food Stamps',
     CNBC, 4 September 2012 <https://www.cnbc.com/
     id/48898378>; Les Christie, 'Number of People without Health
     Insurance Climbs', CNN, 13 September 2011, <http://money.
     cnn.com/2011/09/13/news/economy/census_bureau_health_
     insurance/index.htm>; 'Hedge Fund Managers Set New Payout
     Records in 2009', Reuters, 2 April 2010, <https://www.reuters.
     com/article/us-hedgefunds-payouts/hedge-fund-managers-set-
     new-payout-records-in-2009-idUSTRE6302PP20100401>.

15   Samantha Arfenist, 'Stewart and Colbert's Plea: "take it down
      a notch, America"', *The Current*, 20 October 2010, <https://
      nsucurrent.nova.edu/stewart-and-colbert%E2%80%99s-plea-
      %E2%80%9Ctake-it-down-a-notch-america%E2%80%9D/>.

16   Robert Manne, *Dear Mr Rudd: ideas for a better Australia*, Melbourne,
      Black Inc., 2008.

17   Janet Albrechtsen, 'Under Labor, Elites Will Remain Irrelevant',
      Australian, 27 February 2008.

18   David Marr, 'Glimmers of Hope Survive in the Mush',
      Sydney Morning Herald, 21 April 2008, <https://www.smh.
      com.au/news/national/glimmers-of-hope-survive-in-the-
      mush/2008/04/20/1208629731307.html>.

19   Katharine Murphy, '2020 the Summit: a Kevin Rudd
      production', *Age*, 19 April 2008, <https://www.theage.com.
      au/news/in-depth/2020-the-summit-a-kevin-rudd-producti
      on/2008/04/18/1208025469917.html>.

Chapter Nine: The nature of identity

1   T. Lindsay Baker and Julie Philips Baker, *The WPA Oklahoma Slave
      Narratives*, Norman, OK, University of Oklahoma Press, 1996, 95.

2   Sherry Wolf, 'Unite and Fight?', *International Socialist Review*, 98, Fall
      2015, <https://isreview.org/issue/98/unite-and-fight>.

3   Keeanga-Yamahtta Taylor (ed.), *How We Get Free: Black feminism
      and the Combahee River Collective*, Chicago, Haymarket Books, 2018,
      Kindle.

4   Kathie Sarachild, 'Consciousness-Raising: a radical weapon', in
      Redstockings, *Feminist Revolution: an abridged edition with additional
      writings*, New York, Random House, 1978.

5   Hartman, *A War for the Soul of America*, 21.

6   Taylor (ed.), *How We Get Free*, Kindle.

7   Alex Callinicos, *Against Postmodernism: a Marxist critique*, London,
      Polity, 1990, 168.

8   Salar Mohandesi, 'Identity Crisis', *Viewpoint Magazine*, 16 March
      2017, <https://www.viewpointmag.com/2017/03/16/identity-
      crisis/>.

9   Quoted in Brian Ward (ed.), *The 1960s: a documentary reader*,
      Hoboken, Wiley Blackwell, 140.

10   'Stonewall Anniversary', The Allen Ginsberg Project, 27 June
      2011, <http://ginsbergblog.blogspot.com.au/2011/06/stonewall-
      anniversary.html>.

11   Asad Haider, 'Where Are the People of Color?', *Jacobin*, 27
      February 2017, <https://www.jacobinmag.com/2017/02/left-
      diversity-people-color-white-identitarian-solidarity-difference/>.

12   Verity Burgmann, 'From Syndicalism to Seattle: class and the
      politics of identity', in *International Labor and Working-Class History*,
      67, Spring 2005, 3.

13   Adler, 'Taking Offense'.

14   Martin Luther King, 'Letter from Birmingham Jail in Timothy
      Patrick McCarthy and John McMillian (eds), *The Radical Reader: a
      documentary history of the American radical tradition*, New York, New
      Press, 2003, 366.

15   Taylor, *How We Get Free*.

16   Elaine Graham-Leigh, 'The Return of Idealism: identity and the
      politics of oppression', *Counterfire*, 1 March 2018, <http://www.
      counterfire.org/articles/opinion/19484-the-return-of-idealism-
      identity-and-the-politics-of-oppression>.

17   Quoted in Mohandesi, 'Identity Crisis'.

18   Dan Martin, 'Impassioned Words from Jay-Z in Support of Obama',
      Guardian, 5 November 2008, <http://www.theguardian.com/
      music/2008/nov/05/jayz-falloutboy>.

19   'The Montgomery Bus Boycott — Women's Political Council',
      History Is A Weapon, <http://www.historyisaweapon.com/
      defcon1/wpcmontgomery.html>.

20   Naomi Klein, *No Logo*, Toronto, Vintage Books, 2009, 123.

21   Burgmann, 'From Syndicalism to Seattle', 6.

22   Keeanga-Yamahtta Taylor, *From #BlackLivesMatter to Black Liberation*,
      Chicago, Haymarket Books, 2016, 7.

23   David D. Kirkpatrick, 'Death Knell May Be Near for Public Election
      Funds', *New York Times*, 23 January 2007, <https://www.nytimes.
      com/2007/01/23/us/politics/23donate.html?pagewanted=all>.

24   Michael Luo, 'Obama Hauls in Record $750 Million for
      Campaign', *New York Times*, 4 December 2008.

25   Taylor, *From #BlackLivesMatter to Black Liberation*, 9.

26   Pankaj Mishra, 'Why Do White People Like What I Write?', *London
      Review of Books*, 40(4), 22 February 2018, <https://www.lrb.co.uk/
      v40/n04/pankaj-mishra/why-do-white-people-like-what-i-write>.

27   Andrew Buncombe, 'Barack Obama to Make $1.2m from Three
      Wall Street Speeches', *Independent*, 18 September 2017, <https://
      www.independent.co.uk/news/world/americas/us-politics/barack-
      obama-speeches-fee-wall-street-latest-a7954156.html>.

28   Aidan Mac Guill, 'Late-Night Hosts on Obama's $400,000 Speech:
      "Continuing Hillary's legacy"', *Guardian*, 28 April 2017, <http://
      www.theguardian.com/culture/2017/apr/28/obama-paid-speech-
      late-night-comedians-hillary-clinton>.

29   'Social Reproduction Beyond Intersectionality: an interview',
      Viewpoint Magazine, 31 October 2015, <https://www.
      viewpointmag.com/2015/10/31/social-reproduction-beyond-
      intersectionality-an-interview-with-sue-ferguson-and-david-
      mcnally/>.

30   Tim Hein, 'The 10 Most Publicised Abusive Comments about Julia
      Gillard', *Tim Hein* (blog), 22 May 2012, <https://timhein.com.
      au/2012/05/22/the-top-10-most-publicised-abusive-comments-
      about-julia-gillard/>.

31   Julia Gillard, 'Transcript of Julia Gillard's Speech', 10 October 2012,
      <https://www.smh.com.au/politics/federal/transcript-of-julia-
      gillards-speech-20121010-27c36.html>.

32   Alison Rourke, 'Julia Gillard's Attack on Sexism Hailed as Turning
      Point for Australian Women', *Guardian*, 12 October 2012, <http://
      www.theguardian.com/world/2012/oct/12/julia-gillard-sexism-
      australian-women>.

33   Anwen Crawford, 'This Isn't Working: single mothers and welfare',
      Meanjin, 73(3), 2014, <https://meanjin.com.au/essays/this-isnt-
      working-single-mothers-and-welfare/>.

34   Tim Colebatch, 'Gillard's Fall Is Far Bigger than Labor's', *Age*,
      20 June 2013, <https://www.smh.com.au/politics/federal/gillards-
      fall-is-far-bigger-than-labors-20130619-2ojdv.html >.

35   Amory Starr, *Naming the Enemy: anti-corporate social movements
      confront globalization*, London, Zed Books, 2000, 31.

Chapter Ten: Privilege and inequality

1   'We Are the 99 Percent', Tumblr, <http://wearethe99percent.
      tumblr.com/?og=1>.

2   Mike Davis, 'No More Bubblegum', *Los Angeles Review of Books*,
      21 October 2011, <https://lareviewofbooks.org/article/no-more-
      bubblegum/>.

3   Taylor, *From #BlackLivesMatter to Black Liberation*, 146.

4   Kimberlé Crenshaw, 'Demarginalizing the Intersection of Race and
      Sex: a black feminist critique of antidiscrimination doctrine,
      feminist theory, and antiracist politics', University of Chicago Legal
      Forum, 1989, 149

5   A point made in 'Is Intersectionality Just Another Form of Identity Politics?', *Feminist Fightback*, 11 January 2015.

6   Peggy McIntosh, 'White Privilege and Male Privilege: a personal account of coming to see correspondences through work in women's studies', Wellesley College, Center for Research on Women, 1988.

7   Sean McCann, 'Choose and Be Damned: responsibility and privilege in a neoliberal age', *Los Angeles Review of Books*, 2 July 2017, <https://lareviewofbooks.org/article/choose-and-be-damned-responsibility-and-privilege-in-a-neoliberal-age/>.

8   Asad Haider, 'White Purity', *Viewpoint Magazine*, 6 January 2017, <https://www.viewpointmag.com/2017/01/06/white-purity/ >.

9   Kathie Sarachild, 'Consciousness-Raising: a radical weapon', in Redstockings, *Feminist Revolution*.

10 Kelton Sears, 'A Marxist Critiques Identity Politics', *Seattle Weekly*, 26 April 2017, <http://www.seattleweekly.com/news/a-marxist-critiques-identity-politics/>.

11 Michael Reich, 'Who Benefits from Racism? The distribution among whites of gains and losses from racial inequality', *Journal of Human Resources*, 1978, 524–44.

12 Noel Ignatin, 'Debate within SDS. RYM II vs. Weatherman, Without a Science of Navigation ...', <https://www.marxists.org/history/erol/ncm-1/debate-sds/ignatin.htm>.

13 Phoebe Maltz Bovy, *The Perils of 'Privilege'*, New York, St Martins Press, 2017, 251.

14 Asad Haider, 'Passing for Politics', *Medium*, 15 June 2016, <https://medium.com/@ahaider/passing-for-politics-559e14c813f7#.whuciapyv>.

15 Angela Nagle, *Kill All Normies: online culture wars from 4chan and Tumblr to Trump and the alt-right*, Alresford, UK, Zero Books, 2017, 8.

16 Jon Ronson, *So You've Been Publicly Shamed*, New York, Penguin, 2016, 68.

17 Wendy Brown, 'Wounded Attachments', *Political Theory*, 21(3), 1993, 26.

Chapter Eleven: Trauma and trigger warnings

1   Ethan Watters, *Crazy Like Us: the globalization of the American psyche*, New York, Simon & Schuster, 2010, 101.

2   Ben Shephard, *A War of Nerves: soldiers and psychiatrists in the twentieth century*, Cambridge, Massachusetts, Harvard University Press, 2003, 355.

3   Quoted in Alynne Romo, *VVAW: 50 years of struggle*, Alresford, UK, Changemakers Books, 2017, 25.

4   Shephard, *A War of Nerves*, 357.

5   Institute of Medicine, *Treatment for Posttraumatic Stress Disorder in Military and Veteran Populations: Final Assessment*, Washington, DC, The National Academies Press, 2014, <https://www.ncbi.nlm.nih.gov/books/NBK224872/>.

6   Camilla Turner and Tony Diver, 'Safe Spaces at Universities Are "Fundamentally Offensive", Says Oxford Chancellor', *Telegraph*, 4 November 2017, <https://www.telegraph.co.uk/education/2017/11/04/safe-spaces-universities-fundamentally-offensive-says-oxford/>.

7   'Don't Be So Offensive', *Economist*, 4 June 2016, <https://www.economist.com/news/international/21699903-young-westerners-are-less-keen-their-parents-free-speech-dont-be-so-offensive>.

8   Ali Vingiano, 'How the "Trigger Warning" Took Over the Internet', *BuzzFeed*, 6 May 2014, <https://www.buzzfeed.com/alisonvingiano/how-the-trigger-warning-took-over-the-internet>.

9   Sarah Colbert, 'Like Trapdoors: a history of posttraumatic stress disorder and the "Trigger Warning"' in Emily J.M. Knox (ed.), *Trigger Warnings: history, theory, context*, Lanham, Maryland, Rowman & Littlefield, 2017, 9.

10   Chaim F. Shatan, 'Post-Vietnam Syndrome', *New York Times*, 6 May 1972, <https://www.nytimes.com/1972/05/06/archives/postvietnam-syndrome.html>.

11   Watters, *Crazy Like Us*, 115.

12   Shephard, *A War of Nerves*, 356.

13   Shephard, *A War of Nerves*, 387.

14   Watters, *Crazy Like Us*, 121.

15   Quoted in Watters, *Crazy Like Us*, 123.

16   Jack Halberstam, 'Trigger Happy: from content warning to censorship', *Signs*, 8 March 2016, <http://signsjournal.org/currents-trigger-warnings/halberstam/>.

17   Wendy Brown, 'Wounded Attachments', *Political Theory*, 21(3), 1993, 404.

Chapter Twelve: Them and us

1   Jon Ronson, *Them: adventures with extremists*, New York, Simon & Schuster, 2002, 95.

2   Eric Hananoki, 'Trump Reportedly Praised Alex Jones for Having
     'one of the Greatest Influences' He's Ever Seen', *Media Matters
     for America*, 7 October 2016, <https://www.mediamatters.org/
     blog/2016/10/07/trump-reportedly-praised-alex-jones-having-
     one-greatest-influences-he-s-ever-seen/213616>.

3   David Frum, 'The Great Republican Revolt', *Atlantic*, January/
     February 2016, <https://www.theatlantic.com/magazine/
     archive/2016/01/the-great-republican-revolt/419118/>.

4   Lauren Carroll, 'Ben Carson's First 10 Fact-Checks', *PolitiFact*,
     29 September 2015, <http://www.politifact.com/truth-o-meter/
     article/2015/sep/29/ben-carsons-first-10-fact-checks/>.

5   Sam Clench, 'Donald Trump, Mike Huckabee: weirdest quotes
     from Republican debate 2015', News.com.au, 7 August 2015,
     <http://www.news.com.au/entertainment/tv/the-ten-weirdest-
     lines-from-the-republican-debate/news-story/0e15ba7c765a3c702
     5eeafc81144ca8c>.

6   Igor Volsky, 'Rick Santorum Pledges to Defund Contraception: "It's
     Not Okay, It's a License to Do Things"', *ThinkProgress*,
     19 October 2011, <https://thinkprogress.org/rick-santorum-
     pledges-to-defund-contraception-its-not-okay-it-s-a-license-to-
     do-things-a9a9b04f0761/>.

7   Katherine Stewart, 'Ted Cruz and the Anti-Gay Pastor', *New
     York Times*, 16 November 2015, <https://www.nytimes.
     com/2015/11/16/opinion/campaign-stops/ted-cruz-and-the-anti-
     gay-pastor.html>.

8   Katie Zezima, 'How Ted Cruz Differs from Donald Trump on
     Immigration', *Washington Post*, 5 January 2016, <https://www.
     washingtonpost.com/news/post-politics/wp/2016/01/05/how-
     ted-cruz-differs-from-donald-trump-on-immigration/?utm_
     term=.f8d1bcdcbec1>.

9   Sharon Smith, 'States of Inequality', *International Socialist Review*,
     107, Winter 2017–18, <https://isreview.org/issue/107/states-
     inequality>.

10   Smith, 'States of Inequality'.

11   Thomas Frank, 'The Intolerance of the Left: Trump's win as
     seen from Walt Disney's hometown', *Guardian*, 27 January 2017,
     <http://www.theguardian.com/us-news/2017/jan/27/why-
     donald-trump-win-walt-disney>.

12   Linda Tirado, *Hand to Mouth: the truth about being poor in a wealthy
     world*, London, Hachette, 2014, 169.

13   Kim Moody, 'Who Put Trump in the White House?', *Solidarity*, January–February 2017, <https://www.solidarity-us.org/node/4859>.

14   Christian Parenti, 'Listening to Trump', *Jacobin*, 22 November 2016, <http://jacobinmag.com/2016/11/trump-speeches-populism-war-economics-election>.

15   Matthew Yglesias, 'What Really Happened in 2016, in 7 Charts', *Vox*, 18 September 2017, <https://www.vox.com/policy-and-politics/2017/9/18/16305486/what-really-happened-in-2016>.

16   David Fahrenthold, 'Trump Recorded Having Extremely Lewd Conversation about Women in 2005', *Washington Post*, 8 October 2016, <https://www.washingtonpost.com/politics/trump-recorded-having-extremely-lewd-conversation-about-women-in-2005/2016/10/07/3b9ce776-8cb4-11e6-bf8a-3d26847eeed4_story.html?utm_term=.26cf058f59d3>.

17   Michael Kruse and Taylor Gee, 'The 37 Fatal Gaffes That Didn't Kill Donald Trump', *Politico*, 25 September 2016, <https://www.politico.com/magazine/story/2016/09/trump-biggest-fatal-gaffes-mistakes-offensive-214289>.

18   Frum, 'The Great Republican Revolt'.

19   'Donald Trump Announces a Presidential Bid', *Washington Post*, 16 June 2015, <https://www.washingtonpost.com/news/post-politics/wp/2015/06/16/full-text-donald-trump-announces-a-presidential-bid/>.

20   Robin, *The Reactionary Mind*, 259.

21   'What's Going On', *Economist*, 5 November 2016, <https://www.economist.com/news/united-states/21709596-support-donald-trump-working-class-whites-not-what-it-seems-whats-going>.

22   Alex Ward, 'Why the US Has Trouble Winning Wars', *Vox*, 9 April 2018, <https://www.vox.com/2018/2/15/17007678/syria-trump-war-win-interview>.

23   Charlie Post, 'We Got Trumped', *International Socialist Review*, 104, Spring 2017, <https://isreview.org/issue/104/we-got-trumped>.

24   Amber Phillips, '"They're Rapists." President Trump's Campaign Launch Speech Two Years Later, Annotated', *Washington Post*, 16 June 2017, <https://www.washingtonpost.com/news/the-fix/wp/2017/06/16/theyre-rapists-presidents-trump-campaign-launch-speech-two-years-later-annotated/?utm_term=.3f8296f0a4c5>.

25   Serena Marshall, 'Obama Has Deported More People Than Any Other President', ABC News, 29 August 2016, <http://

abcnews.go.com/Politics/obamas-deportation-policy-numbers/
story?id=41715661>.

26   Allison Graves, 'Fact-Check: Did Top Democrats Vote for a Border
Wall in 2006?', *PolitiFact*, 23 April 2017, <http://www.politifact.
com/truth-o-meter/statements/2017/apr/23/mick-mulvaney/
fact-check-did-top-democrats-vote-border-wall-2006/>.

27   Jenna Johnson, 'A Lot of People Are Saying …': How Trump
spreads conspiracies and innuendoes', *Washington Post*,
13 June 2016, <https://www.washingtonpost.com/politics/a-
lot-of-people-are-saying-how-trump-spreads-conspiracies-and-
innuendo/2016/06/13/b21e59de-317e-11e6-8ff7-7b6c1998b7a0_
story.html?utm_term=.9f008ab234e6>.

28   Dan Roberts, Ben Jacobs and Sabrina Siddiqui, 'Donald Trump
Threatens to Jail Hillary Clinton in Second Presidential Debate',
Guardian, 11 October 2016.

29   Selfa (ed.), *US Politics in An Age of Uncertainty*, Kindle.

Chapter Thirteen: The alt-right and appropriation

1   Justin Wm. Moyer, 'University Yoga Class Canceled Because of
"Oppression, Cultural Genocide"', *Washington Post*, 23 November
2015, <https://www.washingtonpost.com/news/morning-mix/
wp/2015/11/23/university-yoga-class-canceled-because-of-
oppression-cultural-genocide/?utm_term=.5f494e4e641e>.

2   Susan Scafidi, *Who Owns Culture?: appropriation and authenticity in
American law*, Rutgers University Press, 2005, Kindle.

3   Andrew Ross, *No Respect: intellectuals and popular culture*, London,
Routledge, 2016, 68.

4   William Gibson, 'On Evil Yogis and the Icy Silence of Yoga's
Post-Disintegration', *PopMatters*, 11 October 2015, <https://www.
popmatters.com/on-evil-yogis-and-the-icy-silence-of-yogas-post-
disintegration-2495484784.html>.

5   Michelle Goldberg, 'University Canceled Yoga Class: No,
it's not "cultural appropriation" to practice yoga.', *Slate*,
23 November 2015, <http://www.slate.com/articles/double_x/
doublex/2015/11/university_canceled_yoga_class_no_it_s_not_
cultural_appropriation_to_practice.html>.

6   Chris Welch and Sara Ganim, 'White Supremacist Richard Spencer
Speaks at Texas A&M', CNN, 7 December 2016, <https://www.
cnn.com/2016/12/06/politics/richard-spencer-interview-texas-
am-speech/index.html>.

7   Quoted in Shuja Haider, 'The Safety Pin and the Swastika', *Viewpoint Magazine*, 4 January 2017, <https://www.viewpointmag.com/2017/01/04/the-safety-pin-and-the-swastika/>.

8   Neil Davidson, 'Choosing or Refusing to Take Sides in an Era of Right-wing Populism', in Selfa (ed.), *US Politics in An Age of Uncertainty*.

9   Bovy, 'The Perils of "Privilege"'.

10   '"We're Not Going Away": Alt-right leader on voice in Trump administration', NPR.org, 17 November 2016, <https://www.npr.org/2016/11/17/502476139/were-not-going-away-alt-right-leader-on-voice-in-trump-administration>.

11   Richard Spencer, 'Cultural Appropriation', *Radix Journal*, 22 November 2015, <https://www.radixjournal.com/2015/11/2015-11-21-cultural-appropriation/>.

12   Karl Marx and Friedrich Engels, *The Communist Manifesto: with an introduction and notes by Gareth Stedman Jones*, London, Penguin, 2010.

13   David B. Dennis, *Inhumanities: Nazi interpretations of Western culture*, Cambridge, Cambridge University Press, 2012, 50.

14   David Renton, *When We Touched the Sky: the Anti-Nazi League 1977–1981*, Cheltenham, New Clarion Press, 2006.

15   Haider, 'The Safety Pin and the Swastika'.

16   Andy Dangerfield, 'Did Music Fight Racism?', BBC, 24 April 2008, <http://news.bbc.co.uk/2/hi/uk_news/magazine/7351610.stm>.

17   Frank Ross, 'Andrew Breitbart: enemy of the left with a laptop', *Breitbart*, 3 August 2010, <http://www.breitbart.com/big-journalism/2010/08/03/andrew-breitbart-enemy-of-the-left-with-a-laptop/>.

18   Murat Yükselir, 'Who Is Stephen Bannon? How he fits in Trump's unusual inner circle, and why he worries so many', *Globe and Mail*, 14 November 2016, <https://www.theglobeandmail.com/news/world/stephen-bannon-how-he-fits-in-trumps-unusual-inner-circle/article32835619/>.

19   Jake Swearingen, 'Steve Bannon's "World of Warcraft" Gold Farming Inspired Him', *NYMag*, 18 July 2017, <http://nymag.com/selectall/2017/07/steve-bannon-world-of-warcraft-gold-farming.html>.

20   Sean Illing, 'The Woman at the Center of #Gamergate Gives Zero Fucks about Her Haters', *Vox*, 19 September 2017, <https://www.vox.com/culture/2017/9/19/16301682/gamergate-alt-right-zoe-quinn-crash-override-interview>.

21   Steve Hen, 'When Women Stopped Coding',
      NPR.org, 21 October 2014, <https://www.npr.org/sections/
      money/2014/10/21/357629765/when-women-stopped-coding>.

22   Lisa Wade, 'What Happened to All of the Women in Computer
      Science?', *Pacific Standard*, 13 January 2015, <https://psmag.com/
      economics/happened-women-computer-science-98057>.

23   Brendan Keogh, 'Hackers, Gamers and Cyborgs', *Overland*,
      218, Autumn 2015, <https://overland.org.au/previous-issues/
      issue-218/feature-brendan-keogh/>.

24   Dale Beran, '4chan: The Skeleton Key to the Rise of Trump', Medium,
      15 February 2017, <https://medium.com/@DaleBeran/4chan-the-
      skeleton-key-to-the-rise-of-trump-624e7cb798cb>.

25   Andrew Jakubowicz, 'Alt-Right White Lite: trolling, hate speech
      and cyber racism on social media', *Cosmopolitan Civil Societies: an
      interdisciplinary journal* 9(3), 2017, 41.

26   Beran, '4chan'.

27   Zaid Jilani, 'Gamergate's Fickle Hero: the dark opportunism of
      Breitbart's Milo Yiannopoulos', *Salon*, 29 October 2014, <https://
      www.salon.com/2014/10/28/gamergates_fickle_hero_the_dark_
      opportunism_of_breitbarts_milo_yiannopoulos/>.

28   Milo Yiannopoulos, 'Feminist Bullies Tearing the Video Game
      Industry Apart', *Breitbart*, 1 September 2014, <http://www.
      breitbart.com/london/2014/09/01/lying-greedy-promiscuous-
      feminist-bullies-are-tearing-the-video-game-industry-apart/>.

29   Kristen V. Brown, 'The Ultimate Troll: the terrifying allure of
      Gamergate icon Milo Yiannopoulos', *Splinter*, 27 October 2015,
      <https://splinternews.com/the-ultimate-troll-the-terrifying-
      allure-of-gamergate-1793852307>.

30   Ethan Ralph, 'L & O: SVU "Gamer Madness" edition more bizarre
      than anyone could have imagined', *The Ralph Retort*,
      12 February 2015, <https://theralphretort.com/law-
      order-gamergate-more-bizarre-than-anyone-could-have-
      imagined-0212015/>.

31   Jimmy Page, 'Cultural Appropriation, #Gamergate and Why
      Gamers Had to Die', *Medium*, 3 February 2015, <https://medium.
      com/@Dwavenhobble/cultural-appropriation-gamergate-and-
      why-gamers-had-to-die-e745cbebc574>.

32   Milo Yiannopoulos, 'Why I'm Winning', *Breitbart*, 23 November
      2015, <http://www.breitbart.com/big-journalism/2015/11/23/
      why-im-winning/>.

33 Milo Yiannopoulos, 'Meme Magic: Donald Trump is the internet's revenge on lazy elites', *Breitbart*, 4 May 2016, <http://www.breitbart.com/milo/2016/05/04/meme-magic-donald-trump-internets-revenge-lazy-entitled-elites/>.

34 Nagle, *Kill All Normies*, 3.

35 Joseph Bernstein, 'Here's How Breitbart and Milo Smuggled White Nationalism into the Mainstream', *Buzzfeed*, 6 October 2017, <https://www.buzzfeed.com/josephbernstein/heres-how-breitbart-and-milo-smuggled-white-nationalism?utm_term=.bovmd4Wmo#.lh57A587Y>.

Chapter Fourteen: Fascism and democracy

1 Jeffrey A. Tucker, 'Is Donald Trump a Fascist?', *Newsweek*, 17 July 2015, <http://www.newsweek.com/donald-trump-fascist-354690>.

2 Dan Merica, 'Trump Condemns "Hatred, Bigotry and Violence on Many Sides" in Charlottesville', CNN, 13 August 2017, <https://edition.cnn.com/2017/08/12/politics/trump-statement-alt-right-protests/index.html>.

3 Dell Cameron, 'Neo-Nazis Praise Trump's Response to Charlottesville: "He said he loves us all"', *Gizmodo*, 12 August 2017, <https://gizmodo.com/neo-nazis-praise-trumps-response-to-charlottesville-h-1797787685>.

4 Jamelle Bouie, 'Donald Trump Is a Fascist', *Slate*, 25 November 2015, <http://www.slate.com/articles/news_and_politics/politics/2015/11/donald_trump_is_a_fascist_it_is_the_political_label_that_best_describes.html>.

5 Robert O. Paxton, *The Anatomy of Fascism*, New York, Vintage, 2007, 17.

6 Davidson, 'Choosing or Refusing to Take Sides in an Era of Right-wing Populism'.

7 Corey Robin, 'Think Trump Is an Authoritarian? Look at his actions, not his words', *Guardian*, 2 May 2017, <https://www.theguardian.com/commentisfree/2017/may/02/donald-trump-authoritarian-look-actions-not-words>.

8 An early version of this argument appeared in Jeff Sparrow, 'Brexit and the New Hostility to Participatory Democracy', *Overland*, 25 June 2016, <https://overland.org.au/2016/06/brexit-and-the-new-hostility-to-participatory-democracy/>.

9 Edmund Burke, 'Reflections on the Revolution in France', <https://chnm.gmu.edu/revolution/d/563/>.

10   Thomas Jefferson, 'Thomas Jefferson on Politics and Government', <https://famguardian.org/Subjects/Politics/ThomasJefferson/jeff0800.htm>.

11   'Hamilton versus Jefferson on Popular Rule', <http://www.pinzler.com/ushistory/hamjeffpopsupp.html>.

12   Raymond Williams, *Keywords: a vocabulary of culture and society*, Oxford, Oxford University Press, 2014, 96.

13   Gitlin, *The Sixties*, 134.

14   Williams, *Keywords*, 96.

15   Robert McChesney, 'Introduction', in Noam Chomsky, *Profit over People: neoliberalism and global order*, New York, Seven Stories Press, 1999, 6.

16   David Harvey, *A Brief History of Neoliberalism*, New York, Oxford University Press, 2007, 66.

17   Robert Sullivan, 'The Hamilton Cult', *Harper's Magazine*, October 2016, <https://harpers.org/archive/2016/10/the-hamilton-cult/>.

18   Matt Stoller, 'The Hamilton Hustle', *Baffler*, 6 March 2017, <https://thebaffler.com/salvos/hamilton-hustle-stoller>.

19   Andrew Sullivan, 'America Has Never Been So Ripe for Tyranny', *NYMag*, 1 May 2016, <http://nymag.com/daily/intelligencer/2016/04/america-tyranny-donald-trump.html>.

20   James Traub, 'It's Time for the Elites to Rise Up Against the Ignorant Masses', *Foreign Policy*, 28 June 2016, <http://foreignpolicy.com/2016/06/28/its-time-for-the-elites-to-rise-up-against-ignorant-masses-trump-2016-brexit/>.

21   Paul Mason, 'The Leftwing Case for Brexit (One Day)', *Guardian*, 16 May 2016, <http://www.theguardian.com/commentisfree/2016/may/16/brexit-eu-referendum-boris-johnson-greece-tory>.

22   Geoffrey Robertston, 'How to Stop Brexit: get your MP to vote it down', *Guardian*, 27 June 2016, <https://www.theguardian.com/commentisfree/2016/jun/27/stop-brexit-mp-vote-referendum-members-parliament-act-europe>.

23   A. C. Grayling, 'Professor A C Grayling's Letter to All 650 MPs Urging Parliament Not to Support a Motion to Trigger Article 50 of the Lisbon Treaty', New College of the Humanities, 1 July 2016, <https://www.nchlondon.ac.uk/2016/07/01/professor-c-graylings-letter-650-mps-urging-parliament-not-support-motion-trigger-article-50-lisbon-treaty-1-july-2016/>.

24 Abi Wilkinson, 'Leave Voters Are Not All Idiots: some Londoners still don't get it', *Guardian*, 15 February 2017, <https://www.theguardian.com/commentisfree/2017/feb/14/leave-voters-london-voted-remain-eu>.

25 'A Note about Our Coverage of Donald Trump's "Campaign"', *Huffington Post*, 17 July 2015, <https://www.huffingtonpost.com.au/entry/a-note-about-our-coverage-of-donald-trumps-campaign_us_55a8fc9ce4b0896514d0fd66>.

26 Selfa (ed.), *US Politics in an Age of Uncertainty*.

27 *New Yorker*, 27 December 2016, <https://www.newyorker.com/cartoon/a20630>.

28 Abi Wilkinson, 'The Specter of Democracy', *Jacobin*, 1 November 2017, <http://jacobinmag.com/2017/01/bernie-sanders-trump-populism-new-yorker>.

29 Thea Riofrancos, 'Democracy Without the People', *N+1*, 6 February 2017, <https://nplusonemag.com/online-only/online-only/democracy-without-the-people/>.

30 David Adler, 'Centrists are the Most Hostile to Democracy, Not Extremists', *New York Times*, 23 May 2018, <https://www.nytimes.com/interactive/2018/05/23/opinion/international-world/centrists-democracy.html>.

Conclusion

1 Mark Lilla, 'The End of Identity Liberalism', *New York Times*, 18 November 2016, <https://www.nytimes.com/2016/11/20/opinion/sunday/the-end-of-identity-liberalism.html>.

2 Mark Lilla, *The Once and Future Liberal: after identity politics*, New York, HarperCollins, 2017.

3 Margo Kingston, 'Pauline Hanson Takes Centre Stage Again but This Time We Should Listen Not Lampoon', *Guardian*, 4 July 2016, <https://www.theguardian.com/australia-news/2016/jul/04/pauline-hanson-takes-centre-stage-again-but-this-time-we-should-listen-not-lampoon>.

4 AAP, 'Labor Backs Gay Marriage Ban', *Sydney Morning Herald*, 27 May 2004, <https://www.smh.com.au/articles/2004/05/27/1085461884719.html>.

5 AAP, 'Labor Backs Howard's Gay Marriage Ban', *Age*, 1 June 2004, <https://www.theage.com.au/articles/2004/06/01/1086037757556.html>.

6 Meaghan Shaw, 'Labor Backs Ban on Gay Marriage',

Age, 5 August 2004, <https://www.theage.com.au/articles/2004/08/04/1091557919497.html>.

7   Facebook post, Anglican Parish of Gosford, 10 August 2017.

8   Michael Koziol, '"Extraordinary": 100,000 new voters join electoral roll as last-minute surge buoys "yes"campaign', 25 August 2017, <https://www.smh.com.au/politics/federal/extraordinary-100000-new-voters-join-electoral-roll-boosting-hopes-for-yes-campaign-20170825-gy466w.html>.

9   Rob Inglis, '"Dark Days Are Over": Croome and fellow "yes" supporters rejoice', *Advocate*, 15 November 2017, <http://www.theadvocate.com.au/story/5059195/dark-days-are-over-croome-and-fellow-yes-supporters-rejoice/>.

10   Jack Mundey, interview by Robin Hughes, 'Jack Mundey: full interview transcript', 4 October 2000, <http://www.australianbiography.gov.au/subjects/mundey/interview4.html>.

11   'Why Does the CFMEU Support Marriage Equality?', CFMEU Construction and General, 20 September 2017, <https://cg.cfmeu.org.au/news/why-does-cfmeu-support-marriage-equality>.

12   Joanna Horton, '"We Had Marx, They Had Pauline": left organising in poor communities', *Overland*, 13 February 2018,<https://overland.org.au/2018/02/we-had-marx-they-had-pauline-left-organising-in-poor-communities/>.

13   'United States: LGBT Students Face Discrimination', *Human Rights Watch*, 7 December 2016, <https://www.hrw.org/news/2016/12/07/united-states-lgbt-students-face-discrimination>.

14   Marissa Higgins, 'LBGT Students Are Not Safe at School', *Atlantic*, 18 October 2016, https://www.theatlantic.com/education/archive/2016/10/school-is-still-not-safe-for-lgbt-students/504368/.

15   Davidson, 'Choosing or Refusing to Take Sides in an Era of Right-Wing Populism'.

16   Emma Stefansky, 'George Takei Forgives Sexual Assault Accuser After Accuser Retracts Claim', *Vanity Fair*, 27 May 2018, <https://www.vanityfair.com/style/2018/05/george-takei-sexual-assault-accuser-retracts-claim>.

17   Sandra E. Garcia, 'The Woman Who Created #MeToo Long Before Hashtags', *New York Times*, 20 October 2017, <https://www.nytimes.com/2017/10/20/us/me-too-movement-tarana-burke.html>.

18 Stephanie Convery, 'Get your hands off my sister', *Overland*, Autumn 2016, <https://overland.org.au/previous-issues/issue-222/feature-stephanie-convery/>.
19 Hannah Arendt, *On Revolution*, New York, Penguin, 2006, 110.
20 'We Were There — Sydney's Pride History Group', accessed 12 April 2018, <http://www.camp.org.au/100-voices/10-exhibitions/out-of-the-closets-early-activism/97-we-were-there>.
21 *It Was a Riot! Sydney's First Gay & Lesbian Mardi Gras*. 78ers Festival Events Group, 1998.
22 Barbara Ehrenreich, 'Transcendence, Hope & Ecstasy', *Z Magazine*, October 1998.
23 Calla Wahlquist, 'Indigenous Youth Incarceration Rate Is a National Crisis and Needs Action, PM told', *Guardian*, 31 May 2017, <https://www.theguardian.com/australia-news/2017/mar/31/indigenous-youth-incarceration-rate-is-a-national-crisis-and-needs-action-pm-told>.
24 'We Only Want The Earth' in James Connolly, *Selected Writings*, London, Pluto Press, 1972, 292.